BROTHERHOOD

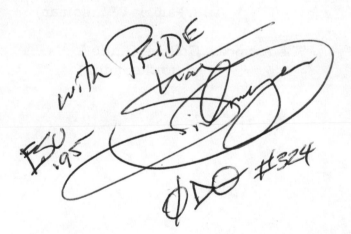

**Also available from Alyson Books
by Shane L. Windmeyer**

Out on Fraternity Row
(with Pamela W. Freeman)

Secret Sisters
(with Pamela W. Freeman)

The Advocate College Guide for LGBT Students
(forthcoming)

BROTHERHOOD

Gay Life in College Fraternities

Edited by

Shane L. Windmeyer

alyson books
NEW YORK
Celebrating Twenty-Five Years

Manufactured in the United States of America.

This trade paperback original is published by Alyson Books,
P.O. Box 1253, Old Chelsea Station, New York, New York 10113-1251.
Distribution in the United Kingdom by Turnaround Publisher Services Ltd.,
Unit 3, Olympia Trading Estate, Coburg Road, Wood Green,
London N22 6TZ England.

First edition: September 2005

05 06 07 08 09 **a** 10 9 8 7 6 5 4 3 2 1

ISBN 1-55583-856-1
ISBN-13 978-1-55583-856-0

CREDITS
Cover photography by Mike Brinson/Image Bank/Getty Images.
Cover design by Tom O'Quinn.
Travis C. Shumake photo courtesy of Brandon Sullivan Photography.

Brotherhood

A family devotion to other men who share a common bond, friendship, and love for their fraternity and welfare of their brothers; a willingness to help or aid a brother in time of need; and shared common values of loyalty, honesty, understanding, and respect.

Shane L. Windmeyer
Founder & Coordinator
Lambda 10 Project

Contents

Acknowledgments xi
Editor's Note xv
About the Lambda 10 Project xviii
Foreword: A Chance to Make a Difference:
Letter to the Lambda 10 Project
by Dwayne Todd xix

Inside the Closet 1

Behind Greek Letters by "Carlos Cervantes" 3
Cry Freedom by "Eric Joseph" 10
From the Haze by "John Welles" 18
Conflicted by Jamison Keller 22
1 John 2:10 by Jonathan Scaggs 26
Sexual Monsters by M. Ducoing 33

Rushing Out 47

The Pledge Jersey by Clay Cunningham 49
My Gay Pledge Son by Benjamin M. Swartz 58
Change Takes Time by Travis C. Shumake 62
Smoking Guns by "Travis Lin" 72
Lifestyles of the Gay and Fraternal by Josh Ney 89
Ordinarily Not Gay by Eric B. Asselstine 98
Spaghetti Dinners by Christopher N. Ho 106

A Question of Love and Loyalty 119

Hide Away *by Chris Zacharda* 121
Lovers to Brothers *by "Michael Goldberg" and "Alan Marshall"* 135
Building a Bridge *by Stefan Dinescu* 145
Brothers Now and Ever *by Jonathan Vogel* 152
Leaving the Door Open *by Raymond A. Lutzky* 165
Bonded *by Michael A. Knipp* 177

Bonds of Acceptance 189

Next on NBC Nightly News *by Gabriel Grice* 191
To Live a Lie *by Joseph Zagame* 201
Two Opposite Tales *by Jack Trump* 207
Standing Tall and Proud *by Richard P. Peralta* 215
Finding Courage *by Adrian V. Herrera* 223
Odd Man In *by Mark Bigelow* 228
The Row *by John Skandros* 237

Conclusion: 245

A Challenge to Fraternities to Fulfill Their Mission
by Douglas N. Case

Interventions & Resources 259

How to Use Stories as Educational Tools
by Pamela W. Freeman 261
The Relationship Between Hazing and Homophobia
by Pamela W. Freeman 272
Trials and Tribulations of Rushing Openly Gay Brothers
by Kelly Jo Karnes 281
How to Come Out of the Gay Greek Closet?
by Tracie M. Massey 289

Biblical Passages to Support a Gay Brother
by Doug Bauder and Reverend Rebecca Jiménez 297
Creating a PILLAR Support Group for Gay Greeks
by Grahaeme A. Hesp 304
Out in Front: Questions, Policy Statements, and Resolutions
Affirming Sexual Orientation 312

Out & Online: Being Gay and Greek
Resources 327

Editor's Note: *Quotation marks around contributor names indicate the use of a pseudonym. All other authors' names are the actual names of the individuals writing the stories.*

Acknowledgments

Ten percent of society is gay, lesbian, or bisexual. I believe that percentage is much higher in college fraternities and sororities. The notion that "he's not gay, he's in a fraternity" has all but disappeared as more people have come out in Greek life. Likewise, the amount of support the Lambda 10 Project has received over the past 10 years indicates that the need for education on these issues is a growing priority.

First and foremost, I would like to thank the men who share their heartfelt stories in this anthology. I recognize how difficult it is to share your lives openly and honestly. Your brave tales of coming out as well as the pain of the closet will undoubtedly help others understand what it is like to be gay and lend strength and courage for their personal journey of self-discovery.

I would also like to thank the many contributors to the other sections of the book. Particularly, I want to recognize the tireless work of the phenomenal Douglas N. Case, who has always supported the efforts of the Lambda 10 Project and me personally. His conclusion truly challenges college fraternities to live up to their promise of brotherhood.

The staff of Alyson books—including Nick Street, Angela Brown, Dan Cullinane, Greg Constante, Matt Sams, and Whitney Friedlander—has stood by my side over the past 10 years. From *Out on Fraternity Row: Personal Accounts of Being Gay in a College Fraternity* to *Secret Sisters: Stories of Being Lesbian & Bisexual in a College Sorority,* they believed in the work of the Lambda 10 Project and have supported our efforts to break the cycle of invisibility. I thank all of you.

Many other remarkable individuals and organizations have also been instrumental to the Lambda 10 Project and helped to make this book possible. I would be remiss if I did not express my appreciation to the following individuals: Bruce Steele, Kathleen DeBold, Kelly Jo Karnes, Tracie Massey, Dan Maxwell, Nita Allgood, Carol Fischer, Doug Bauder, Rueben Perez, Neil Shaw, Christine Shaw, Jon Moore, Candace Gingrich, Tom Jelke, Judy Riggs, Dwayne Todd, Mitchell Gold, Nick Geimer, Elizabeth Couch, Dave Podell, Brian Bradley, Jeremy Podell, Laura Podell, Bryan Podell, Grahaeme Hesp, George Miller, Sue Rankin, Reverend Rebecca Jiménez, Rick Myracle, Dan Bureau, Judy Shepard, Joni Madison, Sue Kraft Fussell, Amanda Greer, Paul Maierle, Mudhillun MuQaribu, Rob Rosen, David Katzin, Mitchell Gold, Bert Woodard, and Richard McKaig.

Several organizations also deserve special recognition: Chi Epsilon Fraternity, Tyvola Design, the National Consortium of Directors of LGBT Resources in Higher Education, Phi Delta Theta International Fraternity, Association of Fraternity Advisors, Human Rights Campaign, STOPHATE.ORG, the Matthew Shepard Foundation, Association of College Unions International, Campus PrideNet National Online Network for GLBT Student Leaders and Allies, National Gay and Lesbian Task Force, *The Advocate,* the *Washington Blade,* Parents, Families, and Friends of Lesbians & Gays, Indiana University, North-American Interfraternity Conference, Center for the Study of the College Fraternity, American College Personnel Association, Brandon Sullivan Photography, and National Association for Student Personnel Administrators.

And I cannot forget my personal cheerleading squad, who gave me energy and a sense of spirit when I needed them most. The cheerleaders are: Thomas Feldman (my partner), Fred Windmeyer (my dad, who recently passed away and now watches over me from above), Diann Windmeyer (my mom), Jennifer Windmeyer (my sister), Paula Podell, Kelly Greemore, Phillip Wells, Jay Biles, Rodney Tucker, Rodney Hines, Regina Young Hyatt, Janis Singletary, and Tyvola (my lovely shih tzu). I wish to give my special thanks to all these wonderful individuals and organizations for their personal and professional support of the Lambda 10 Project.

Special acknowledgment goes to the men who started this—my fraternity brothers in Kansas Epsilon of Phi Delta Theta Fraternity. Their love, acceptance, and brotherhood gave me the courage to be another "famous first" for our fraternity. Those brothers made all the difference in my life and proved that the bonds of brotherhood can prevail over homophobia. The fraternity taught me the valuable lesson: "To do what ought to be done but would not have been done unless I did it, I thought to be my duty." Together we did it. We fulfilled the duty and promise of brotherhood to one another. Thank you.

A special woman and a special man have been there from the beginning of the Lambda 10 Project. The woman is Pamela W. Freeman, whom I convinced 10 years ago to believe in one of my small ideas—to write a book about being gay in a college fraternity. The idea started as a semester practicum experience during my master's program at Indiana University. She always said I had a knack for thinking big.

Last but certainly not least, the special man is my partner in life, Thomas Feldman. He is my personal dream maker and miracle worker. When we met over 10 years ago, we gave birth to the Lambda 10 Project. He designed the logo, the Web site, the book promotions for the "Call for Writers," and continues to support the Project today. He makes all my dreams come true every day, and I love him beyond words.

The Lambda 10 Project has been blessed over the past 10 years. We would like to pay tribute to the many people who have lent support, created visibility, and assisted in spreading the word about our educational efforts in Greek life. I personally thank all of you who have been a part of the Lambda 10 Project along the way. You believe in what we do and together we have made a huge difference in Greek life on college campuses. Thank you!

Editor's Note

Ten years ago Pamela W. Freeman and I initiated the Lambda 10 Project to collect the stories of gay and bisexual men in college fraternities. As a result, *Out on Fraternity Row: Personal Accounts of Being Gay in a College Fraternity* was published in 1998. The book, the first of its kind, single-handedly knocked down the Greek closet door, breaking the cycle of invisibility for gay men in fraternities. No longer could anyone ignore the fact that gay men have always been brothers and were an intricate part of the history of the college fraternity.

Surprisingly, the book quickly ascended to the top of the nonfiction gay best-seller list and exceeded all of our expectations. In 2001 the Lambda 10 Project extended our efforts to compile a companion anthology for lesbian and bisexual sorority women titled *Secret Sisters: Stories of Being Lesbian and Bisexual in a College Sorority.* Both books shattered any silence that lingered about sexual orientation issues and started a vast ripple effect of positive change in Greek life across the country.

I often think back on the last 10 years and cannot believe how the initiative all started with a small idea, the Lambda 10 Project, that grew bigger and bigger. People are shocked when I tell them that we owe the books and the work of the Lambda 10 Project to straight fraternity men. It seems odd, I guess, to most. But to me, it makes perfect sense. My choice to come out to my fraternity and their response made all the difference in my life.

In the early 1990s, I came out to my fraternity brothers at Emporia State University in Emporia, Kan. It was my junior year, and I was serving as vice president of Phi Delta Theta fraternity. Coming out to my fraternity was by far one of my most rewarding undergraduate experiences. The members' overwhelmingly supportive responses were absolute proof that fraternities could rise to the challenge of accepting a brother who was gay. If only others knew that there were indeed gay brothers and that a brother could be openly gay in a fraternity. The spark had been ignited. Shortly thereafter, the Lambda 10 Project was born.

Today I am often asked one main question: "What made your brothers accept you for being gay?" My answer is simple: "Brotherhood." Not the kind of fraternity brotherhood that is solely based on getting drunk and partying but the type of brotherhood that is founded deeply on values of loyalty, honesty, understanding, and respect. Fraternities can welcome openly gay brothers if they have a strong brotherhood—a shared bond and love for the welfare of a fellow brother.

Brotherhood is presumably the promise that all fraternities offer. Unfortunately, we seldom discuss the challenges and responsibilities of brotherhood, especially around sexual orientation issues.

Unlike *Out on Fraternity Row,* this book includes profiles of men whose experiences illustrate changes over the past 10 years as well as the challenges that still exist today. Some of the writers chose to use pseudonyms due to their current life circumstances. Also, several of the stories discuss often taboo or controversial topics such as hazing, sexual experimentation, suicide, religion, rushing openly gay, negligent use of alcohol, and falling in love with another brother.

As a result, *Brotherhood* delves deeper into issues of sexuality and male friendship and reveals the truth behind the promise of brotherhood. The book will be useful to men seeking membership in a college fraternity, men currently in a fraternity, staff members and alumni who work with fraternities, and those who wish to understand more about fraternity life for gay and bisexual men.

While the stories reflect a diversity of experiences, it is not a national research study. The Lambda 10 Project will be launching such an online national study with the release of this book in fall 2005.

Brotherhood reminds us that being gay in a college fraternity presents many obstacles and opportunities. The times are definitely changing in college fraternities. The idea of rushing openly gay was hardly a possibility 10 years ago. Today it is a reality—a reminder that fraternities are increasingly willing to confront issues of sexual orientation head-on.

When we published *Out on Fraternity Row,* we printed an anonymous letter in the preface titled "A Chance to Belong." The letter shared the emotional pain of being closeted and feeling alone and isolated within a college fraternity. The Lambda 10 Project had received this anonymous letter when we began collecting stories 10 years ago. We had no idea where this letter came from or that we would ever know the outcome of the man's personal struggle.

Today we know the writer as Dwayne Todd. He was asked to write another letter for the foreword of this book titled "A Chance to Make a Difference." Dwayne broke his personal cycle of invisibility and has become a leader within his national fraternity. His story describes how coming out to his fraternity changed his life, and how together we can all make a difference.

I invite you to share this book with others, straight and gay alike. Read the stories to better understand the meaning and the promise of brotherhood. Donate the book to your fraternity, your college/university, or to the fraternity brother(s) who made all the difference in your life. Use the book to demonstrate that the cycle of invisibility has been broken and we are here—Greek and queer! Together, let us take the first step to be a brother to one another—to be better people, to be better fraternities, and to live up to the ideals of brotherhood! No matter the letter, let us never forget that we are all Greek together!

About the Lambda 10 Project

Begun in the fall of 1995, the Lambda 10 Project National Clearinghouse for Gay, Lesbian, and Bisexual Fraternity and Sorority Issues provides support, education, and visibility for gay, lesbian, and bisexual members of college fraternities and sororities. Several initiatives, resources, and educational materials related to sexual orientation and the fraternity/sorority experience can be found on the Lambda 10 Web site and are specifically tailored to the Greek community. Lambda 10, through its educational efforts, works to create a stronger Greek community based on the founding principles of fraternal life and open to anyone regardless of sexual orientation.

Lambda 10 Project
National Clearinghouse
for Gay, Lesbian, & Bisexual Fraternity & Sorority Issues
Office of Student Ethics & Anti-Harassment Programs
Indiana University Bloomington
705 E. Seventh St.
Bloomington, IN 47408
(812) 855-4463
Fax: (812) 855-4465
E-mail: info@lambda10.org
http://www.lambda10.org

The Lambda 10 Project

Foreword

A Chance to Make a Difference

Dear Lambda 10 Project:

If our brothers could see what goes on in the minds of closeted gay members when homophobic slurs fly around the [fraternity] house, would they care? If I was truly a brother when I was seen as straight, why can't I be as homosexual as well? My deep friendship and unquestioning loyalty were never suspect before; why would my being gay change anything?

Many years ago, I sent you an anonymous letter asking these questions and describing my experience as a closeted gay leader of my fraternity chapter. I was both stunned and excited when reading *Out on Fraternity Row: Personal Accounts of Being Gay in a College Fraternity* to find that my letter titled "A Chance to Belong" was used in the preface of the book. As I read more of the stories from *Out on Fraternity Row*, I began to feel a deep sense of gratitude for the opportunity to share my experience along with many other fraternity men.

So much has changed in my life since I wrote that letter. I came out of the closet about five years ago, and I am now out of the closet in practically every area of my life. I work in higher education, and in that capacity I advise the Gay and Straight Student Alliance on my campus. I also serve on the board for a GLBT organization that helps people who have been hurt and confused by religious organizations (like I was) to reconnect with their spirituality. And for the first time I have discovered true romantic love, and I have been in a committed relationship for almost five years.

Never could I have imagined that I would be comfortable with my sexuality and be visible as an out gay man in my personal life, professional life, and local community. After years of acting straight, I finally learned to embrace myself as gay. No more hiding. No more acting. No more lies. I gained the courage to come out and the love to accept myself for who I am. My family and friends now knew me—all of me. I had chosen to be open and honest, shattering my fears of the closet. But what about my fraternity? What about the questions from my first letter?

The answers came steadily after I chose to come out. When I accepted my first volunteer leadership position with my national fraternity, I was still in the closet and unsure how my homosexuality would be regarded by others. There was one individual who demonstrated great courage by being out at a national level. But he was essentially the maverick for many years. He and I developed a close friendship, and it wasn't long before I was ready to come out to the national fraternity as well. With the words "I am gay," I broke my personal cycle of invisibility within my fraternity. There was no rejection, only brotherhood and acceptance.

The ripple effect began as the number of out gay men quickly multiplied in the fraternity. Amazingly, more fraternity alumni and active brothers came out, only to find that the bonds of brotherhood withstood the fears of homophobia. Recent graduates who were already openly gay were hired into national headquarters staff positions and were readily accepted by alumni and undergraduate brothers. Then, believe it or not, just a few years ago, our national fraternity assembly of all undergraduate chapters voted to include "sexual orientation" as a component of our fraternal statement of diversity.

To think this all started for me almost 10 years ago with my anonymous letter. My journey began when I read *Out on Fraternity Row* and continued with the steadily increasing visibility of gay and bisexual men in college fraternities. I realized that, indeed, we were everywhere—even in fraternities—and we were your brothers! I was no longer alone. The stories lent me the hope and instilled within me the courage to be who I am today and to challenge my fraternity to do more on sexual orientation issues.

Brotherhood: Gay Life in College Fraternities will further inspire hope and offer courage to those today who suffer from real or perceived rejection within their own fraternities for being gay or bisexual. There is still plenty of hatred and prejudice toward gays within college fraternities. But the landscape is changing, and there is a strong and growing acknowledgment and acceptance of sexual orientation issues within Greek life. And most of the time, our undergraduate members are leading the way for fraternities to uphold the promise of brotherhood for every brother—gay, straight, or in between.

Together we have the pride and visibility to create positive change simply by being who we are. The stories in *Brotherhood* not only reflect the overwhelmingly supportive environment that fraternities can be for gay brothers but also the intense, pervasive homophobia that still permeates college fraternities. If you are straight, realize that your gay brothers desperately need your support and need you to be an ally for them. If you are gay, bisexual, or not sure, realize that you aren't alone. It took time to acknowledge who I was both to myself and to my fraternity, but I eventually got there. I wish the same for all who read this book and share my experience.

I had written in my anonymous letter that I was among the many closeted fraternity men who "continue to live a lie among their chapters, trading their true identity for a chance to belong." Thankfully, that is no longer the case. Today instead of "trading my true identity for a chance to belong," I have instead chosen to break the cycle of invisibility in my own personal way for a chance to make a difference. One person, a group of people, a book can make a difference. Indeed, it already has in my life.

The letter is no longer anonymous. My name is Dwayne Todd. I am a gay fraternity man along with thousands of others who are gay and bisexual in college fraternities. I stand proud with my Greek letters. May this book help others on their journey and grant them a chance to make a difference.

With Pride,
Dwayne Todd
Brother of Pi Kappa Phi Fraternity

Inside the Closet

Behind Greek Letters

by "Carlos Cervantes," the Midwest

It was over. I pulled the T-shirt over my head and opened my eyes. Greek letters stared back at me. I was complete. I had overcome every trial set in front of me by the fraternity. Disciplining myself to take orders and never being allowed to refuse these orders, I passed the tests set forth by the brothers no matter how rigorous they were or how exhausting. The most difficult task was to depend solely on the brothers and to cut off everyone else outside the fraternity. Finally, I reached what I once thought would be an impossible goal for someone like me. In the middle of the hugs from all of my new fraternity brothers, I wiped the sweat from my forehead. I was now a brother in a national Latino-based fraternity. I had achieved what I wanted my whole life—the support and friendship of men, of brothers, my fraternity family.

I gazed into the mirror across the room. I'd hoped that I would see a proud, good-looking, slender Latino with dark brown hair and light brown eyes. Instead, I saw the quiet, self-conscious high school kid who lost himself in books to escape being taunted every day. I desperately did not want to be the reflection of my past; I wanted to change all that. I told myself that the past would no longer haunt me, but the reflection showed an individual who felt so out of place with other young men that he had never been able to get close to males—not even his brothers and father. I had found a new mask for my identity, but there in the mirror I could still see my undeniable secret deep within, now hidden behind the letters.

As a freshman, far away from home for the first time, I wore my fraternity letters and drew instant acceptance. The only thing I cared to be was a fraternity man—my classes were secondary. The campus was a typical large state school in the Midwest. The land surrounding the school was flat with cornfields, the nearest city was an hour away, and the student body was predominantly white. That year I slept with several women on campus to gain the acceptance of my fraternity brothers. I acted the straight role perfectly. It came too easily. The Latino fraternity was the epitome of a testosterone-driven, women-objectifying, *machista* collective. The fraternity was the perfect cover-up: No longer could anyone question or doubt that I was heterosexual.

There was just one small problem. His name was Alexander. He was the first openly gay brother in the fraternity and had pledged two years before me. He was the stereotypical gay man—well-dressed, intelligent, with feminine mannerisms, and not at all into sports. Alexander loved fashion and gossip. He was very popular across campus and involved in many leadership activities. He did not have to hide his sexuality; he was just flamboyant Alexander. He came into the fraternity a year after it was founded on campus. The brothers needed quality pledges to establish a strong foundation; Alexander was active in extracurriculars and had a strong grade point average. As a result the brothers looked past his sexual orientation and focused on his connections.

Alexander, with his whimsical gestures and flashy couture, made me shudder every time he was around me. I felt as though he could read me like an open book. I attempted to get to know all the fraternity brothers, but with Alexander it was different. I felt like he could smell the homosexuality beneath my skin. I would try to mask it with ample sprays of my Dolce & Gabbana cologne. Nothing stopped Alexander. I was so frightened that he would call my bluff that I took the offensive and avoided him like the plague.

One Saturday night, three of my brothers—Juan, Chuey, and Gato, the three brothers I was closest to in the fraternity—stopped by my apartment to pick me up on our way to a nightclub. Those three spent so much time together that they even began to look alike in their dark polo shirts and jeans. Gato filled his polo out the best with his muscular arms and chest. Juan was the traditional Mexican: short and round with dark brown skin. Chuey was the one in the trio who really stood out. His strong jawline, flawless physical proportions, and hypnotizing blue eyes speckled with hazel made me wonder if he had been airbrushed by God.

As I was getting ready in my room the guys started talking about sex, of course. It was an almost unavoidable topic among fraternity men. The subject provided the perfect means to harass a brother who was not getting any lately. Then it suddenly got heated. Gato started messing around with Juan on a sore subject. Gato had heard that Juan's girlfriend tried to finger him in the asshole while giving him head. Juan was shocked that Gato knew these details and tried to deny everything.

"Fuck, no! She tried—but you know I wouldn't do that. What do I look like, a fag or something?" said Juan, trying to salvage his pride.

"Bro, I was gonna say that…that shit is sick," said Chuey. "How can homos do that? I mean, you take a crap out of there. That's what God intended it for…that's why they are all goin' to hell."

I listened to the homophobic tirade as I tucked my shirt into my pants. Standing in front of the mirror in my jeans, still undone at the waist, and my blue Express dress shirt, I listened more intently.

Then Chuey targeted Alexander. "I'm sorry, but every time I look at Alexander I see him bending over and taking it up the ass. He disgusts me," Chuey said, then chugged his beer.

This was the first time I had heard the fraternity brothers make cracks about Alexander's sexuality. Alexander was usually untouchable because he was a likable, smart, charismatic guy. Comments about his sexuality were generally taboo among brothers. I had thought so anyway.

Gato quickly responded, "Yeah, Chuey, you're right. I can't help thinking of that when I see him. That queer shit is gross. I bet Alexander screams like a girl when he's getting boned."

Chuey stood up and started to walk around the room bowlegged. "Yo, have you guys seen Alexander walk around like this? You know that's a sure sign that he got lucky. That shit is sick."

Listening to this trash talk about Alexander, I began to feel disgusted by their words and their laughter. It was as if every comment was being redirected toward me. I chugged a beer to regain my composure. I tried laughing, but it was hard. I finished buttoning my shirt and shook it off as best I could. I never realized until this point that my fraternity brothers, for whom I cared so deeply, harbored such feelings about gays—even about Alexander, another brother.

My second year in the fraternity, I was elected to the executive board. I was eager to lead and contribute to the success of the fraternity. I had the neophyte fire burning inside me, and I was going to use that flame to recruit new members for our pledge line. These men would be the future of the fraternity and continue our legacy on campus. I wanted to ensure we got the best men possible. I plugged the brotherhood at every opportunity.

That fall semester, during the first few weeks, the fraternity held an open information meeting for potential new members. I arrived and saw the room packed full of prospective pledges. Still, I noticed some strange looks on the faces of some of the brothers. *The turnout is awesome,* I thought. *So what could be up with the attitude in the room?*

I pulled Chuey aside and asked what was wrong. He replied, "Carlos, take a good look at our turnout."

"What? I think it looks great. We have a great number—more than when I came to the informational last year," I replied.

"Really, c'mon, take a hard look," he said. "We were supposed to recruit *men* for the fraternity."

"Sorry, Chuey, I don't follow…there aren't any women as far as I can tell," I said jokingly. Chuey did not even crack a smile.

"Might as well be—there are two fags in there," Chuey said. "Two that we know of for sure."

I couldn't say anything. I looked back into the room and saw myself in those faces.

The red alert was sounded. The presence of two openly gay individuals at our informational meeting shook the entire fraternity. No one wanted the stigma of being known as the gay fraternity. It was bad enough to have one gay brother; they could not fathom having more—it would ruin the fraternity.

"The jokes, the ridicule, the loss of clout on campus would be too much to bear," Juan explained. "There are the jocks, the smart fraternities, the womanizers, the dorks, the drunks, the thugs, the well-rounded pretty boys, and the fags."

"We don't want to be known as the gay fraternity," responded Chuey. "Can you imagine all the jokes that will be made about our organization?"

Gato chimed in, "I've worked too hard to allow it. People love us now, and they respect us on campus. All that would be lost; people would turn on us and think we were gay just by association. We can't have that."

The situation compelled me to do something I had avoided most of my life—take a deeper look inside myself. Alexander was in full commando mode after hearing what had happened. The gossip had spread on campus and he was disgusted to hear such blatant prejudice among the brothers. He couldn't believe that brothers would act this way. Alexander called an emergency meeting to discuss the issue openly and to resolve the matter. I was afraid to go to the emergency meeting—I knew the meeting would force me to look at myself more closely. Still, there was no way I could come up with a convincing justification for my absence. I had no choice but to go.

The air in the room was very stale, and the tension was high. Nobody wanted to be there. The brothers did not want to face this issue head-on, much less face their own homophobia. I hoped nobody would notice my unease. I greeted no one.

When Alexander walked into the room, all eyes were on him. I took another deep breath before he began talking, as if I were about to receive an injection at the doctor's office.

"Brothers," Alexander began, "I called this emergency meeting to dispel some of the rumors I've been hearing about you guys having an issue with pledging gay men. If this is true, then you must also have an issue with *me* as a brother. So, brothers, what's going on?" Alexander looked out into the faces with one eyebrow raised, waiting for their response.

No one dared speak, so Alexander prodded some more. "What's going on here? Will someone please have the balls to speak up?"

And so began the downward spiral. Gato began by telling Alexander that although he had tried to set aside the gay issue, it was impossible to change 20 years of socialization, and he couldn't help his feelings. Other brothers quickly agreed. They talked about the importance of image and their clout on campus. Then they started talking about how they never really felt close to Alexander.

The attack was merciless. The brothers said his being a part of this fraternity was more about his involvement on campus, his grade point average, and what he could do for the fraternity. To them, Alexander was not a brother; he was always "the gay guy" they tried to tolerate. There was nothing he could do to make the brothers look at him any other way.

Every time Alexander spoke, he made direct eye contact with me. I could tell that he wanted me to speak out. He knew I was closeted and that this incident affected me too. I tried to gather the courage to speak. But I was afraid the brothers would reject me. I'd devoted a lot of energy to hiding my true self and avoiding that reflection in the mirror. I was not going to let it all go to waste. Surely somebody else would speak up. The meeting fell quiet, and Alexander stood alone in the haunting silence.

Then Alexander called me out in front of everyone. "Carlos, you're being very quiet. What do you think about all of this?"

I looked up at him in horror. My worst nightmare was coming true. I felt everyone's eyes on me. My heart beat furiously, and beads of sweat drained from every pore in my body. The brothers were all waiting for my response.

"Al-Alex," I stuttered. "I agree with Gato." My voice trembled with every syllable. "I mean, you ask us to be tolerant and understanding of you all the time, but you need to practice what you preach." The words came too easily. I was justifying the homophobia I had felt toward myself for a long time. "This is tradition, this is how we were raised—take that into consideration. We can't do away with our values with the snap of a finger." I looked away, wringing my hands, and continued.

"I love the fraternity too much, and I'm not going to lose respect on campus or potential members because they think we're a gay fraternity, or we only pledge gay members. Sorry, Alex, but you need to see it our way as well."

Alexander's eyes reddened with rage and filled with tears. I took another deep breath and tried to give him a look to say, "I'm sorry— please understand." I could tell that he did not accept my apology. I was so ashamed of my cowardice—and I had kicked him while he was down. I regret it to this day.

Shortly thereafter, Alexander dropped out of the fraternity. He had every reason to leave. On the other hand, I stayed deep in the closet. With Alexander gone, there was an opening for another "gay brother." The fraternity actually pledged one of the interested gay men. He was told that we were very tolerant and his sexuality was not an issue. All the brothers chose this new gay member supposedly because he truly represented what our fraternity stood for—though he was the more masculine of the two who had shown up at the informational meeting.

My fraternity valued brotherhood above all else, but I would often wonder why that didn't apply to a gay brother like Alexander. Ironically, I was chosen as president of the fraternity for the next two years. I was the voice of the fraternity, the leader.

Alexander was the true leader. He confronted the trials of the fraternity and lived his life openly and honestly. Still closeted to my brothers, my friends, and my family, I sometimes venture onto the Internet to find other gay Latinos. These men are also hiding behind different masks: varsity jackets, thug wear, and—of course—Greek letters.

Cry Freedom

by "Eric Joseph," Hofstra University, New York

I watched my family mourn my Uncle John. Seeing him lie motionless was unreal—I was used to seeing this dark, bearded, flannel-clad man drinking his beer at the dinner table. All of us wept as if our hearts were broken. Although my family was far from religious, the powerful chords of funeral hymns and our memories of John simply overwhelmed our souls.

When I got the call about Uncle John, I could not believe the news. I hung up the phone and turned to my coworker and said flatly, "My uncle was just found dead. He slit his wrists in some hotel room in Jersey." I had not seen my uncle since I was about 14 years old. His death was a complete shock.

The church was just minutes away from where he had ended it all. As I looked at John's body, I thought that my mother could have been sitting in the front row of that church, destroyed over the death of her son. The phone call and now seeing John lying there made my thoughts drift to a time when I considered taking my own life.

In the fall of 1995 I was a completely different person than I am today. Back then I lacked self-confidence and was not ready to leave Long Island. I stayed close to home and decided to attend Hofstra University. At 18, I stood a towering 6 foot 4, with a physique that had filled out nicely. My boyish face, dark hair, and good looks made it easy for me to attract women. I wanted nothing more than to blend in.

When I attended Hofstra, I was already dating a sophomore girl on campus named Vanessa. She had magnificent green eyes, flowing auburn hair, and unforgettable breasts. Gay or not, I loved boobs. Vanessa was sweetly innocent, and we always had a wonderful time together. On top of it all, we had a great sex life. Dating Vanessa gave me an extra edge on campus. I had feelings for her, but she also was the perfect excuse to keep my closet door firmly locked.

By the time I was a junior, everyone on campus knew me. I was vice president of my fraternity and the resident assistant of my building, and I hung out at all the regular college bars. Nobody questioned that I was heterosexual. I was popular and funny, and my sexual desire for men was not remotely detectable. Most of the guys assumed that I was most certainly banging any girl I was talking to. Here I was, this awkward and shy kid thrust into the alpha-male role. I acquired a reputation as a player. I didn't deserve it, but I liked it.

Almost subconsciously, I decided to join a fraternity to cover up my attraction for men. I also hoped the extra time commitment would distract me from the growing pain inside me. Truth be told, rumors of hazing always turned me off to the idea of going Greek. I never really planned on joining a fraternity. But after getting to know some of the men from the Sigma Phi Epsilon fraternity, my perspective changed.

One night I was out at McHebe's, a Hofstra watering hole that soon became my Friday afternoon party spot. The name of the bar was derived from the name of its two owners—an Irish guy and a Jewish guy. I was shooting tequila with Mike and David, two older Sigma Phi Epsilon brothers. Both of them were telling me about the fraternity and had bought me a drink or two…or eight. After a long conversation with Mike and David about "Sig Ep," as the fraternity was often called, I began to wonder about this whole frat gig. *Could this be me?* I asked myself.

The Sig Ep guys had a 40-man chapter, which was large for any Long Island campus. The men had a lot going on: They were involved in all areas of campus life, from noble philanthropic endeavors to heavy partying. They were the most diverse bunch of guys I had ever met. Sig Ep even had three Turkish brothers.

Nevertheless, being ordered around like a slave as a fraternity pledge was not my idea of fun. *I do not need friends this badly,* I thought. Then I learned about the fraternity's Balanced Man Program, which was worlds away from the typical *Animal House* hazing rituals. I soon figured that the brotherhood of a fraternity was the opposite of what I had imagined. What Sig Ep fraternity stood for, and the friendships I had begun to develop, led me to decide to pledge.

I was still dating Vanessa at the time, and my soon-to-be Sig Ep brothers were, shall we say, inspired by her. Vanessa would wear this tight black shirt with a clear plastic heart-shaped window in the center of her chest, revealing just enough cleavage for boyhood imaginations to run wild. Vanessa's breasts made me the envy of the chapter and were a favorite topic among the brothers. I often heard comments like "You're the man" and "Just wait for all the other sorority girls you'll bag." I responded with a smirk and a nod. Deep down I thought, *I could never let my fraternity brothers down. I could never let them see who I really am.*

Then I met Rob. He was a brother in another fraternity on campus, Sigma Chi. He was a good-looking guy who suffered a bit of a Napoléon complex—he was short in stature but loud. Everybody knew who Robby was, probably because he had slept with half the student body. Rob was openly bisexual. Supposedly he had been hawking me since I was a pledge. One night at McHebe's he made his move. Rob followed me into the men's room, where he could finally get me alone.

"You're pretty hot," he said from the urinal beside me.

"Excuse me?" I replied as I turned to the sink to wash my hands. My face was red with embarrassment, anger, and bashfulness.

I turned back to see Rob watching me in amusement. "Is that the best pickup line you've got?" I asked coyly. He smiled and said, "I've seen you around before." He looked me up and down. I was not sure if I liked this or not. But I was transfixed. "I've been waiting for you to finish pledging," he continued, "and I think we should hang out." The next thing I knew, Rob's tongue was down my throat. I was terrified of being caught but strangely wanted more. The thrill of being naughty was a total turn-on.

Rob actually turned out to be a cool guy, and despite my fear of being labeled gay by association, we had fun together. Before long, Rob and I were into a regular routine. We would meet on the weekends at a bar on campus called Hofstra USA, where one Greek organization or another was always throwing a party. We would both proceed to get trashed with our fellow brothers and other college friends. Once everyone was drunk enough, Rob or I would give the signal to the other. We would then sneak out separately and meet back at his dorm room, all the while hoping that none of his roommates would catch us together.

My sexual encounters with Rob frightened me, and my feelings became more intense. I was enjoying the sex but I was not at all ready to have the label *gay* or *boyfriend* attached to me. Plus my own brothers were starting to ask the obvious questions. "You guys are spending an awful lot of time together, Skee-lo," they'd say, addressing me by my pledge name with raised eyebrows. "What's up with you and Robby? I heard he's gay." The risk was too high. I decided to cut all ties with Rob.

That is, until a few months later. Rob resurfaced, but this time with a girlfriend named Laurie. Together they were an ominous, alluring pair. Laurie wore black leather thigh-high boots and skirts that did not leave much to the imagination. She was painted up like a whore and had floppy tight red curls reminiscent of Raggedy Ann. "Pleasure to meet you," Laurie squeaked in her trademark voice when Rob introduced me. Laurie was simply fabulous, and Rob had laid his plan wisely. Laurie was introduced into the picture to provide me with cover and to allow for a threesome. Rob was successful in his ploy and received his compensation in full that night.

Soon Laurie and I had become very close. She introduced me to all her queer friends, and I was suddenly thrust into the glittery world of gay, bisexual, and questioning people like myself. Laurie took me to Chameleon's, a gay bar outside of Long Beach. I simply loved it. That was just the beginning for both of us. Laurie and I served each other well, as she was not exactly straight either. Laurie was my "beard," and likewise I was her "purse." My fraternity brothers assumed Laurie and I were a couple, and so did her sorority sisters. I don't think her sorority would have given her a bid otherwise. We were the perfect heterosexual accessories for each other.

Now, let's not forget the gay 10% rule. My pledge class had 17 guys, which increased our fraternity to about 60 guys. Statistically, the 10% rule would mean that there were five or six gay brothers. The 10% rule was dead-on. There was not only closeted me; there were about five more gay brothers. How much the straight brothers in the fraternity knew about us gay brothers was vague at best. Luckily for me, my sexual escapades with Vanessa, Laurie, and other girls solidly slammed my closet door shut for most of my straight brothers.

For the other gay brothers, this was not necessarily the case. The "potentially gay" or "thought to be gay" brothers were often alluded to by certain brothers as something that Sig Ep should be ashamed of or disgusted by. The word "faggot" was definitely thrown around a little more often than I could tolerate. I never joined in the gay bashing, but I still lacked the courage to defend myself or say anything. The experience only pushed me deeper into the closet and deeper into shame about who I was.

I began to contemplate suicide my junior year, even though I was successful as a student leader on campus and vice president of the fraternity. I thought that being gay would be the end of the world and would bring everyone close to me more shame than I could imagine. When it came down to it, I would rather have died than have anyone—my family, my fraternity brothers—know I was a "faggot."

The date I chose was Sunday, February 22, 1998. That was a particularly rough weekend for me—I felt acutely lonely and depressed. I was waiting tables at Pizza Hut that night, and on my dinner break I walked across to Rite Aid to purchase the aspirin I planned to use to kill myself.

Once I got home to my empty dorm, I swallowed the first 10 pills and began writing a letter to my family. Stopping and starting the note many times, I hunched over my desk wondering, *Am I really going through with this?* I tried to talk myself out of it several times but ended up in the same frame of mind. Ten more pills down the hatch and the spark of a match to light the joint I rolled to cope with the nausea. I continued to write, first listing several details, including that I wanted my brother to have my car and where I had some money to leave for my mother. Tears welled in my eyes, and I gagged as I tried to swallow 10 more aspirin.

I finished my letter, left it on my desk with the lamp shining on it, and lay on my bed. Over the 30 minutes it took me to write the letter, I had ingested 55 maximum-strength aspirin.

The light was bright when I woke the next morning. I opened my eyes not sure if I was dead or alive. There was a horrible ringing in my ears. I decided to dial poison control. The person I talked to insisted that I be admitted to a hospital immediately and offered to send an ambulance. There was no way I was going let my failed attempt at suicide become campus news. I decided to drive myself to the nearby hospital.

My inner drama queen emerged at this point. I grabbed my keys, ran feverishly out to my car, and drove to the edge of campus toward the hospital. Considering all the aspirin I had put into my stomach, I was surprised that I had no urge to puke. But then suddenly, waiting at a stoplight, I had the urge. I opened the car door and let the vomit flow. When I finished, I shut the door and made a left turn. A few blocks later, waiting at the next light, I opened the door a second time and puked. I noticed the same car was behind me and saw me spew again. Two more traffic lights and two more gag sessions: Stop, open door, puke, shut door. After having seen this four times now, the man in the car behind me got concerned and walked up to my window.

Boom, boom, boom—he pounded on my glass. "Are you okay?" he said.

Wiping the tears from my eyes, I managed to reply, "Almost there," and sped off as the light turned green.

Finally I got to the hospital. I parked the car in the middle of a helicopter landing pad and stumbled towards the E.R. entrance. A security officer yelled from across the lot, "You can't park your car there."

I shouted back, "Then you park it," and threw him my keys.

The nurses hooked me up to every hose and tube you can imagine, including a catheter in my penis. My system had already absorbed the aspirin, so it was too late for a stomach pump. I was served a charcoal cocktail: thick, black, and disgusting. I could barely keep the atrocious stuff down. Sipping that was supposed to neutralize the drug in my body.

Despite all the drama, I never told my family, my fraternity, or my friends the real reason for my attempted suicide. My closet door remained tightly locked.

The day after I was discharged from the hospital, I jumped back into my routine working at Pizza Hut. That night one of my coworkers accidentally hit the panic button behind the cash register. Responding to the alarm call, to my delight, was a police officer by the name of Mangrove. I had always thought cops were hot in general, but Officer Mangrove was sizzling. As I tended to my customers, I noticed his roving eyes scan my body and land on my apron. My interest in him must have been apparent too. He raised his head to lock his eyes with mine. Shyly, I diverted my stare and went quickly back to work.

Officer Mangrove left the building after he confirmed the false alarm. I watched him through the window as I wiped down one of the booths, and our eyes met again. We exchanged smiles. Sure enough, Officer

Mangrove found an excuse to come back into Pizza Hut and flirt with me some more. His first name was Craig, and we made plans to meet after work in the parking lot of the Starbucks down the road.

At midnight I completed my work shift and showed up at Starbucks. Craig had changed from his police uniform to street clothes and was waiting for me in his beautifully restored blue '66 Mustang. I parked next to him and accepted his invitation to "jump in his ride." He made me laugh and feel good about myself. I desperately needed someone to talk to—someone who could just listen to me and not judge me. I could tell that Craig was hoping for a lot more action than he got that night. The sex would have been wild. Instead, Craig gave me exactly what I needed. In tears I poured my heart out to him over the next hour.

Craig and I continued our friendship and met often over the next couple months. Our long discussions gave me hope for the first time in my life that being gay was okay. I could identify with Craig, and that helped me to accept who I am. Craig also introduced me to some of his coworkers and friends who were all comfortable with being gay. These men were exactly the kind of community I had been searching for. *I can be gay and okay if they can,* I thought. My closet door crashed open.

"Animal" and "Chopper" were the nicknames of two of my closest fraternity brothers. I decided they would be the first brothers I would tell that I was gay. There was no turning back. Telling "my boys," as I liked to call them, was one of the hardest things I've ever had to do.

That summer I invited "Animal" and "Chopper" over to my apartment to barbeque and get a buzz on before we went out to the bars. While we were sitting outside, drinking beer, I said, "Hey guys, remember when I was out with the flu for that week in February?" I took a deep breath. "Well it wasn't the flu, and I'm not straight either." Silence. I had managed to completely stun my brothers.

"What?" they exclaimed in unison.

I had their complete attention and slowly began to explain. It felt so good to be coming out of the closet. When I was done, they made me promise that I would never do anything so stupid again. Then, both brothers made it clear that all that mattered was our brotherhood—not my being gay. This strengthened our friendship tenfold. The sense of freedom I felt was immeasurable.

To my surprise, both "Animal" and "Chopper" agreed to go that night to a gay bar in the Village called Pieces. I could not believe it. We rounded up

12 other friends, piled into three cars, and headed into Greenwich Village.

The night out at the bar was outrageous. I was in great spirits, then all of a sudden I was in tears. Out of nowhere, I heard my name called for the karaoke contest. I wiped away my tears and got up on the stage with my boys "Animal" and "Chopper." We all sang like idiots for the crowd. And wouldn't you know it, we actually won! I could not have asked for a better coming-out party.

Over the next year, I said the words "I'm gay" many times to my family, friends, and fraternity brothers. Every time I came out to someone new, I felt that much stronger—I was developing a sense of freedom. My need to uphold some pseudomasculine straight image gradually disappeared, along with my depression. My fraternity brothers stood by me throughout the process. Coming out was the best thing I ever did, and the responses I received from those who loved me were more positive than I ever could have imagined. I was finally free of all the lies. I was a new person.

From the Haze

by "John Welles," upstate New York

I joined the most *Animal House* fraternity imaginable, where hazing was considered an important measure of character. I had received bids to join a couple of fraternities, but I chose the one with the most diverse mix of athletes and burnouts, jokers and fighters, urban sophisticates and hicks. There were the scions of Park Avenue millionaires as well as first-generation college attendees. Despite these differences, what impressed me was the brotherhood. That is what I desired.

College was my opportunity to forget the past, and the fraternity was the vehicle. I chose a small liberal arts college in upstate New York. The campus was a beautiful combination of green quads and fields that pushed up against a promontory above a vast lake.

The fraternity house was an enormous 19th-century mansion built by a corrupt Civil War profiteer. The brick facade faced the main street, and a large back lawn covered a rise above the lake. Inside the fraternity house there were incredible formal rooms with fireplaces and warrens of bedrooms. For generations the fraternity house had been the setting for parties, dances, concerts, secret rituals, fraternal traditions, camaraderie, and general mayhem. While the house was always decked out for special occasions, it was normally littered with cups and cans, cigarette butts, pizza boxes, BB pellets, and liquor bottles. Then there was the odor: a mix of old beer, whiskey, smoke, vomit, dog shit, bleach, and sweat.

Just a few months earlier I had considered coming out, but now I was prepared to sacrifice honesty for the chance to live in a mansion on a lake with 33 of my best friends. I had my whole life to be gay, but you can only be in a fraternity once.

There was only one other fraternity on campus that had admitted a gay pledge. It was the least popular and most ridiculed fraternity. Many people joked that only fraternities who were desperate to fill their membership gave bids to gays. Quite frankly, gays were not welcome at the other fraternities. One fraternity even went as far as remaining exclusively white while the other fraternities had begun accepting blacks in recent years. My fraternity was on the forefront of the racial issue; I knew that being gay would not be acceptable, however.

As a pledge I was amazed at the camaraderie and closeness of the brothers. These guys truly were best friends and rarely hung out with people, besides girls, outside the fraternity. It was not that the brothers were not liked on campus—just the opposite. These men were campus leaders as well as sports team captains. The brothers simply had more fun together. Even in bad times they were there for each other. When the mother of one of the brothers passed away after a long illness, the entire brotherhood traveled five hours to New Jersey to attend the funeral services. That's what brotherhood was all about. As a pledge, I wanted to prove myself worthy of this bond.

Exotic rumors of hazing rites circulated among the pledges. These acts ranged from eating vomit to being sodomized with lacrosse sticks to fucking a goat. The pledging process lasted two and a half months. Both psychologically and physically draining, it was calculated to keep us reliant on the brothers and each other. We never knew what to expect at any time. We suffered injuries and humiliations along with intense bonding rituals. The average night consisted of standing in place for up to 10 hours while being lectured by brothers who were in various states of inebriation.

The rituals contained a lot of homoeroticism. One night the entire brotherhood got naked and had a huge "beer-slide" across the floor of the basement. A beer-slide is basically an improvised Slip 'N Slide across linoleum on a mix of lathered dish soap, beer, and urine. The slide ended abruptly and dangerously at the base of a large wooden bar. The edges of the linoleum tiles were unfriendly to the genitals. The only thing funnier than a brother trying to bandage his damaged penis was hearing his cries when he had to remove the bandage the next day.

Finally my dream of fraternity life came true. I was initiated into the fraternity and swung—or ranked—second in the pledge class of 19. I was so proud: Among all these straight dudes, a closeted gay guy had ranked ahead of all but one of the pledges.

When I moved into the fraternity house, I accepted the fact that I was not going to have much of a personal life. Still, I would fantasize about sexual encounters with men—even brothers. I knew these were wild, unrealistic yearnings, and I fought their intensity. I had some minor relationships with girls to curb my desires. There were a handful of openly gay students on campus. I had a class with one guy named Ezra. He was a stereotypically flaming gay guy. Ezra was not my kind of guy, but in class I would enjoy his company and his laughter. Ezra's honesty and openness shamed me but also reinforced my reluctance to do anything to betray my brothers.

I began to do cocaine, acid, mushrooms—anything I could find, really. If I was busy doing drugs and getting drunk, no one bothered to ask whom I was hooking up with. And anyway, my friends were engaging in the same behavior. I could not imagine my life without my brothers. They were my family.

By my senior year, I was finally ready to tell a few brothers. The first one was Alex, the captain of the soccer team. He was widely respected in the fraternity and was politically pretty liberal for upstate New York. Alex and I had been close friends since freshman year. I hoped he would support me.

One evening Alex and I were sitting on a balcony drinking bourbon as we watched the sun set over the lake. Down below one of our brothers was driving golf balls into the water.

I said, "Alex, I've wanted to tell you this for a while, but…um…ah, you know how you like girls?" I took a breath and paused. "Well, I like guys."

Alex smiled at me. He understood. Alex said he knew my secret and I was still his friend and brother. He even asked, "So what dudes are hot in the house?"

The courage I got from telling Alex helped me tell another brother.

The next brother I chose was named Russell. He was a tough redhead and my frequent partner in crime in the bars downtown. We had become close after many nights drinking and partying together. One night on our way back from the bars, we were walking along the shore when we stopped for a smoke.

"Russell, I got to tell you something," I said.

"What, Welles?" Before I had a chance to reply, Russell said, "You're not going to tell me you're a fag or something?"

I was stunned, remained true to my intention.

"Actually, dude, yeah, I am," I stuttered.

"Holy shit!" he shouted. Then he asked, "Are you sure?"

We depleted the six-pack of beer we had brought from the bar as we talked. Finally he said he didn't have a problem with my being gay. Again, I had been honest, and he was still my brother.

The spring of 1999 was bittersweet for many reasons. I had finally come out to a few of my brothers, and graduation signaled that my time in the fraternity was over. None of us wanted to graduate and leave—especially me. Brotherhood without deceit felt incredible.

Conflicted

by Jamison Keller, California State University, San Bernardino

You're pathetic! Look at you cowering behind that phony fraternity man image, a voice inside me said. *If they really knew who you were, they would probably bash your head in and leave you somewhere in the hills behind campus.*

Stop, I pleaded silently as I walked down the narrow aisle toward the stage. Being selected Greek Man of the Year was the highest honor a fraternity man could receive. This was supposed to be one of the happiest moments of my entire college career. I was miserable.

Katie was sitting in the second row with all of her sorority sisters. She was my beautiful girlfriend—blond hair, blue eyes, gorgeous body, and huge boobs. Katie and I had been together for two years. We always had magnificent sex together. Surely that meant I wasn't gay. Katie and I were the perfect Greek couple: I was fraternity president and she was our fraternity chapter sweetheart.

On stage, our Greek advisor motioned for me to take the microphone. My fraternity brothers screamed my name and beamed with excitement—yet another Sigma Nu had won this distinction. My brothers were considered the all-around gentlemen on campus—the best mix of leaders, jocks, and face men. We strove to be better men living by our fraternal values of "love, truth, and honor." My conflicted voice told me I was not worthy of these values or this honor. I desperately wanted the voice to go away.

One night soon after Greek Week, Kyle, one of my closest fraternity brothers, spent the night at my place. He was definitely one of Sigma Nu's face men. He was tall, had dark hair, striking eyes, and a well-built physique. He was the ideal model for the all-American fraternity man. He was also the friendliest brother in the fraternity and made people smile. Since Kyle lived far from campus, he often spent nights at my place and even borrowed my clothes. That night I cried myself to sleep. I was deeply disturbed by my sexual attraction to Kyle.

Our White Rose Formal was a few weeks later. For the event we traditionally had a huge dinner and party at a nearby hotel. The formal would mark the end of my life as an undergraduate fraternity brother in Sigma Nu. I continued my heterosexual act and tried to share the excitement my fraternity brothers felt. Inside, however, I was being eaten alive by my emotions and by the guilt I felt because of the lies I told myself and others. That evening I was named Sigma Nu Man of the Year and inducted into the Sigma Nu Alumni Hall of Honor. Again I performed my phony fraternity man role perfectly, accepting the honors with appreciation while secretly believing I was unworthy of them.

After the fraternity formal, I went to my hotel room and cried. Tears were streaming down my face when I looked up to find Kyle watching me. He sat on the floor beside me and put his arms around me. Kyle told me that he understood and let me cry on his shoulder. I wondered what exactly he understood.

One night a week later, I was alone in the fraternity house finishing a paper. As I recalled how good it had felt to be in Kyle's arms, I typed the words "naked men" into the Web browser. I jumped from one link to another. Then I clicked on a gay chat room. I was terrified but incredibly horny.

Searching online I found several pop-up ads for "live all-male" phone chats. For the next hour I just listened as men spoke while they jerked off. It was like a drug—I was so high and excited. At the start of the second hour, I reached inside my shorts. The release I felt was unlike any I had had before.

Phone sex and online porn became my only means of satisfying my sexual urges. Every night I would rack up $300 or more in phone and credit card charges. And, of course, I felt horribly guilty and was constantly afraid of being found out.

Graduation day came and went, and I struggled to figure out my next step in life. I was accepted to a graduate program in higher education. Still, I believed that my desire to be a professional fraternity advisor was foolish. Who would hire a gay fraternity advisor?

The graduate program in higher education I chose to attend was at a nearby private Christian university. My last hope was that religion would ease the stress of my internal war. Somehow I hoped God would deliver me from my feelings toward men. The first semester everything seemed to work as I had hoped—I didn't have time for much besides my course load and getting settled into a new place.

Since it was a Christian school, we began each class with a prayer. One day as we began our personal leadership class, a guest lecturer led the class in a prayer followed by a devotion. The lecturer encouraged us to speak aloud to ask God for assistance and guidance with pressing matters in our life. I remained silent. I heard my classmates mention things like making it through midterms and papers, family security, and success in life. I silently prayed that God would lead me out of my unhappiness.

The next day I decided to see a counselor. I finally chose to deal with my sexuality and find acceptance. I spent an entire year learning about myself and facing my fears. There were horrible days when I would blame the world for making me gay and other days when I was happy to be who I am.

I realized that to find real peace I was going to have to tell my fraternity brothers. The values of Sigma Nu fraternity are love, truth, and honor. Still, I was afraid my fraternity brothers would reject me because I had been lying to them for so long.

One night I invited my seven closest brothers to go barhopping on Sunset Boulevard in Los Angeles. One of the brothers, Alex, arrived early. I admired his sensitivity and understanding. As we sat in my apartment waiting for the others, I went to the kitchen to get us each a beer. When I handed him the cold bottle, I just blurted out, "Alex, I'm gay."

He looked at me with a long inquisitive gaze and said, "Oh, I kind of figured that. It's cool." Then he opened his beer and took a drink. He went on to ask some questions and reaffirmed that he would always respect and look up to me.

I could not believe that I told him I was gay and it was simply "cool." I had dreaded this moment for such a long time, and sharing my true feelings with Alex gave me the courage to tell more of my brothers.

Soon the other six brothers arrived at my apartment. When I had their attention, I announced, "I'm gay." Like Alex, the brothers were "cool," and to my surprise, most of them had always guessed. After we talked for a while, they said, "Now can we get to the strip already?"

At that moment, I realized I was no longer alone. The bonds of brotherhood enabled me to accept who I was as a gay fraternity man. Today, as an openly gay Greek advisor, I have seen many students who struggle with their own internal conflicts. They ask, "Can my fraternity accept a gay brother?" The response of your fraternity to that question is the true test of brotherhood.

1 John 2:10

by Jonathan Scaggs, Indiana University, Bloomington

Alpha Sigma Phi could never be classified as a typical fraternity at Indiana University. We never had more than 40 members, and during my involvement we functioned without a fraternity house. Our motto was "We are more than bricks and mortar," and that held true for almost every brother. When Alpha Sigma Phi was founded at Yale University in 1845, it was a literary society, although many of its secrets and traditions are based on Christian principles and ideals. Perhaps the most common thread that wove the tightly knit group together was our shared faith in Christianity. Almost everyone identified as Christian—in fact, the fraternity had only one Jew during my undergraduate years. So when my pledge class was recruited and initiated, most of us had been involved with Campus Crusade for Christ. Every Thursday evening we could be found leading the Bible discussion at the weekly crusade meeting. In addition, I could also be seen singing in the praise band called Vandy.

The Indiana University campus revolved almost entirely around Greek organizations. One of the qualities of Greek life I was attracted to was the simple fact that thousands of men had done the same thing before me. It was the place to be. The Greek system included athletes, 4.0 students, and many of the student government leaders. So after my first year I decided to go through the traditional men's recruitment for fraternities. Many of the fraternity houses welcomed us with blaring music and by playing pornography on a big screen. Most fraternities were a blur of smoke and beer. There were the houses that were strictly Jewish, and of course, the "face frats" where everyone looked like they shared the same DNA. Only one fraternity made me feel at home: Alpha Sigma Phi. These men were not like the rest. The brothers made me feel comfortable and part of something special.

Joining a fraternity was exhilarating. The best part was becoming one of the founding fathers of the newest fraternity on campus. Within our first two years we won the major campus singing competition twice and earned countless awards during Greek Week. Soon after, we finally gained our charter and became Chapter of the Year. Alpha Sigma Phi stood proud for brotherhood. Never could there be a bond stronger than Alpha Sigma Phi—25 young men striving to breathe life into the fraternity and a cause they believed in.

Still, the fraternity cultivated an atmosphere of compulsory heterosexuality: There was always pressure to date and socialize with women. Many times when the brothers would get together off campus this was apparent with remarks like "Don't forget to bring the *girls!*" Such comments were constant reminders that I felt different inside. I was still closeted, but I was aware of my sexual inclinations toward men. The fraternity environment made me realize that I would always be the odd man out. Nevertheless, I grew to love the guys in the fraternity—in a platonic sense. As the fraternity chapter consultant would tell us: "You can love your brother—you just can't *love* your brother." This comment was meant for everyone; however, I always felt like the joke was directed straight toward me.

Later that year, Alpha Sigma Phi fraternity finally had the opportunity to have a house on fraternity row. It was a huge three-story U-shaped brick building. Each wing had six rooms, and the house could easily hold over a hundred men. Our fraternity crest was etched in glass on the front door to welcome everyone. The library off the formal lounge was filled with towering bookshelves full of out-of-date academic class tests and books. The lounge was devoid of furniture, which had been stolen by the former occupants. The dining room had broken chairs and large holes in the walls from rowdy fights. Still, the brothers were proud to have our first house. We cleaned up the hallways, put the legs back on the pool table, painted our rooms, and made the mansion our home.

There was plenty of space for everyone. I chose room 46, not because of its size but rather the location. There were five other rooms on the same wing, but they were all unoccupied. Secluding myself allowed me to be a part of the fraternity and still hide relatively easily. Outside my room I had to be Jon the straight guy. Inside I was free just to be me.

I had a steady boyfriend named Mike. As far as the fraternity was concerned, we were just best friends. Mike was the all-American guy, with blond hair, blue eyes, and a smile that could take your breath away. He was a member of another fraternity on campus. Most nights I would leave my fraternity house to hang out with friends off campus or to go over to Mike's fraternity house. Mike was also in the closet at his fraternity, and we were always scared of being discovered together. Mike was in a "face frat," so being homosexual would have been highly frowned upon. Fortunately, we had the same classes, so we saw each other every day. Every so often I would sneak Mike into the house and we would spend the night together. Of course, we would wake up early so he could sneak out the back without anyone seeing him.

Living in that house taught me many things: how to share one fridge with 15 guys, how to steal the neighboring sorority house's furniture at 4 A.M., and of course how to deal with a broad range of people. The fraternity had an eclectic mix: Republicans, Democrats, musicians, football jocks. I found myself being the diplomat in many situations. Deep down, I believe some of the brothers had probably figured out I was gay, even though I would have flatly denied it.

Many of the concerns I had about being gay were from my beliefs and Christian teachings regarding homosexuality. Most ultraconservative churches preach that God hates homosexuality, making their case by citing one Bible verse, Leviticus 18:22. It says, "Thou shalt not lie with mankind as with womankind. It is an abomination." Of course, I figured my fraternity brothers, from a similar conservative Christian background, might share this belief. Many of us attended church together regularly.

One Sunday evening one of the fraternity brothers, Adam, strongly urged us to try a new church. He had been going to this church and figured some of us would like it. Adam was definitely more conservative and had a devout religious faith. I never really thought much about his motive before that Sunday.

Then came the moment that changed everything for me: After a few minutes there I finally understood why Adam asked us to come to this new church. In big letters the caption on a video screen read, HOMOSEX-UALITY: A CHOSEN SIN. I sat there and thought that I was truly fucked: My cover was blown. Somehow Adam—and who knows how many others in the fraternity—knew my secret. I slowly gathered my things and got up to leave the church. In the foyer, Adam confronted me.

"Hey, Jon, where are you going?" he said.

"Uh, I just remembered I have a test tomorrow," I replied.

"Oh, well, I thought you might be interested in this topic," he said.

Trying not to explode, I asked, "Adam, why did you ask me to come here? Was it just for this topic?"

"Jon, I just thought you might like this church, and it did have a little to do with the topic."

"Why tonight? Just go ahead and ask me what you want to know," I said, almost yelling at Adam.

"I just know you have some gay friends, that's all. I don't need to know anything else, man," he said. His voice sounded conciliatory.

"Well, my friends and my life are my business, so stay out," I said.

From that moment on I constantly worried about who knew that I was gay. My discomfort in the fraternity grew steadily. Brothers would stop to ask where I was going at night or whom I was going to be with. It was a living hell for a young closeted gay man. Room 46—my closet—had been my sanctuary, and now the door was propped open. I wanted to live my life outside the fraternity without anyone watching. And I desperately wanted a fraternity brother to stand beside me and tell me that God loved me for who I am. Being gay was not a choice; that is the way God made me.

Several weeks later a few of the brothers were hanging out at the fraternity house when the topic of homosexuality arose. Weekly conversations on the Bible were common in the fraternity, and I assumed speculation about me had inspired the brothers to address this particular topic. The argument over what the Bible actually says was arduous and long. Many other brothers came by to join the discussion and offer their strict, one-sided interpretation of the Bible. Out of nowhere, brother Sam—a short, scrawny guy with curly blond hair—stood up and handed a Bible to one of the brothers who had been most vocal in his opposition to homosexuality.

"Find where it says God hates gay people in here," he demanded.

Everyone sat there in shock. Sam was the total opposite of me. He was an officer in the Air Force, very politically active, and most definitely not gay. We had never been close in the fraternity. I was confused as to why Sam was taking a stand for gays. *What does he have to gain?* I asked myself.

When the argument was over, we all went our separate ways and I ended up in room 46 alone, as usual. Surprisingly, many of the brothers had had their notions about Christianity and homosexuality challenged. Maybe, like what Sam had said, this was a sign from God that now was the time.

That night I tried to sleep for hours before I finally got up, walked down the stairs, and knocked on the door to Sam's room. He groggily opened the door in his pajamas, but I could not manage to get a damn word out of my mouth. After about a minute of Sam staring at me, I opened my mouth and softly stuttered, "Th-th-thank you."

"For what?" he said.

"Well, for um...for just saying what you did earlier," I replied.

"Jon, I know you have gay friends in choir and stuff," he said yawning. Sam finally remembered the earlier conversation.

"No, Sam," I interrupted, "it's more than that. Sam, I'm gay."

I expected Sam to react in shock. Instead, he said, "Um, okay." His response seemed totally ordinary. Then he said, "Can I go back to bed now?"

Sam said good night and closed the door. I stood outside his room for over five minutes. What I had done began to sink in. I could not believe I had told a fraternity brother that I was gay. Never had I admitted that aloud to any other person. I was perplexed and relieved at the same time. My coming out to Sam was met with acceptance. The only weird thing was that I knocked on his door at 3 A.M., and then after I told him he merely wanted to go back to bed. Still, his response was comforting, and I had taken the first step in coming out of the closet. A couple of weeks would pass before I chose to share the news with the rest of the fraternity, my family, and the rest of the world.

Reactions were mixed but overwhelmingly positive. Coming out to my fraternity became a fun puzzle to put together. Piece by piece, one by one, I let the brothers know. Sometimes I would tell large groups all at once during dinner in the cafeteria downstairs. Other times I mentioned it in everyday conversation. For instance, one brother was telling several of us about something weird that had happened on campus. To drive home his point, he said, "Man, that's so gay."

I leaned into the conversation and said, "No shit? Me too," and then went on with my business, leaving the brothers in complete shock.

As I had expected, many of the brothers had already thought that I might be gay. Several brothers said, "Thank God! We already knew." Others were more reserved, and I always allowed ample time for them to ask questions. Some were even excited when they asked about Mike and I confirmed that we were more than best friends. Room 46 was no longer my hiding place. Coming out opened my heart to faith in the brotherhood.

I left a close fraternity brother named Jeremy out of my coming-out puzzle. I had hoped he would learn the news from someone else. Jeremy was one of the many high school football stars who lived in the fraternity house, and he had the confidence to back up every single pound of his muscle. Maybe I was worried about telling Jeremy because his mood could change from friend to foe in 2.2 seconds or less. Finally, after much consternation, I worked up the courage to tell him. I walked into his room and noticed he was alone watching television.

"Jeremy, can I talk to you for a second?" I asked.

He turned his head slowly from the television. "Uh, what do you want?"

I reached for the remote, turned off the television, and sat down. I turned to Jeremy and said, "I know you've probably heard the rumors by now."

"What rumors?" he replied.

"The, uh, rumors about me," I said.

"Oh, well, I didn't know what to believe. I just wanted to hear the truth from the source, but yeah, I've heard some things," he said, looking concerned.

"Ah, well they're...they're true," I said.

Jeremy looked down at his hands and said, "Jon, you know I don't agree with homosexuality, but you are still my brother." Then he looked up and said, "Love the sinner, not the sin."

"Well, I appreciate your honesty," I said as I reached out to shake his hand.

"Just know that if you need anything, I'll be here. Nothing has changed." Jeremy grabbed my hand and hugged me. I left with the biggest grin on my face.

Many of my brothers were incredibly positive and showed their support in every facet of my life. The fraternity continued to grow stronger, recruiting more men. My being the token gay guy in the fraternity was short-lived, however: Over the next two years other men in Alpha Sigma Phi came out about their homosexuality. Having other openly gay fraternity brothers was wonderful.

There were challenges among the brotherhood, but the real backlash started outside the fraternity. Other fraternities considered our house the gay fraternity on campus. The atmosphere changed rapidly among the younger brothers, who were largely in charge of the leadership of the fraternity; they were more homophobic than previous brothers. They felt it necessary to demean gay people in order to defy the "gay fraternity" label. "Faggot" became a common word thrown about the house.

I always felt that as the first out gay brother I had a responsibility to the others. The older brothers who had joined me tried to defuse the situation with the younger brothers as best they could, but before long the other gay brothers chose to leave the fraternity. But I remained. Sometimes I blame myself for being too forgiving of the name-calling and joking. Gay jokes never really bothered me; hell, I can tell some of the best gay jokes. But I knew that some of the gay brothers were uncomfortable.

The lessons I learned from Alpha Sigma Phi fraternity are definitely a central part of my life today. Fostering friendships with men, gay or straight, is an essential aspect of a healthy male identity. The fraternity and my relationships with those 25 men changed my life. The brothers immediately loved me for who I am and gave me strength to find that same love and acceptance from God. When I look back on my fraternal experience, one particular Bible verse comes to my mind. I hold this verse close to my heart when thinking about my fraternity brothers. 1 John 2:10 reads: "Whoever loves his brother lives in the light, and there is nothing in him to make him stumble." My fraternity brothers live in the light, and they forever will not stumble.

Sexual Monsters

by M. Ducoing, Cornell University, Ithaca, N.Y.

As a boy I had often been warned that there were monsters in my closet. Images of horrible creatures with terrible growls, sharp teeth, and frightening and distorted expressions would fill my deepest thoughts. The monsters I experienced in college were real—and different from the outwardly grotesque beasts that had haunted my childhood. These creatures were beautiful, masculine, and desirable. They represented the true horror I had still to discover.

My nightmares began during my freshman year at Cornell University in 1999. It was a time of mixed emotions. Fear, anxiety, excitement, and confusion all danced in my mind. I was thrilled to finally have more freedom. The campus was enormous, and the possibility of disappearing among the masses was real. Dozens of freshman dormitories dotted the north campus in a vast labyrinth of students, rooms, and mortar. October brought the constant cold that seemed to last as far into the future as anyone could bear.

Despite the overwhelmingly expansive campus and the frigid temperatures, I was determined to find my place and fill every moment with some sort of activity. Drama troupes, protests, water polo, tennis, school clubs, it didn't matter: Every moment I had to be busy, every moment needed a distraction of some kind. But even as I succeeded in filling my time, there was still a nagging emptiness that I knew from high school. It had been a constant burden. All my life I had made a pact to hide an important detail of my life: I was gay. At times my world would become suffocating and lonely. Keeping busy was the only way to alleviate the despair. It was only a matter of time before the eerie scratching of monsters at my closet door became overwhelming.

My freshman year had been full of pointless meanderings, but my sophomore year was full of new discoveries—including my decision to rush a fraternity. I had avoided the prospect of Greek life my first year because the stereotype I had of fraternities was that they were insidious social clubs that bred alcoholism, violence, and most important, a lust for women. I was afraid that such an environment might uncover my secret. Nevertheless, I had become lost and alone, disappearing, fading into a black abyss on campus. At my huge university, I had been told that a fraternity was a good way of finding a niche, a sense of belonging.

Several of the fraternity houses simply reinforced my preconceived notions. I felt like Rush Limbaugh at a Democratic convention. I was shy and awkward while the fraternity men were obnoxious and conservative. I was on the brink of giving up, not having found what I had hoped for, but then I came across an old high school acquaintance, Kevin. He always had a certain magnetic appeal; he was a large guy with dark hair and a round face. His sense of humor was a mirror image of my own. So when he mentioned his fraternity, I was immediately interested, even flattered.

Kevin invited me to a fraternity party at his group's annex that evening. I spent the rest of the day preparing mentally for the excursion. Nevertheless, I had no idea what to expect when I arrived. The annex was located in a remote part of the college town and was used for overflow housing outside the fraternity house. I had to wander through a *Blair Witch*-like forest behind a dorm to get there. It was dark and eerily quiet. Not until I was standing on the porch was I certain that I was in the right place.

Kevin greeted me and instantly introduced me to several of his brothers. They all seemed more than happy to hang out with me. Phil was the first to swoop down and introduce himself. He was a short, thin brother with a large nose and sunken eyes. His hair was buzzed short, and he wore a sweat jacket and loose jeans. Even though we had different majors and interests, I was able to talk to him comfortably for over an hour.

"You live here?" I asked, pumping the keg for my fourth beer.

"Yeah. It's cool, I guess," Phil replied.

"Yeah, it's, um, it looks nice. Who else lives here?" I fumbled. The annex was a hideous hole-in-the-wall apartment on the first floor of a dilapidated building. Thankfully I had just gotten a tetanus shot.

"Rick and Jake live here too. It's cool 'cause we're all different years but we get along well," Phil replied. "I actually prefer living in the house, but there's not enough room."

"Really? What's the fraternity house like?" I asked.

"Much nicer. You can always be sure to have a great time there. Everyone's all over the place, and there's always someone to hang out with, something to do. All the brothers become close." We both surveyed the annex, looking at the disarray. I wondered if they had considered painting the place or just accidentally burning it down to collect insurance. "It's definitely an experience living in the house. That's why we need brothers to step up and live out, so we all get a chance. I'm moving back in next semester."

The fact the fraternity house was full and everyone seemed desperate to be there reflected highly on the brotherhood. I asked, "But it's still cool living in the annex?"

"Yeah, I've got brothers here too, and we all go together for dinner at the fraternity house every night anyway. We just want to be there; it's not really this place. No matter where we live, the fraternity house will always be home. Some of my best memories are with brothers in that fraternity house. A bond, a closeness, something I'll take with me forever."

Hearing Phil speak so passionately about the fraternity house and the bonds of brotherhood made me desire the same closeness. I wanted those memories, those experiences, and those brothers who could make my life better, more bearable. I had finally found a place to belong on campus.

Over the next few weeks I spent plenty of time at the infamous "fraternity house." I had decided that I would go through fraternity rush. Somehow being there made me feel revitalized as I learned more about the brothers. The house itself was not what made the fraternity; rather, the brotherhood represented the soul of the fraternity. Each of the brothers contributed unique qualities that were magnified in the context of the fraternity house. I was impressed with what I saw: a group of men who cared for one another like family.

Then came my most embarrassing moment at a rush party. I was drinking some random alcoholic shots in Mark's room. He was a relatively small brother, a Jewish guy with a razor-sharp wit. After the vodka shots came the White Russians, evidently Mark's specialty. I had never had one before, but as soon as I chugged my first one I knew the introduction would be remembered the next day.

By the time I got downstairs from Mark's room, I was drunk and rowdy. David, another brother, was already stumbling about the dance floor with a half-empty bottle of Clan MacGregor's. David was tall, with a shaved head and quite a large build and green tattoos all over his body; one was prominently displayed on his stomach. Those tattoos were often visible since he rarely had a shirt on, and tonight as soon as the booze flowed he tore off his shirt. His breath always reeked of gin, whiskey, vodka, or some other lethal combination.

We all danced, the music pumped, and the room began to spin faster and faster. The drinks and the dancing all blurred together. I woke up on the fraternity house couch the next morning, completely disoriented and covered in vomit. My mind exploded with possibilities, and my body went numb with horror. *What had I done?*

In horror I fled as quickly as I could. It was 6 A.M., and by 6:20 I was hiding in my bathroom, gasping for air, with a dreadful hangover.

After several hours of recuperation and a hearty breakfast, the horror began to fade away. At least I had only humiliated myself. Then as I walked to town, I ran into Kevin. He looked at me with a knowing smile.

"How are you feeling this morning? I woke up and you weren't on the couch anymore," he said. "Where did you go so early?"

"I…I needed to go home; it was obviously a bad night. I had fun, but I think it got out of control," I said. I was still recovering from my hangover and wore an expression of humiliation.

"You know you threw up on one of my brothers," he said.

"What?" I was shocked. I had no memory of this.

"You know you threw up on one of my brothers," he repeated.

Falling to my knees out of dramatic embarrassment, I pleaded, "Oh, my God! Tell me you're kidding." I almost burst into flames on the spot.

Evidently I had puked all over David with a stream of vomit that the makers of *The Exorcist* would be proud of. Oh, my God—David. He was much bigger and could easily beat the shit out of me. I could feel the half-empty handle of a Barton's crashing down on my head over and over again.

Two days later at the next party, after I had crawled out of my hole of fear and humiliation, I was quickly taken to David's feet like some kind of sacrificial offering. Instead of slaying me, he laughed.

"You threw up on me, dude."

I stared in horror. "Yeah, I'm a tool, it was…" I tried in vain to defend my horrific actions.

"It's cool, man. It's happened to me before too. In fact, I think it happened to me a few minutes ago." He smiled drunkenly, putting his burly arm around me. There was definitely gin on his breath. "I like you, but don't throw up on me again. It's my turn."

Whew! Everything was all right. For a moment I thought he was going to throw up on me right there. He didn't. His message was clear: You are forgiven, but maybe one day the favor would be repaid. The fraternity brothers, including David, made me feel welcome and undeniably part of something bigger than myself.

That semester I began pledging the fraternity. The experience was torture for the pledges and fun for the brothers. Several events that involved only brothers and pledges helped bring us all closer together, to create a familial bond of brotherhood. All the events and experiences were within the context of tradition. Only we knew and shared those experiences. To an outsider this appeared to be an absurd idea: Who cares about tradition when I'm trapped in a small room and screamed at for hours? We were becoming brothers, sharing our best moments as well as our humiliating disgraces with the backdrop of the ageless traditions and secrets of the fraternity. Along with these experiences came an undeniable connection. Together we would be there to help one another: to fight, to care, to support, and to simply be a brother. I began to find my place.

The brotherhood, it was made clear, did not end with graduation from Cornell. No matter how far you went, your link to the fraternity was eternal. Homecoming and other alumni events were perfect examples. Alumni like Teddy, a short but muscular Asian man, were widely considered to be the epitome of brotherhood. When I first met him I knew why. After going out of his way to meet me at my first homecoming fraternity event, he pulled me aside, wineglass in hand, and made his position clear.

"How much do you want this?" he asked.

"Want what?" I wondered aloud.

"To be here, to be part of this fraternity, this brotherhood?"

"Badly. It's been rough, but I want to be here," I said.

"Best decision of my life. All this, you always have—no matter what. You're always a brother, always. Most people never have that. One day soon you'll understand."

I had promised to be one of them, a brother—a promise I had already broken. I had repeatedly promised myself to lie to my brothers about who I was. I could not tell them I was gay because of my self-hatred, fear, and shame. The slightest hint of my truth might shatter the brotherhood. As each day passed my confusion and instability grew. No matter how hard I tried to deny my sexuality, the monsters in my closet did not ever let me forget. They whispered in my ear, "What's worse, the lie or the truth?"

That sophomore year I not only found the fraternity, I discovered the gay underground: the Internet. Online there was a vast network of gay men who were searching for many different things—friendship, conversation, relationships, and of course, sex, which seemed to be the main impetus: I wondered if that was all anyone was looking for online. That three-letter word was on my mind too.

The fraternity offered me unquestioning loyalty and brotherhood, but I needed more. I needed to find my soul, my identity—who I was. The Internet offered an outlet to explore the unknown gay world anonymously. The whole process seemed harmless. I figured that I had suffocated in my closet for far too long; the Web would be my escape. The wall of fear that had surrounded me cracked, if only ever so slightly.

For the first two weeks I lived in anxious trepidation. I explored various rooms, including "older for younger," "bears," "oral only," "top for bottom," "bottom for hot hung top" and countless others. Any fantasy or fetish was at my fingertips. Each time, a tingling of anticipation grew inside me and my breathing got heavier as I logged on—quietly, terrified of what would happen next. My screen names were reflections of my interests, attributes, and desires. They were always different but somehow also the same: "waterpoloboy19," "fratboycu19," "fitguy20," along with a dozen more. The online world was about fantasy. Hard bodies and muscular physiques were coveted, and masculinity was an absolute necessity. Frat boys were solid gold too. The opportunity to live out my sexuality became available in the hidden online closet. I broke through my silence and began chatting. I opened the closet door just a crack, only to unwittingly let the monsters out.

Many men who were out had pictures online; you could use these to gauge general attractiveness. For those who were closeted, there were no pictures. Instead there were descriptions, stats that would give height and weight, hair and eye color, skin tone, and cock size. Some men included stats like "six-pack abs," "hot body," "bubble butt." Descriptions of sexual interests were included as well: "Top looking for oral, vocal bottom" or "Just looking to give head." The most misleading were the sexual acronyms: "VGL ISO hot bttm for fun—LTR oriented." The translation was: "Very good-looking in search of hot bottom for sex, but also looking for a boyfriend."

For two weeks I fumbled through chat rooms, barely speaking to anyone. My first hookup was a dreadful horror. His description read, "VGL 23 y.o., junior, 5 foot 9, 155 lbs., hard body, 6-pack, bl/bl, discreet white frat boy." I met him late one night at a corner near my fraternity house. He drove up in a black Ford Mustang. Instantly, I knew I had been a fool. The monster in front of me had lured me out of the closet just long enough to reveal his ghastly demeanor. He was clearly over 60; his skin was withered and diseased. His teeth were jagged and cluttered in his mouth. I ran away as he cursed into the night. Lucky to be alive, I did the only logical thing: I went back online. It was like an addiction; I succumbed to the online world being my only way to be gay.

Another late night, under the shadow of the luminescent computer screen, I discovered CUFratStud02. The green glow opened another possible doorway and the prospect of someone like me. The terror from my first encounter had worn off. Finally I had acquired the confidence to figure out who was real, with probing questions about academic majors, fraternity involvement, campus activities, and classes. If they were not real, I would surely catch them in their lies. And most important, I eventually needed a picture. CUFratStud02's stats read:

6'3", 200 LBS., MUSCULAR, BROWN/BLUE, CLOSETED FRAT GUY

The fact that he played rugby enticed me further. I breathed heavily and typed:

CUSTUD19: HEY, WHAT'S UP MAN?
CUFRATSTUD02: YO. WHAT ARE YOU UP TO?

CUSTUD19: CHILLIN. SEEIN WHAT'S GOIN ON...WHAT ABOUT YOU?
CUFRATSTUD02: U LOOKIN MAN? YOU SOUND HOT.
CUSTUD19: COULD BE COOL. INTO?

After a few more minutes of chatting and after my questions were satisfied, he suggested we meet, anonymously and discreetly. The risks were high. We were both closeted men in fraternities, and we could potentially know each other. The thought was frightening. We decided that nobody should know who we were, not even ourselves. The location for our hookup would be the bathroom in the basement of the campus library; isolated, quiet, with a lockable door. We were both risking a lot, but quite frankly we were horny. We chose the most ridiculous time: the middle of the day, when other students were sure to be everywhere. But I could taste the sex; I could taste him even before I smelled his masculine scent, even before I felt his body. I could picture us together all in my mind. My first real sexual encounter would be perfect. I only hoped that he would not be another vile monster.

I arrived in the main public bathroom of the library. I was to stay in the far stall and wait for him to enter the adjacent stall. Then he would give the signal. I would then go to the private bathroom and wait for him to come. As I sat on the toilet in the semicrowded bathroom, sweat streamed down my forehead. I took deep breaths, trying to calm my apprehension. Suddenly the toilet next to me was occupied. Under the stall a hand came and directed me to go. I touched his hand to confirm as I opened the door.

The halls were fairly empty, but like roaches people appeared everywhere. I went into the private bathroom and flushed the toilet, as the last occupant had forgotten. It still reeked unpleasantly. I turned off the light. The room was moist and strangely quiet in the desolate dark. Then there was a knock. The door opened and a sliver of light fell onto the tiled floor below. I was still in the shadow. He secured the door lock behind him. For a few moments we fumbled clumsily like two blind men. Fears that he was like the previous creature plagued my mind.

Suddenly, we touched. His sweatshirt was soft. I could tell from his shoulders that he was huge, as I had imagined a rugby player to be. He was strong, with bulging biceps and a hard muscular upper body. He wrapped himself around me and kissed me frantically, as if we were lovers reunited after a war. His jeans felt cool as I ran my hands along them, massaging them. He unzipped my pants. His lips were soft. I could tell, even in the shadows, that he was beautiful. I could only think how fortunate I was to find him. He forced me out of my pants, cautiously stopping every other moment to hear a phantom sound outside. He dropped to his knees. I put my hands on his broad thick shoulders, occasionally grasping the back of his head. The pleasure I experienced next was a mixture of physical and emotional ecstasy. This new, amazing man of my dreams could not be described in words alone. After groping and intense mutual oral sex, we both climaxed. In the dark there was an awkward, anxious moment. Then he pulled me to him and held me tightly. It was a forceful hug, one a family member might give after an intimate moment. Then he let go, touched my hand, and left. The door closed behind him. His departure made me realize that I had never once heard him speak, only groan in pleasure. All alone, I stood there in the cold darkness.

We met three more times on campus anonymously. Each time the cycle was the same: burning anxiety followed by pure ecstasy, then the cold loneliness afterwards. We had so much in common and had shared intimacy, but we knew nothing about one another. The paradox was odd, and I had hoped that as fraternity men we could support each other. None of my fraternity brothers had any clue as to my secret sexual encounters, and the pain of my lies grew steadily. I lived two separate lives.

One afternoon, mesmerized by the computer screen and drunk with a desperate desire for more than anonymity, I initiated a new conversation with CUFratStud02. I typed:

CUSTUD19: CAN I FINALLY MEET YOU?
CUFRATSTUD02: DO YOU WANT TO? IT'S DANGEROUS.
CUSTUD19: I WOULD FEEL BETTER ABOUT IT. I'VE REALLY LIKED OUR MEETINGS. I THINK THEY'D BE EVEN HOTTER IF I COULD SEE YOU.
CUFRATSTUD02: WHEN? I'M NOT TOO SURE ABOUT THIS, I LIKE ANONYMITY.
CUSTUD19: I'D FEEL BETTER. I DON'T USUALLY MEET GUYS I NEVER SEE. HOW ABOUT TOMORROW AT 2:00P AT THE LIBRARY. THE STACKS ON THE SIXTH FLOOR. IT'S USUALLY EMPTY.

I braced myself for his response to appear on the screen. I wanted this so badly. I needed to be honest and acknowledge who I was. But I feared I would scare him off. He gave me such relief to know I was not alone.

CUFratStud02: I'm not sure. Ok. Bathroom on the sixth floor, 2:00p. This time we'll keep the light on.
CUSTUD19: OK. COOL :-)

Eager with anticipation, I went to the sixth floor. All night I had envisioned how he looked and how we would be able to support one another. Our self-disclosure would bring us together and take the sex to a deeper level. Twenty minutes passed, then an hour, and he had still not shown up. I went back online to find not only that he had stood me up but that his screen name had been abandoned. His closet door had slammed in my face. Afraid, he had slithered back in.

The loss sent me into a tailspin, hurt my self-esteem, and fueled my self-hatred. I had hooked up with someone I had never seen, four times, and now I would never know him. He could sit next to me in class; he could be at the next fraternity intramural game. I would never know. I stopped knowing myself that day. Deep in my closet my monsters howled, "What was I becoming?" I had no idea.

Fraternity life had become a wild party. A keg stand, a wine stand, shotgunned beer, whatever it took. Double-fisting the whole night was commonplace. I would often drink so much that I was awake late into the morning, but I only could remember what happened before 11:30 P.M. the night before. Being drunk was a liberating escape and became my way of coping with the fraternity and my fears.

The irony was bitter and devastating: Brothers had stood by me in so many ways, but my secret, deeply hidden, kept the fraternity at a distance. I couldn't get the support I longed for, the acceptance I needed to break free of my closet.

Sometimes I would fill one-liter bottles full of rum and soda and drink them all night long. For a while that helped me fit in with the fraternity. My brothers seemed to genuinely care when I was the partyer: I was a "good" dancer, but after a case of beer I was a "great" dancer. My reputation had become that of the fun or crazy drunk. I made others laugh, often purposefully, to drown my inside. The idea of occasionally hitting on women to hide my homosexuality seemed more plausible when I was heavily intoxicated.

All that changed after losing CUFratStud02. I was in a dangerous spiral. Online I met more men, trying to form connections after sex, but each time was more of a failure than the last. Fraternity life became a drunken depression where my actions became steadily aggressive and angry. Brothers would whisper about how mean I had become. Some feared me and avoided me during parties. Alcohol ruled my life.

In my mind I had begun to destroy my straight world, so I had to salvage the online gay world. Sex lost all emotional value—it was meant to exploit, to use another for pleasure. Sometimes I would set up multiple encounters online; the hotter and nastier the better. Rarely did I ever look in the mirror and see anything I recognized. I had become what I had despised: I was the monster now, hideously deformed and armed with deceit and lies, merely a prostitute who traded my self-respect instead of money for sex.

Kevin often came to my room to rouse me from my computer. I told him I was very sick and could not be bothered. He persisted: "Come on, man! We're going out. It'll be fun. You have to come—we haven't hung out in days."

"I'm sick. I can't go," I sputtered.

"No, you aren't," he said, laughing.

"Shut up!" I turned away, hiding my face from the light. My body now stank like a carcass. "Go away," I demanded angrily.

"Dude, what's wrong? Do you need to go to the hospital or something? You've been like this for a while," Kevin replied.

I responded only with a callous grunt, though inside I was screaming for help. I was weak and broken, and worse, I was ashamed.

My brotherhood in the fraternity suffered, my grades suffered, and I was crying incessantly, alone. Crying was a routine: right after breakfast and right before English class. Often I cried until my eyes stung. Loneliness and sorrow led me to withdraw from both my worlds. I fell asleep for days at a time. Only occasionally I would wake myself long enough to drag my body to the bathroom or take a sip of stale water. I finished out the semester in a constant state of depression. I still drank, but now I was alone without my brothers. Somehow I had survived the semester, but I was a shell, a corpse.

That summer I managed to get away and attend a summer internship program. I almost didn't go, but I hoped the experience would be a refreshing break from the insanity. My roommate at the internship, Ryan, was a gay guy, a chunky black fashion designer from Brooklyn. He was flamboyant and more confident about his identity than anyone I had ever seen. Instantly I knew we would be friends. I was not out in any way, but for some reason Ryan lent me the courage. After two days, as we lay there talking before bed, I told him that I was gay. It was the most liberating moment of my life. The release granted me the acceptance I so desired. My closet door flung open.

I told others in my summer internship program as well. Each responded with complete acceptance, praising me for my courage. Their compliments made me feel special, like I was indeed someone. My self-hatred was replaced by a sense of self-worth and pride. We partied harder than I ever had before, but now I was happy again: I smiled, I laughed. For a month and for the first time in my life I was open and honest about who I was.

"Why are you not out at school or at home?" Ryan asked in his lovable way.

"I don't think I'd be accepted. I can tell they're homophobic. They'd hate me," I growled, an emptiness in my words.

"So you're judging them before they judge you, huh? Why do you get that power? Why is it okay for you to do that?" he asked, indignant but still with his friendly smile. I shrugged.

"If you want to be accepted, you need to accept them. If you think they won't accept you, it's because you haven't shown them it's okay, that you're still a good person, a great person," Ryan said, pausing. He smiled. "I don't hang out with losers." We both laughed. "You don't need friends who don't like who you are, but at least give them that chance or you're as bad as they are. Maybe worse," he finished. He made perfect sense, and I knew I was ready now.

I promised Ryan and my other new friends that I would return to campus and come out to my fraternity. I was prepared for possible rejection and to move out; either way, I knew I had Ryan and others who would stand by me. No matter what, I had found the confidence to know that I was indeed worthy of the brotherhood. Now the fraternity brothers needed to prove that the brotherhood was true.

For two months after returning to school I remained closeted. Then came the fateful evening when I mustered up my courage. After a party I brought one of my brothers, Matt, into my room. He and I were close because we had been fellow pledge brothers. He had always worried about me and genuinely cared for me as a brother. We sat, drank, and laughed together. In previous conversations I had asked him what he thought of gay people. He had always been indifferent but generally supportive. So, in a drunken yet eerily calculated moment, I let go.

"Matt, I'm gay," I blurted. There was a pause. He choked on his beer.

"Really?" He laughed.

"Really," I laughed back, uncomfortably.

"Really?" He repeated, head tilted. I nodded.

"You're for real. You're not playing a joke on me?" he implored, wondering about my real intentions.

"Really!" I said resoundingly.

Back and forth, we went on for some time. Nevertheless, when Matt left that night, I knew everything would be okay. He gave me a hug that showed our brotherhood was true. The brothers cared for me regardless of my sexuality. His acceptance had begun to bring my gay world and my fraternity world together. The ball was rolling.

Word spread to several other brothers, who began asking about my sexuality. I decided I would be honest from this point forward, no more lies. The brothers would almost always ask when they were under the influence of alcohol, I suppose to take the edge off. Kevin asked me at a sorority crush party, where, after several tequila sunrises, he confronted me indignantly in a whisper.

"Why couldn't you tell me you were gay?"

"Why didn't you ask?" I replied.

"I was afraid. Imagine if I'd been wrong?" Kevin said.

"But you weren't. I was afraid too."

"I'm just upset you didn't tell me, that you didn't feel comfortable," he said.

"I was afraid of your reaction. I had a lot to lose if you didn't understand."

I told him how difficult the process of coming out had been for me. I told him that I had truly wanted to tell him, but losing his friendship would have been too much rejection. I could not have handled that kind of loss. He finally understood and reached out to give me a long hug.

"You're still my brother, man," Kevin replied.

That night Kevin learned my secret, and he still called me his brother. Finally, I was free—my closet door was opening and the monsters were slowly fading in the light. The entire fraternity soon learned that I was gay. While not everyone "understood," they did accept me as a brother. This acceptance gave me the strength to form a campus support group for closeted gay fraternity and sorority members. My hope was that CUFratStud02 and other Greeks might one day find the same acceptance.

From time to time I am still confronted with monsters, online and in person. But the way they affect me has changed. No matter what my fears, I have a fraternity of brothers who are there for me. I can stand up to any monster. I am no longer afraid.

Rushing Out

The Pledge Jersey

by Clay Cunningham, Texas A&M, College Station

I still remember the overwhelming sight of a thousand rowdy, crazed Texas A&M fraternity men hollering, whistling, and chanting cheers for the fall 2002 pledge class. I stood there momentarily stunned and eager with anticipation along with hundreds of other new pledges. The huddled crowds of over a dozen fraternities seemed immense from atop the steps of the Administration Building, with its Corinthian columns lining the front entrance. In the A&M Greek rush tradition, hundreds of pledges then rushed down the 20-plus steps into the crowd. Every pledge had on his pledge jersey, fraternity letters emblazoned across the chest, proudly declaring his allegiance. The fraternities each held high their 15-foot Greek letters. I was indeed claimed that day, and it felt really good. We were all still drunk or hungover from the night before, but it didn't dampen our spirits. The experience was simply awesome, exhilarating, and one that I will never forget.

I was 19 years old and a junior majoring in political science. I had graduated early from high school, and I looked more like a junior in high

school than one in college. At 5 foot 10 and 145 pounds, with a buzz cut
and naive blue eyes, I was hardly an intimidating character. I was out as
gay on campus, but I would not say I was proud. Some would have called
me "straight-acting." I had marched in the Houston Gay Pride Parade, I
knew about Fire Island, and I had read books on gay theory, such as *The
Culture of Desire*. There are many things that describe me as a person,
and being gay did not seem to be one of my more important qualities.
Up until my junior year I had been involved in campus organizations,
but never in a fraternity. Texas A&M is not a liberal oasis of understanding when it comes to the acceptance of gays. Frankly, I did not know what
to expect from a fraternity in that regard. However, I did know that I
wanted the friendship, the camaraderie, and the promise of brotherhood.
Desperately, I tried not to stereotype fraternities into the conforming
mold of Texas A&M. I had hoped that I could find one fraternity where
being gay would not matter. I wanted the men to get to know me for who
I am, not just for the gay label. I decided to give fraternities a chance.

Along came rush week with its parties, socials, and mingling with all
the fraternity guys. I had made my mind up: I was rushing, and nobody
was going to stop me. Each night the fraternities would have their events,
and it was hard to know exactly how to act in any given situation. In a lot
of ways the rush events were like mingling at a gay bar. Groups of people
would be talking; one person would introduce himself and start up a
conversation. Each guy was seeing if the other would be a good fit. I
found it engaging, and though I was nervous I worked hard to open up,
relax, and be myself.

I quickly realized there was a general format to the conversations:

"Hey, what's up? My name is [insert frat guy's name]."

I would respond: "Hi, nice to meet you, [insert frat guy's name].
I'm Clay."

"Nice to meet you. So what year are you, Clay?" He would ask.

"I'm a junior. You?"

"I am a senior, but I rushed later too, when I was a sophomore. So
what made you decide to rush?"

"Well, you guys always seem to have a lot of fun, and I want to get
more involved on campus, so I thought I would check out fraternity life."

Mostly we talked about football games, A&M politics, what their fraternity is like, and what sports I played. I avoided talking about girls, dating, sex, and the guy I was seeing at the time. Like I said, I wanted the

men to know me first as Clay, then later as gay. I was determined not to let homophobia get in the way. Sometimes they would ask questions or make comments about girls, and I was careful to maneuver around the question while managing not to lie.

"So, Clay, how are the ladies treating you these days?" one fraternity guy asked.

"Well, it's been a while since I've had a girlfriend, but I hear a lot of guys meet girls through their fraternity parties and stuff, " I replied and smiled.

"Yeah, the chicks are a lot easier after a few glasses of the trash-can punch. You'll have no problem," he joked and jabbed me in my side.

I did do a lot of sidestepping and used tactics of distraction to get through all this. Despite my attempts to not stereotype the fraternities, I worried that if I admitted to them I was gay, there was absolutely no chance they would accept me. I hoped I was wrong. But all the while I was thinking, *What if they knew?* or worse yet, *What if I look gay?*

One fraternity stood out in particular—Tau Kappa Epsilon, otherwise referred to as "TKE," pronounced "teke," for short. Even before rush week had officially started, the men of TKE called and invited me to the A&M football game. They did not have the typical clean-cut, polished, preppy look of the other fraternity guys. Their fraternity house was reckless and looked like it was on the verge of being condemned.

That Thursday night before rush week I met Peter, the rush chair. He was a constant fixture throughout the entire week. He took me under his wing from the start and personally took me on a tour of the fraternity house, making sure I felt comfortable, always ensuring that my beer wasn't getting warm. He made me feel good about TKE, and he was a really cool guy. As rush chair he was second in command only to the TKE president. I thought he was the perfect guy to have on my side to get me into the fraternity.

I ended up going to the Texas A&M football game with TKE. It was a blast: We all stood there yelling the A&M Aggie cheers, wearing our maroon shirts (A&M's official color), and singing the Aggie fight songs. The TKE brothers had an "anything goes" attitude, so being among them gave the football game an extra edge. Of course, charismatic Peter was there making sure everything went smoothly. He stood next to me and somehow knew just what to say to reassure me about my future fraternity experience.

"So what do you think about TKE?" asked Peter above the noise of the crowd.

"I like it. Y'all seem like pretty cool guys," I replied instantly, then paused, grinning. "But the whole thing about getting a bid is kind of weird."

"Well, don't worry about that, you'll get a bid," he reassured me.

Despite the stereotypes about fraternities, TKE seemed diverse and accepting. There was a Jewish guy, an Asian guy, some Hispanic guys, and I thought, *Why not a gay guy?*

And I was right. Why not a gay guy? I soon got a bid from TKE, just as Peter had said. It was a huge surprise, despite Peter's reassurance— something I never thought would happen to me at Texas A&M.

I was thrilled with my bid and had no doubt that I would join the fraternity. All the men seemed eager to have me as a brother, and the gay issue had not come up once. I had done it: No lies, just Clay, and they liked me for who I was—no gay stigma or gay label to cloud the issue.

All of the TKE brothers celebrated at the fraternity's "invite only" dinner and after-party. The dinner was more formal, with all of us dressed in khakis and collared shirts. Brothers sat around the tables eating, talking sports, joking, many of us asking about the big day to come. Only guys who were to be pledged the following day were invited and treated to the formal dinner.

Virtually all the guys had brought dates except me. I made a joke: "Everyone I asked had to wash their hair tonight." The brothers all laughed, and I don't think anyone thought anything of it. I ate a big fat meaty steak and a baked potato, then went on to the after-party, held at one of the brothers' houses. All the TKEs and their dates came to celebrate with the guys who had received bids to join the fraternity. We played drinking games, filling our red plastic cups from the refrigerator-turned-keg while music blared and the men bonded. I was on cloud nine, high on fraternity life.

Before the night was over the rush chair, Peter, pulled me aside to talk to me. "Hey, come with me for a minute to my truck," he said nonchalantly. I followed him, and when we got to his truck he pulled out a crisp new white T-shirt with the Greek letters TKE sewn on the front. He handed it to me and said, "Put it on."

I did, and we walked proudly back into the party together. Some of the fraternity brothers saw the jersey and responded almost as if they objected to me wearing it. "He's not supposed to have that until tomorrow," one said to Peter.

"Dude, chill, it's no big deal," Peter replied sharply.

As the rush chair, Peter had the power to decide much of the fate of the pledges. For whatever reason, I still don't know, Peter had decided to give me—only me—a pledge jersey that night. All the rest of the guys were to get theirs the following morning. But as drunk as I was, I didn't really think anything of it.

I woke up the next morning passed out on the floor of the apartment of one of my future TKE brothers, still half drunk and devastatingly hungover from the night before. Still, my stupor was eclipsed by the excitement of the TKE jersey and the day to come—Bid House. Little did I know what excitement was in store.

All of TKE was at the Administration Building for the start of Bid House. It was the site of the ritualistic display of fraternal bliss and a powerful show of the force for A&M's fraternities. This is a time I will never forget. The rest of the brothers had received their pledge jerseys, and together we waited to run from the top of the steps of the Administration Building down into the chanting of thousands of fraternity men, all whooping and hollering for their respective new pledges. TKE pledges were accepted with open arms, cheers, and yells by our fellow brothers as the 15-foot tall Greek letters, Tau, Kappa, and Epsilon, led each of us to our newfound brotherhood. I was now a TKE.

All in all, the TKE brothers seemed like standout guys. I thought that these guys could be friends and extend the lifelong fraternity promise of brotherhood. I believed that somehow they knew I was a little different but were still cool. *I don't have to be just like them—I can be who I am,* I told myself. Nevertheless, I had hoped that perhaps one day I would come out to the fraternity. Maybe they would just figure it out and not care. They liked me as a brother—as Clay—not gay. I still remember thinking, *This is the happiest day of my life.*

Exhausted, tired, hungry and still hungover, I decided to head back to catch my breath at my off-campus apartment. I was all pumped up from Bid House and knew that a weekend full of fraternity parties would be on the way.

Remember we're in Texas when I tell you this, but that afternoon the brothers met at a college hangout known as the Dixie Chicken. Many students call it "the Chicken" for short. The bar is about as country as you can get and even featured a caged rattlesnake. I found it easy to identify the brothers in the bar: We were all still proudly wearing our TKE Greek-letter pledge jerseys. The jersey meant a lot to me, and I had taken it off only to take a shower. I was not going to part with that jersey and would wear it until it reeked of sweat and beer.

I headed toward the back of the Chicken, where Peter was playing a game of pool with one of the girls who always hung around with the TKEs. Peter was an imposing 6 foot 3 and had probably been a lot cuter earlier in his college life. The toll of the fraternity drinking routine had not been kind to him. He was always a very charming guy; his smile and all-American frat boy look made you feel like you could let your guard down. While I didn't have any kind of physical attraction to him, I did feel more camaraderie and more of a special connection with him than with any of the other brothers.

I sat on the bench next to the pool table. Peter immediately approached me as if he had something to tell me.

"You know there's more than one Clay Cunningham at Texas A&M," he said with a grin, standing in front of me, leaning against the weathered wood that lined the walls.

"No, I didn't know that," I replied with a smirk.

"Yup, there is." He patted me on the shoulder. "He's in the Texas A&M Gay and Lesbian Association here," he said, as if the point was of little importance to him.

Grinning from ear to ear I responded, "I think there's only one Clay Cunningham at A&M."

"I know, I know," he said. He placed his pool cue beside me along the bench and asked me to follow him to the back of the bar.

I thought nothing of his request and followed him without question. His tone was calm and charming as usual. He wasn't angry, nor did he seem bothered by the way I replied to his comments. As it got darker toward the back of the bar, I thought, *Okay, this is easy…now they know me for being Clay, and at least one of the guys knows that I'm gay. Perfect.*

The back of the Chicken was empty, just Peter and me. We sat across from each other at an old weathered and splintered wooden table with names and dates carved in it. The benches on either side of the table were equally rugged, much like Peter's appearance that day. His breath smelled of alcohol. He was sweating a little, but perhaps it was just warm. His TKE jersey, like mine, had been through a rough 24 hours, and it appeared that Peter had probably not taken a shower since last night.

Peter sat there glaring at me. Then, with an apologetic sigh, he slowly managed to explain that I could not be in the fraternity. I was in complete shock and asked him to repeat himself. He said again that I could not be in the fraternity and went on to say that it would ruin TKE's reputation at A&M to have a gay guy.

I sat there stunned, gripping the bench with my hands. I was upset, heartbroken, utterly destroyed by what Peter had said. I began to beg, pleading with him to change his mind and just give me a chance. Peter looked down without knowing what to say other than what he considered to be the final verdict: "No gays in TKE."

"Isn't there any way?" I pleaded again.

"No." His answer was firm. He then compared the situation to an incident a few years back when the fraternity had a black guy who tried to pledge. When it came down to a vote, many brothers said that they would leave the fraternity if he was allowed to join. The verdict: "No blacks in TKE."

My jaw dropped. I grabbed the bench tighter in frustration, anger, and despair. My voice rose. "I can't believe you're actually saying this. This is unethical. This is wrong."

Peter said it was quite simple and became noticeably angry. "The principle is one of sacrifice—a few for the good of many." His tone became increasingly sharp. "As I said, a gay brother would ruin TKE. The only way is to kick you out now."

I became even angrier and struck back. "If you do this, your fraternity is ruined anyway. The first thing I'm going to do is go to the university; then I am going to my lawyer, then to the press," I said. "This is wrong."

Peter stood up and shouted, pointing at my chest, "Take off your pledge jersey." He could see I was frightened by his sudden movement. He was going to literally rip the fraternity letters off me. My pledge jersey was the one material connection that I had to TKE. Peter knew it would be over by taking the jersey—he was taking away my membership in TKE.

"No," I said firmly, standing up, both of us straddling the bench. At this point he looked as if he might punch me at any moment.

"Take off your pledge jersey," he said again, even more enraged. He yanked his own pledge jersey over his head and stood there, bare-chested, sweat dripping all over his face, glaring in rage. I didn't know what was next. I stepped back from the bench. I thought to myself, *Oh, fuck, he's going to beat the shit out of me.* Before I had time to say anything, Peter pulled it back on and threw an undershirt he had been wearing on the tired wooden table between us. I stepped farther away.

He then demanded, "Now take off your pledge jersey and put this shirt on. Do it!" I saw the hate in his eyes, and it was clear to me that Peter was not going to let me leave the Chicken with my TKE pledge jersey, even if that meant beating the shit out of me and tearing it off.

Despite that, I was not going to take his sweaty undershirt handout. I would not give him the pleasure of seeing me cower. I yanked my jersey off, staring at him in disgust. I threw it on the bench, turned my back to him, and headed out of the Chicken shirtless. Peter knew I was afraid and upset. I walked out as quickly as I could without looking at any of the TKE brothers. I wasn't sure if the other TKEs knew what had happened in the back room, or if I was going to make it out of the Chicken alive.

Shaken by the whole ordeal, I was barely able to drive back to my apartment. If they had the balls to blatantly kick me out of the fraternity, perhaps I should be fearful of what might happen next. I could hear Peter again in my mind, loudly, over and over, "Take off your jersey!" I was frightened for weeks and couldn't sleep. I shuddered every time I saw fraternity letters. I felt victimized by the whole fraternity experience: It had cost me my sense of safety on campus. I could not believe this had happened to me.

Throughout that entire rush week, I had hoped I was wrong about the stereotypes of fraternities and Greek life at Texas A&M. I wanted to believe that I could be Clay first and then be gay. Nevertheless, everything was worse now than I could ever have possibly imagined.

Later, after my nerves had begun to settle, I told the university administration about the TKE incident. I also shared it with the press in the hope that something would change at conservative Texas A&M. As a result, TKE was ultimately suspended on campus for several years. The reputation of the TKE fraternity as well as that of the entire Greek system was damaged, making headlines statewide and nationally. Texas A&M's ongoing reputation as an unwelcoming place for gay, lesbian, bisexual, and transgender students was reinforced. Sadly, nothing more seems to have changed since then in the Greek system to educate or to create awareness on sexual orientation issues. The traditional A&M rituals of fraternity life continue.

Even today I fondly remember the thrill of Bid House—running down the steps of the Administration Building in anticipation of new-found friendships and the promise of fraternal brotherhood. Images of a thousand rowdy, crazed A&M fraternity men are etched in my mind. I thought it was the perfect introduction to fraternity life and brother-hood. Instead, the Bid House is a reminder that gay people are every-where. There were closeted gay men in those fraternities who were cer-tainly fearful of coming out at Texas A&M and being labeled as gay. Each of us runs forward to find brotherhood and acceptance for who we are.

My Gay Pledge Son

by Benjamin M. Swartz, University of Connecticut, Storrs

Sheltered. That's how I would describe my upbringing. Hidden away in suburbia with all the other middle-class white folks, far from diversity and difference. I was far from an imposing figure: A little above average height and skinny as a rod, I blended right into my surroundings. My high school was a ridiculously small place full of totally ordinary people. I can remember being thoroughly amused by all kinds of derogatory humor. We laughed at blacks, Asians, gays, and Hispanics from the fast-food joints, none of whom we'd ever really met. As a town we were safe from these unknown people. We were immune to the cultural integration that we had carefully built defenses against. Looking back, it is eerily funny how blind we were to the hidden diversity around us.

College was different. It was impossible to block out the different cultures, races, and lifestyles that passed by every day. When I chose the University of Connecticut, it surprised a lot of people, even me. It was big, in the middle of nowhere, expensive for a state school, and not a place I would have been expected to spend four years of my life. I suppose it's not surprising that Greek life drew me in. There was always a lot of the "same" in a fraternity—but I would soon be surprised. As far as I knew, I had never met a gay person before; now I would be pledging with one.

"Hey, you know that kid from pledge class?" a pledge brother asked me. "Is he, you know...?"

"Gay?" I said. Apparently it was a difficult word for some to say. "I don't know. I assume so."

"I guess that makes sense," the fellow pledge said.

"If you want, you can ask him to make sure," I suggested.

"No, that's all right," he said. "We can just assume."

I guess I knew from the first time I saw him. He strutted into the room wearing a bright yellow Playboy visor, and with a high wave of his hand he declared his professor a "ho-bag bitch." He was not flamboyant, but he had his moments of drama. We were pretty sure that he was gay, but we were not about to question him. Maybe we thought that if he wasn't gay, he might be insulted by the question. Or maybe the topic itself was so foreign that the awkward feeling of it outweighed our desire to know. I suppose that implies that I thought being gay was a negative thing. To tell you the truth, I cannot put my finger on what I thought, but I do know that I was not the only one who felt at a loss about what to do or say. I guess my excuse at the time was simply that we were not close, but mostly I just didn't have the balls.

Less than a semester passed before I got my first "pledge son": somebody for whom I had the responsibility to teach the ropes, hang out, and help adjust to fraternity life. Coincidentally, he happened to be gay too. We were we an odd pairing. At the time, we allowed our pledges to list which brothers they wanted for pledge fathers. He did not even know my name, so he wrote on his list, "the tragic Caucasian kid who always wears a hat." Everyone knew who he meant, and the expression became the subject of many jokes and led to my temporary nickname of "Tragic."

"Why did you pick me?" I asked him later in private.

"I don't know," he said. "You seemed friendly."

I did not get it. It didn't seem like enough to base that sort of decision on, especially since he knew other brothers in the chapter.

That semester did not go the way I had planned. My excitement at being a pledge father was not enough to overcome our busy schedules, and we were barely together at all. I felt disappointed and truly hoped we would be able to bond.

As luck would have it, the next year we were both living in the same dorm. It was a slow start, but after a few lunches together I finally was able to get to know him beyond a brief remark now and then. The conversations began much like those with any other friend or brother. But the closer we got to one another, the more I was able to ask questions that I would never dare ask anyone else. If it had not been for our fraternal bond, I would undoubtedly still be in the dark on much of what I learned about being gay. We stood outside while he smoked his cigarettes, and I would wait for a lull in the conversation.

"So…you want to get married?" I asked.

"Yeah, someday," he replied with a shrug and a puff on his cigarette.

"To a guy?" I questioned.

He looked at me, tilted his head, and after a pause said, "Um…yeah."

And so it went. Slowly, I bumbled my way through what for me were once foreign topics. "So you don't ever want to have sex with girls?" I asked incredulously.

"I almost did once," he said, as if it were an unimportant event.

I pushed on, trying to understand. "But you didn't want to?"

"No way!" he cried out. "I took one look at that thing and said 'gross!'"

"Really?" I wondered aloud. "Interesting."

As the year went on, the conversations became deeper, and I began to meet a lot of his gay friends at the university. I discovered how similar people can be despite differences in sexual orientation.

My pledge son and I formed a close bond of brotherhood that year. So close, in fact, that the lines of our relationship often seemed blurred to others. A perfect example was when my pledge son went abroad to study for the next semester. Before he left I went to say goodbye. His older brother was picking up his stuff, and my father was collecting my things. The four of us met, and after introductions I gave my pledge son a hug goodbye and wished him well. My pledge son later told me that when my father and I walked away, his brother turned to him and asked, "Does his father know he's gay?" We both had a good laugh about that. A few months earlier I don't know if I would have had the same reaction. That change demonstrates how getting to know someone gay really did change my outlook on life and my comfort level about sexuality. I did not care what people thought. We were fraternity brothers. He was my pledge son.

It wasn't all good times, though. No matter how close we became, there was still a difference between us and a stigma that followed my gay pledge son. I couldn't always understand what it felt like to be gay. It was difficult to relate to the persecution he felt from people who did not understand. Once he and I were watching TV and one of the brothers remarked that something on the show was "so gay." I didn't laugh and in fact became uncomfortable, but I didn't say anything either. My pledge son looked directly at me like it was me who had made the remark, and then he stormed off. It took me a while to figure out what had upset him so much. There is an implication of agreement in the absence of confrontation. I quickly learned that "silence speaks louder than words."

I was ignorant, and I still am, but I am learning. That is what college life is for: to learn, to become better. It is incredibly easy to make assumptions about what you don't understand. You cannot simply apply blatant assumptions as truths without further investigation. Exposure is the best cure for ignorance, which I have learned from my fraternity brother, my pledge son. Every person needs to have experiences like mine, and if fraternities are a vehicle to make that possible, then every fraternity should have at least one gay brother. Gay people do not detract from your fraternity or the bonds of brotherhood. On the contrary, fraternal diversity can enhance brotherhood by adding a whole new dimension to lifetime friendships, to the growth of individuals, and to the fraternal values of humanity. My brother, my pledge son, taught me valuable lessons about diversity. Through his eyes I was able to see his reality, and as a result I am a better brother and a better person.

Change Takes Time

by Travis C. Shumake, Northern Arizona University, Flagstaff

I did not think twice about going Greek when I got to college. My father was a Sigma Chi, and that made me a legacy. I thought of myself as the ideal college fraternity man. My high school student government shirt said MR. PERFECT, I lettered in three sports, was president of my senior class, and sat on homecoming and prom court every year. I was your stereotypical good-bone-structure A-crowd member. The only difference between me and the star quarterback was that I was gay. Gay was okay for my generation of teens. My entire high school knew, so why would college be any different?

Northern Arizona State University was a huge change from my home in Phoenix. Though it was only two hours away, there were pine trees and green grass but no familiar cacti or palm trees. Wearing a jacket in August was all too common. Snow started early in Flagstaff, 7,000 feet up in the mountains of Arizona.

When I arrived on campus that fall my dad took me to the Sigma Chi fraternity house. The Greek system at Northern Arizona is unlike any other. There are not any fraternity houses per se. Instead, fraternities and sororities are housed together in a state-of-the-art university-owned megaplex known as Mountain View. My father and I toured the five-story building. The accommodations were like those of any regular fraternity house. Each fraternity had its own wing with individual suites and a large, nicely adorned chapter room. The Sigma Chi wing was beautiful, with bright blue and gold stripes down the wall and a glass bridge that overlooked the scenic mountain landscape.

Walking down the Sigma Chi wing, my dad told me stories of his good ol' days in the fraternity.

"They made us swallow a goldfish with our water every night at dinner," he said gleefully.

The sound of boxes dragged across tile mixed with the screams of reunited sorority sisters. We went into the fraternity chapter room and I felt like I was in a movie. It had a fancy old-fashioned pool table, a big-screen television, couches, and enough composites to wallpaper the entire building. I was impressed, and it was just as I had imagined—perfect.

My being a Sigma Chi fraternity man would give my dad and me common ground to bond over. He was excited that I would be following in his footsteps. He spoke about fraternity life with pride, but there was hesitation in his voice. The "openly gay son" thing was new to him, and I could tell he was concerned that my being gay might not mix with the traditional ideas of fraternal brotherhood.

Fortunately, the Sigma Chi brothers had e-mailed me several times over the summer. The brothers all seemed eager to meet me. One brother even offered to take me to lunch while a couple of others said they would help me move into the dorms. I was assured by e-mail that my many high school accomplishments would be an asset to the fraternity. Reading over the e-mails, all signs seemed to indicate that the fraternity wanted me. Never did I consider that the brothers had not even met me yet.

Some high school friends believed that anyone could tell I was gay. Physically, I look like an Abercrombie model, with wavy highlighted hair, brown eyes, and dark skin. But my outward attitude, mannerisms, and tone scream "gay." Plus, I loved cheerleading and had chosen to come to Northern Arizona for its cheer program. I am who I am, and nothing would change that about me.

Before I had time to be concerned, it was rush week, the first formal step to going Greek. I was finally going to meet the men of Sigma Chi fraternity. Together with my new roommate and some other guys from my dorm floor, we walked to the first rush forum. It was comforting arriving with a large entourage.

The rush forum was in the Skydome, the indoor football stadium on campus. The vastness of the stadium was awe-inspiring, a perfect backdrop to Greek life. Overall there were probably 200 guys there. The stage was set up on the 50-yard line of the field. Each fraternity had its president come to the podium and brag about its philanthropy and leadership on campus, then drop a subtle hint about its awesome parties. The speeches were like a revolving door of guys in khaki pants. The whole process reminded me of one of those reality dating shows where you have 12 episodes to choose someone to be with for the rest of your life. Our task was to choose the right fraternity in 90 seconds or less. When it was all said and done, nobody had mentioned kegs, beer, or female strippers. Omega Delta Phi stood out by saying, "If you want to drink and party, don't come here." I thought about checking it out, but it is a national Hispanic fraternity. I figured being a gay guy in a regular fraternity was going to be hard enough.

After the litany of speeches, the rushees marched around to visit each fraternity booth. Some fraternities had pictures of famous alumni and gave out food and drinks. The Sigma Chi booth was hard to miss. It had two pop-up tents with big blue awnings that stood out vividly on the green Astroturf.

As I approached the Sigma Chi tent, my palms broke out in a sweat. Each of the Sigma Chi brothers was amazingly good-looking. I stepped closer and was greeted by a brother who helped me sign the interest list.

"Oh, you're Travis, the legacy, right?"

In an effort to give off straight vibes, I replied, "Uh, yeah."

Otherwise I typically would have said, "Oh, my gosh, that's me! I am so excited to finally meet you," and shaken his hand with giddy excitement.

Gesturing for the other Sigma Chi brothers to come over, I was knocked over by the wave of testosterone. A punch in the arm from one, a strong handshake from another; these guys were as straight as they came. They were not only supermasculine but also outrageously nice. They all seemed so genuine, so all-American. I felt like a movie star on the red carpet with all eyes on me. They invited me to a list of Sigma Chi events.

Trying not to look overly desperate, I took off early and checked out a couple of other fraternities that caught my eye. I would hate to go Sigma

Chi without seeing what everyone else had to offer. One in particular that I had chosen as my backup was Delta Tau Delta. These were the student government officials and the movers and shakers on campus. I had a lot in common with the Gucci-wearing, platinum-highlighted Delts.

The week of rush flew by. Sigma Chi called every day, reminding me of events and checking to make sure I was adapting well to college life. All this time Delta Tau Delta also had become interested and was pursuing me just as strongly. I was thrilled to have both fraternities vying for me. Being gay had never come up, so everything seemed okay. Either they did not care or they were clueless.

The last event of rush was the preference dinner, where fraternities extended invitations to those they are most interested in. Both Sigma Chi and Delta Tau Delta gave me invites. I could not attend both dinners. The choice had to be made—just like on the reality dating shows. Thinking long and hard, I chose to be with the men of Sigma Chi. No doubt remained in my mind as to where I belonged. The tradition would continue. I put all my faith and attention into going Greek as a Sigma Chi legacy.

Dinner was awesome. The invitation was to one of Flagstaff's classiest Asian restaurants, Monsoon. I volunteered to drive a group of rushees from my dorm to the restaurant. Sitting down at the dinner table, I had wonderful company with some promising pledge brothers and the fraternity president. After learning about my past high school involvement, one of the guys mentioned that I would be the "perfect pledge class president." Wow, I already had a nomination. Hearing the constant chatter and deep laughter of the brothers made me feel safe and comfortable. I could see myself enjoying many good times in the fraternity, just like my dad.

Slowly, as the tables cleared, the brothers began to leave the restaurant. Before we left, each rushee had to do an impromptu video interview. The videos would aid the brothers in making their final choices. Questions like "Why do you want to be a Sigma Chi?" and "What is brotherhood to you?" were mixed with things like word associations for the word *fork*. Driving back to the dorms, we all reveled in the excitement of receiving our bids next day. We decided that we would go together first thing at 8 A.M.

My alarm went off at 7:30. I reached over and turned it off. Four hours later my door went off: "Bang! Bang! Bang!" The guys were pounding loudly. As I opened the door, one of them said snidely, "Eight o'clock huh?" They had already picked up their bids and were proudly wearing their matching Sigma Chi T-shirts. Realizing that I had not picked up my bid and T-shirt, the guys came back to wake me up. There was an intramural game that day, and all the pledges had to attend. So off we went together to Mountain View.

I was more anxious than nervous. My main concern was that I got the correct T-shirt size—"small, please." The tighter the better; I like my arms and abs to look like they are ripping through my clothes.

"Shumake," I said, giving the guy behind the table my last name. We then proceeded to the table marked with the letter S. I quickly noticed that the S table did not have any of the Sigma Chi fraternity-colored shirts. He came back and checked the spelling. Checking three times, he then told me that there was not any bid for me. One of my friends piped in and said, "He's a legacy, check again."

The Greek life representative assured me that there must have been a mistake, promising that every fraternity takes its legacies with almost no exceptions. He said that he would call the fraternity president, and if things changed, he would give me a call. I was upset and frustrated, but there was nothing else I could do.

Nevertheless, the guys invited me to come along to the intramural game. I hesitated for a second, thinking maybe I really did not get a bid. I told them to go along without me, hoping things would get straightened out.

Back in my dorm I waited for the phone call explaining the mistake. I showered, took a nap, color-coded my closet, checked my e-mail, showered again, and then went to the student union for some dinner. I took my best friend, Robin, with me as a security blanket. Robin was 51% of the reason I came to Northern Arizona. Besides being homecoming royalty together and being voted "most spirited" in the high school yearbook, we had one thing in common that could not be matched: cheerleading. We had both chosen the university based on the cheer program and had made the team a week earlier. Together we had often dreamed of being college cheerleaders.

That day, entering the student union, I felt exposed. A sea of blue T-shirts came into focus as we got closer to the eatery. The familiar sound of deep laughter and masculine voices rang out. There sat the 40 members of Sigma Chi who had turned their backs on me.

"There you are," yelled one of the new pledges from my dorm. The active brothers quickly whispered something in his ear. All the heads at the table sunk toward their plates. Every eye stared downward. Nobody would even look in my direction. In my mind, everyone in the union knew I did not get a bid to join Sigma Chi. It was like I was wearing a shirt that said WANNABE FRAT BOY.

Less then 24 hours ago these guys were fighting over me with Delta Tau Delta. Now they pretended not to know my name. Could this be because the brothers thought I was gay? Afraid of the answer, I didn't ask any questions. I did not want to hear the truth. Instead, I made up my own excuses, like *Maybe they have too many class presidents* or *My 4.0 GPA would have really brought the chapter down.* I e-mailed the president and he beat around the bush, inviting me to get to know the guys better and rush again in the spring. His e-mail was a polite way of saying, "From what we've seen, you suck."

My dad told me he was not disappointed, but I had reason to believe differently. He really did want me to be a fraternity man, a Sigma Chi. I felt like a failure. My friends were careful not to mention fraternity life in front of me. Nobody would dare tell me what really happened. When everyone disappeared on Sunday nights without a goodbye, I tried to not remember that they were headed to fraternity meetings.

Things were better being openly gay in high school. Why not college? As the semester progressed I met more Greeks on campus, especially sorority women. They all seemed to love me and before I said my name—they knew exactly who I was from the horrible rumors. Every time I ran into a cute Gamma Phi or a crazy Tri Delt at a party, she would say things like, "You know, we all hate those Sigma Chis for what they did to you." This comment was followed closely by "You don't want to be one of them anyway." I appreciated their support and friendship. But the truth was I did want to be one of them.

Finally someone said what I had expected all along. It was like hearing nails on a chalkboard. As I was talking with a group of guys at a party one night, one of the guys said, "I can't believe Sigma Chi didn't give you a bid because you're gay. It's not like most fraternity men aren't anyway."

Never did I want to face the ugly truth for what it was. I had made up excuse after excuse. I always tried to tell myself that there had to be other reasons: I had a bad video interview, or the fraternity thought I was going with another chapter. But it was strikingly obvious: Gay and Greek don't mix.

The drama continued over that semester. Mountain View was like a small high school, where everyone knows everything about everyone.

Slowly I became the most popular person in the Greek system without ever being in a fraternity. My story traveled fast through the giant Greek dormitory. As a result, the Sigma Chi men faced the wrath of angry sorority girls over the next year. The girls were like an army. "I met a Sigma Chi yesterday, and I told him he couldn't sit with us," one foot soldier reported back to me.

Day after day it was a new story about how a Sigma Chi was kicked out of a party or lost his girlfriend because of me. I didn't know which ones to believe, really. Everyone knew what the fraternity had done was wrong, but nobody did anything to make it right—until one day when another fraternity jumped on the anti-Sigma Chi bandwagon.

That spring my roommate and nine other guys in my dorm had joined Phi Delta Theta fraternity. Already I had a good relationship with these men, and my being gay had never been an issue with them. Phi Delta Theta seemed to accept me unconditionally for who I was. I did not go through formal rush; in fact, I was given the bid by the drunken rush chair one night at a party. That probably says a lot right there.

Phi Delt was really not my style. I found myself many times earlier in the semester making fun of my friends for being in the "white trash" fraternity on campus. Every Phi Delt brother had two or more tattoos, no sleeves on anything, and at least two pairs of cowboy boots. Such jokes made it easier not being in a fraternity and feeling left out. Maybe I was desperate, or maybe I wanted a place to fit in with some Greek letters on my chest. Either way, Phi Delt at least seemed interested in me.

Unfortunately, things came crashing down once again. I had come to Mountain View for my weekly pledge class meeting. We met in the fraternity chapter room and were going to be tested on the Greek alphabet. I could do it backward and forward in seven seconds—alpha to omega. Our pledge class educator came into the room and asked to talk to me outside. Since we had a social coming up, I assumed he wanted my help with advertising or decorations. Instead, I was led into a room with the president and my big brother, Sonny. I knew Sonny better then anyone else in the fraternity. He and I were very close, having met my first day on campus. I looked up to him and could not think of anyone better to be my big brother.

The fraternity president then proceeded to explain the blackballing process. Sonny sat across from me at a desk with tears in his eyes. I knew what was coming. I could not believe I was hearing this. The formal reason I was given for being "let go" was that I was "breaking down the brotherhood." Bullshit! I had become the brotherhood. What was he talking about? In shock and dismay, I left without any further discussion. I was outraged and tired of being mistreated for being gay.

Forget it. I turned in my pledge pin. The fraternity became split over the whole ordeal, and some brothers came to my defense. When all the dust had settled, three brothers dropped out of the fraternity because they believed that I had been wronged. Phi Delta Theta also came under review by Greek life. Tensions ran high in Mountain View for weeks between the sororities and the Phi Delts. Tired of the drama, tired of the rejection, and tired of trying to fit in, I gave up. Fraternity life was no place for an openly gay guy.

Despite my disdain for fraternities, I was still a permanent fixture in the Greek system. The sororities made sure of it. There was not a sorority formal or date dash that I was not invited to. I was every sorority girl's perfect date. Cute, well-mannered, drove a nice car, and could carry on a conversation about almost anything—politics, fashion, you name it. As a result, Gamma Phi Beta sorority recognized me as its "Gamma Phi Guy," the one man the sisters always hold closest to their hearts. Just as in high school, everyone knew me, and the girls loved me for being gay. However, everyone also assumed I was Greek. And the bell rang for round 3.

Sigma Chi had been trying to make amends. Perhaps it was social pressure or their own moral fiber that led the brothers to admit what they had done was wrong. I gave them the cold shoulder, thinking they were only interested in clearing things up to save their image. Then something big happened: I met Cole.

The Sigma Chi mailbox was in the student union, and Cole often came by to retrieve the fraternity's mail. I had known Cole's girlfriend, Sarah, for a couple of years. She was my instructor at cheer camp in high school and a member of the cheer squad on campus. One day while chatting online I received an instant message from a guy who said he had seen me around campus and thought I was cute. Conversation naturally turned into descriptions and statistics. I knew where the conversation was headed, but this guy did not seem gay. I never suspected that it was Cole. When he told me he was a Sigma Chi, I did not know what to think. I knew of him, and I knew his girlfriend.

Cole and I met for the first time and spent hours getting to know each other. From there our relationship became physical, and we often hooked up. I began to hang out at the fraternity with Cole and the other brothers. Cole was very closeted within the fraternity, and none of the brothers had any idea what was going on. Oftentimes an unlocked door was all that separated Cole and me from a party or a group of brothers watching *The O.C.* The sex was intense, and it gradually faded into a friendship over the course of several months.

Fortunately, I had the chance to meet each of the brothers personally during this time. Many of the brothers would invite me out on weekends. During the day I started eating lunch with the brothers, and I felt like things had changed. These brothers liked me. It felt like a true brotherhood. Or at least that's how I imagined one to be.

People change. By this time, a year later, only four brothers from the first time I rushed were still around, and Sigma Chi was a completely different fraternity. The few brothers who knew of my past with Sigma Chi held no grudge and welcomed me with open arms. When I was asked if I would accept a bid to join Sigma Chi, I did not immediately know the answer. Instead of an answer, the question was, "Why would I go back to this fraternity after all they put me through?" The answer was not black-and-white. Sometimes you can just feel a click.

Chapters change, year by year, semester by semester, pledge by pledge. When I felt ready I told Cole that I would probably accept a bid to join Sigma Chi. Nobody in the fraternity knew Cole was gay. Eventually I figured it would come out, but I did not want to hurt Cole or lie about our sexual affair. Instead, the only thing I wanted was to join Sigma Chi as a brother.

Shortly thereafter, the fraternity offered me a bid. I chose to decline the bid and wait for formal rush in the spring. After all I had been through, I wanted to do it right this time.

Eighteen months later, I wholeheartedly signed the bid to join Sigma Chi at 8 A.M. on bid day. I was treated like every other pledge. No exceptions, no special treatment, and no more mention of the past. The legacy lived on, and I was prouder than ever to be a Sigma Chi.

I have some pretty deep battle wounds from my first two years in fraternity life. I have rushed three times with two different fraternities. I have had two groups of great pledge brothers whom I know are different now because of me. I have had two big brothers who have changed my outlook on life. Through it all I followed my heart and knew where I belonged, but it took time for fraternity guys to get used to homosexuality. I have one fraternity, one home, and one place where I can feel comfortable being me—Sigma Chi.

Smoking Guns

by "Travis Lin," University of California, Los Angeles

There was never a choice to be out with my family. I grew up in a strict Chinese household, and my immigrant parents worked every day at a local Chinese eatery, not by choice but out of duty to the family. My father constantly reminded us, "To eat bitterness is to create opportunity." My mother was quick to translate: "We work hard, so you must study hard." As the eldest son I was expected to capitalize the most from their hard work. I was to fulfill the dream for our family. Quite simply, three tasks would rule my life. Number 1: I should graduate from a prestigious university. Number 2: I should secure a financially lucrative job. Number 3: I should carry on the family name through marriage. Success would be measured by my ability to fulfill all three. Since being gay was not part of this well-defined equation, I kept my sexuality from my family and my high school. I desperately wanted to make my parents proud and to bring honor to the family name.

Number 1 was easy for me. I gained admission immediately to the University of California, Los Angeles. My first day on campus was for orientation. Nestled below the stately red brick halls, the trimmed green lawns of Westwood Plaza hosted a sea of incoming freshmen for the official Welcome Assembly. Before us sat five student orientation counselors. Each stood up to tell how much UCLA meant to them. My attention quickly turned to the fifth counselor: a tanned, muscular Asian boy with sunglasses and long sideburns. He sported a short-sleeved UCLA shirt that showed off his biceps and clung tightly to his chiseled chest. *This was something worth looking forward to,* I chuckled to myself.

When the time finally came for number 5 to speak, he took off his sunglasses and stood up confidently.

Squinting in the sunlight, he spoke in his deep voice, "Hey, everyone, I'm Steven. Since I'm last, I'll try to make this short. As Joe, Cindy, Betty, and Mark have already let you know, UCLA is great, and we're happy you'll all be joining us. I just wanted to add that UCLA is also very accepting. You see, I'm gay."

My jaw literally dropped, along with countless others. A hush fell over the audience as they shook their heads in disbelief. My eyes and ears were fixed on his words, his square jaw, and his slightly crooked smile.

"And I came out because UCLA helped me. My friends, my professors, and our administration have created an environment that promotes tolerance and acceptance for everyone. I'm not afraid to stand here and welcome you, because UCLA has welcomed me. Just be yourself. Have a great orientation!"

This is my chance, I thought, as my defining moment was lost in the rousing applause. *If this school could give someone like Steven the strength to grow and come out, then why couldn't I have the same experience?*

Disappointed that I had not been assigned to Steven's orientation group, I made it my personal mission to talk to him and get a little more input. The opportunity finally came when we took a combined tour of campus. I noticed Steven was bringing up the tail end of the tour, so I deliberately fell to the back of the pack until we were side by side. He was a head taller than me, and his forehead glistened from the August heat. He caught my gaze and smiled.

"You going to keep up with us, little man?" He taunted coyly.

"Definitely," I breathed. My palms got sweaty, but I managed to get my words out, "Hey, you know what you said at the assembly? That was pretty cool. Took lots of guts. I don't know if I could ever do that."

Steven raised his left eyebrow.

"So you're part of the family?" he asked matter-of-factly.

My nervousness stifled my reply. "It's okay—you will," he winked. "One step at a time, and you will."

The rest of the afternoon, Steven and I spent time together. He shared his experience of coming out as a freshman to residence hall neighbors and how their positive support pushed him to work in student orientation for the past two years. He had hoped to challenge stereotypes and give students that extra nudge to come out on campus. Sadly, Stephen had just graduated from UCLA and would not be around campus any longer. His encouraging words that day stuck with me. He said, "Just be yourself. Don't worry, you can handle it."

Three weeks later, my first day on campus was a swirling mix of tanned athletes hiking around campus with backpacks, frumpy bio students in white lab coats, and lean Asian boys zipping around in fixed-up imported cars. UCLA had room for everyone, and they all existed together. I remembered Steven's words over and over: "Just be yourself." I was determined that I would be honest about being gay with anyone I met.

Making friends seemed easy enough, and I even stayed friends with a few girls from my high school who now went to UCLA. None of them really seemed to care that I was gay, and their responses were comforting. Helping matters immensely, my family lived 50 miles away. The distance gave me a security and freedom I had never felt before. I figured that I could at least fulfill my family's expectations of number 1 and 2—and be openly gay.

My first week of classes I made many friends. Some I would tell immediately that I was gay while others I would wait until they knew me better. One of my close friendships began that week with Michael Yu. We were sitting in a history class lecture, both apparently trying to fight the fatigue brought on by the ramblings of an aged professor. I had rested my head on my left arm and attempted to scribble into my notebook. My eyes fell shut. Plop!

"You dropped this," Michael chuckled as he handed me my pen. "Good thing you did, because it woke me up as well."

Michael smiled and ran his hand through his bleached surfer-looking bangs.

"Man, I have to get out of here. Want to bounce?" Michael asked.

"Sounds good." We quietly packed up our books and sneaked out the back exit.

Lighting up a cigarette, Michael motioned the pack to me.

"It's all right." I declined his offer.

"That's cool. I'm trying to quit, but I can't." He puffed away. "Need a ride up to the dorms?"

"You have a permit? But I thought freshmen never get parking," I said.

"Simple: doctor's note." Michael flashed a sneaky grin and unlocked the doors to a sleek new silver Lexus with a high spoiler and shiny rims.

"My graduation present. I made a few adjustments, of course." He put in the faceplate to an aftermarket hi-tech stereo system. "Nice, isn't it?"

I was impressed. I had driven my father's 1980 Toyota back home, but driving his car in Los Angeles was completely out of the question. Now this kid had both, a new car and the freedom to drive all over L.A.

"Jeez, I've been missing out," I drooled.

"No problem. Just hang with me, and you'll be good." Michael oozed confidence. "What are you doing tonight? Come meet my friends."

Michael and I exchanged numbers and made plans to hang out. Of course, I had still not told Michael I was gay. I figured I would do it in due time, but for now I wanted him to get to know me first. His flashy demeanor and his Lexus had completely caught my attention.

That night I piled into Michael's car and headed off with the rest of his gang: Terrance Chan, Ben Wong, and James Pan. I had no clue where we were headed, but I didn't care. These guys were cool, and I was equally enthralled with the prospect of getting to know them.

"All right, fellas," Michael said. "There are a couple things going on tonight. This Asian fraternity is going to host a party downtown, or this Chinese-American student group is throwing a mixer at this billiards joint. What are we up for?"

"Hmm, those fraternities…man, I've heard some jacked-up stuff about them," said James as he squirmed in the seat next to me.

"Right, something about getting into fights and stuff. I don't know about you guys, but I'm made for loving, not for fighting," Terrance snickered as he flipped down the passenger side mirror to readjust his slickly spiked hair. "I mean, why mess up this face?" he asked playfully as he winked at his reflection.

"Seems like those Asian fraternities are bad news," Ben added from beneath his green Oakland A's hat. "Probably should stay away from them."

The campus buzz was that the fraternities had an extremely macho aura. That really put me off. I hoped that the fraternity option would disappear. I wanted to build an honest foundation with these guys by telling them I was gay. I was not ready for a fraternity as well.

"Yeah, I could shoot some pool," I added.

"All right, the fraternities will always be throwing parties anyway, so let's move on," Michael bellowed over his turned-up speakers. We zipped off to the billiards joint five blocks down the road.

From that night at the pool hall, the five of us became really close friends. Each of us had very different personalities and traits that seemingly brought us together. Terrance was the "Ladies' Man." Some might call him a player, with his sharply defined jaw, high cheekbones, and impressive height. Ben was the "Rock." He never said much, but he was always down to hang out with his signature green A's cap. James was always "Mr. Funny." He had an impressive build, cracked jokes, and shared slightly naughty stories, never taking life too seriously. Michael, of course, was the "Ringleader." Confident and the only one with a car, he had the authority to call the shots and often did just that, pulling rank on everyone. Nobody ever seemed to mind. Terrance did not complain as long as he had his girls; Ben and James just bumbled along. I felt indebted to Michael, of course, for inviting me into their group. Together, the five of us made the perfect mix of friends.

Michael finally named our group "the Smoking Guns" after this Cantonese action movie about a rebellious gang of five teens who ravaged Hong Kong by causing trouble, having fun, and most important, just by being best friends. They did everything together because their style was "all for one." Of course, Michael named the lead character after himself, and we all somehow filled the supporting roles. That was not a surprise to any of us. Michael was our leader and we were the Smoking Guns—a true group of friends who were always there for one another.

Never had there been a perfect opportunity to come out to the Smoking Guns. I knew I had to come out, and the clock was ticking. I did not lie about my sexuality to any of them, but I was not completely honest either. I figured the Lexus, where we were confined to talk with one another, would be the best place to come out.

One night we were all meeting to go out to a special event at a Hollywood bar. I sat on the bench in front of my residence hall scanning the dark night for Michael's Lexus to pull into the driveway. My nervousness ate away at my stomach and I felt more afraid than ever. Soon the bright glare of the superwhite Lexus headlights broke the black night. I heard the familiar blare of techno music ripping through the parking lot. *This is my first step. Just be yourself,* I thought as the car came to an abrupt stop in front of me.

"Hey, fellas, right on time," I yelled as the door opened.

James hopped out of the car to let me into the backseat.

"Yo, Travis!" James stuck out his hand to grip mine in our familiar greeting.

As Michael pulled out of the lot, I cleared my throat and tried to control my unsettled nerves.

"Yo, Terrance, can you lower the sound?" I asked as beads of sweat collected on my forehead.

Terrance obliged, and as the engine purred I said, "Hey, guys, I have something that I thought you should know."

There was no turning back now. I cleared my throat again to make way for the words. Then I said, "I'm gay."

"Ha, ha, ha! Right, man!" James burst out laughing, "Very funny, Travis."

Laughter was not what I had expected, so I responded with a nervous chuckle and then said, "No, guys." I looked in the rearview mirror at Michael. "I'm serious." My insistence created a crisp silence. Michael's lips were pursed and his face looked stern.

A moment of quiet awkwardness swept over the car.

"Oh…whoa! Sorry, dude," said James. His cheeks turned pink from embarrassment.

Still sensing some discomfort, I said, "So, guys, are we cool?"

My face was hot and I doubted myself, but I kept thinking, *Just be yourself, it will be okay.*

My eyes were locked on Michael's. He ran his hand through his hair and muttered something under his breath in disbelief. Then he paused. "Man…some people were asking questions. But I didn't think anything of it." He looked at me. "Wow, but that's cool. We're good, right guys?"

"We're good," said Ben casually nodding under his familiar green cap. "You're a Smoking Gun always, man."

"Right. Yo, as long as you don't go after any of us," Terrance joked, holding up his index finger. He laughed and leaned back to pat me on the leg. "I know some girls that might help, if you're not sure." He winked in his usual playful manner.

"Nah, I'm okay. I don't need that," I replied weakly. I had not yet recovered from the agony of the awkward, unknowing silence.

"Don't worry, Travis, it's cool. You're still a Smoking Gun, and you always will be." Michael had sensed I was still nervous. "All right, fellas. Enough with the small talk! We're here to have fun!"

Michael parked the car and motioned to the line of Asian-American teen girls dressed in short skirts around the corner of the bar. As we walked to the club, Michael placed his hand on my shoulder and repeated, "Don't worry, Travis. We're good, man."

Michael's matter-of-fact tone said that all was okay. Their relaxed acceptance confirmed the open-minded label Steven had given the UCLA campus. I was just myself. I never pressed the issue again.

As the year continued the Smoking Guns' weekly excursions grew less frequent. The parties all started becoming the same, and the guys were growing restless.

"We need a change," puffed Michael during our summer break. "Second year will be different. We just have to think how."

Nodding, I acted like I agreed, but I did not share the same desire. The Smoking Guns did not need anything else. Our territory was clear; we had one another.

Classes started the following September, and our gang walked down the familiar red-tiled main path on campus. Yet something was amiss with the Smoking Guns. The warm autumn wind was going to blow something unexpected my way. Michael had said they wanted a change, and change was coming.

"Hey, guys!" yelled a tall, slightly built Korean guy. "Come and check us out," he pointed to the Greek letters on his dark blue shirt as he ran up to our group and handed us fliers. "Are you guys affiliated?"

"Nah, we're not affiliated," said Michael, taking the flier as the rest of us shook our heads in unison.

"Well, I'm Jeff, and we've been having rush all week," he explained as he shook Michael's hand. When he looked over and saw Terrance's athletic warm-ups, his voice perked up, "You play ball at the Rec Center, right? Yeah, you guys should definitely party with us."

"Right. Yo," nodded Terrance.

"Thanks." Michael examined the flier more closely.

"Yeah, thanks," I breathed deeply.

As the guy disappeared behind us, the Smoking Guns analyzed the detailed rush flier announcing a number of fraternity events. Most of the events had already passed.

"Man, they're the big one. They have chapters all over California," Michael said, sounding impressed. "The other one doesn't have other chapters, right?"

"Nah, I don't think so," replied Terrance. "Dang, look at these pictures. Hot girls! These guys are major players."

"They have this party tonight at a club downtown. It's free if we go to this rush event before the party," read James.

"Hey, aren't they the ones that got into trouble last year? It was all over school," I said, reminding the guys of our previous discussion about Asian-American fraternities. "When the news came out, we decided to avoid them and stick with clubs and student groups. Right?"

"Yeah…but we never did get around to any of their parties," said Michael, brushing aside my concern.

"They must have fixed up their beef. We haven't heard anything else," responded James.

"Dang, they look like that have a hell of a lot of fun. I need some ladies," said Terrance, whistling aloud.

"It's free, Travis. It's the last event. We should check it out, or we won't get another chance," said Michael, deciding that we should all go. "All for one, right?"

Nodding and smiling, I agreed to go along to the rush event. The fraternity did not know I was gay, so what did I have to worry about? I could tell them when I was ready after they got to know me first. *All for one is right. It'll be okay. Just be yourself,* I thought.

At 9 o'clock the Smoking Guns pulled up to a swanky building with a red carpet entrance and a huge sign that spelled out the same three Greek letters. A dozen clean-cut, well-gelled Asian fraternity guys in sharp, dark-colored suits buzzed around. Immediately we recognized Jeff, who had given us fliers on campus. He quickly came up to greet us.

"Glad you guys could make it. I knew you'd show up," Jeff said. "Let me get your names on these tags and show you fellas inside." He pulled out a marker and started jotting down our names.

"Wow, there are a lot of people here," James said, sounding overwhelmed as he scanned the walkway.

"So what are we supposed to do?" Michael asked intently.

"Oh, it's fairly simple: We're just going to show you guys a little more about the fraternity. You guys can see if we're right for you." Jeff motioned for us to follow him to an open booth.

"Just take a seat, and we're going to get started in a little bit. Here are some applications to check out." Jeff left the applications with us and went back to preparing for the event with his brothers.

As we slid into the plush leather chairs, a goateed Japanese guy with two long bangs approached our table. "Hey, fellas!" He read our name tags off as he shook each of our hands. "I'm Brad, and I'm going to be this quarter's pledge dad."

"How's it going?" Terrance asked casually.

"I just wanted to personally welcome you guys to our rush event. Jeff over there said you guys came in as a group, right?" Brad was remarkably calm and cool talking to new people.

"Right. We're all friends," explained Michael. "So, what are we here to do?"

"Well, we're looking to recruit fine gentlemen such as you." Brad put an emphasis on the word *gentlemen*. "So have any of you come to check us out before?"

"Well, no," I said ready to lodge a complaint. "We heard you guys got into some fight—"

"Right, Travis," Brad interrupted, picking up the ball. "Yeah, that was unfortunate. We actually had a misunderstanding, but that's all water under the bridge now. We're competitive, but we're not crazy."

"I heard it's pretty hard to get a bid. You're pretty selective," Terrance said.

"Right. Well, we select the best. But we're pretty open-minded. We have diverse brothers from all over the country. You know we even have African-American brothers in Texas and Puerto Rican brothers in New York."

Brad was a salesman and knew exactly what to say. He continued, "You guys shouldn't be worried about that at all."

"We're all friends. So how does that work if we don't all get bids?" asked James. He had remembered our agreement—"All for one."

"Right," said Brad. His bangs bounced as his head nodded. "I'm sure we're going to want all five of you. We like recruits who come out together."

"But this is our first time at one of these things, " I said. He was making it sound easy to get into the fraternity.

"Yeah, usually we like rushees to come out a few times more so we can get to know you. But Jeff said he knows Terrance from before, so it's cool, don't worry," Brad reassured us. "Hey, it looks like we're getting started."

Jeff was at the microphone. "Hey, everyone! Thanks for rushing fall

2000. I'm Jeff, and on behalf of our brothers I'd like you all to enjoy your-
selves on our last night. But let's make sure we understand the purpose
of our fraternity: our brotherhood."

The throng of suits clapped and shouted madly as the lights dimmed.
At the front of the room, Jeff was working a laptop that controlled the
image projected on a large white screen. Hip-hop music blared from the
giant speakers as a wave of visuals exploded. BROTHERHOOD was spelled
out boldly in front of the fraternity's three Greek letters. Spinning crazi-
ly, the wild montage portrayed brothers shooting hoops, downing shots,
and mugging for the camera. Then appeared the word SOCIAL. Clips
flashed on the screen of scantily clad girls dancing with the brothers and
huge composite shots of the fraternity through the years. Then the screen
read NATIONWIDE. Brothers from different campuses across the United
States were featured posing for various group shots. The next words, IN
SYNCH. popped up with video clips of the fraternity brothers dressed uni-
formly doing stomp performances. Then the word LEADERSHIP appeared
with shots of individual fraternity brothers, including both Brad and Jeff.
The parting shot of the fraternity's three Greek letters faded into the
words FOR LIFE. As the lights came up, the suits burst into roars and
applause. The room buzzed with rushees all talking to each other at once.

"Man, this sounds pretty tight," sighed Michael. "This is what we've
been looking for."

"Yo, these guys are so cool. They're all so slick," said James, impressed.

"Dang, and the girls were even hotter than on the flier," replied
Terrance, excited by the prospects.

"They all seem to be good buddies," said Ben in agreement. "We must
have been wrong."

Jeff came up to our table. "Well, guys, what did you think?"

"Awesome," said Michael, providing our response without any second
thought.

"Great! Well, the party is just starting. The ladies have been waiting
outside." Jeff motioned to the door, where a number of girls were starting to filter in. The lights began to flicker and the music began to blare.

"I thought I'd help you guys get started a bit," announced Brad as he
brought over a pitcher of beer. "On the house, fellas." He began filling
glasses.

"Just fill out the interest applications real quick. A formality, really,"
said Jeff, winking. "Just pass them to Brad when you're done."

The Smoking Guns had smoking pens as they scribbled their contact info and little blurbs onto the one-page application. We were convinced this was the place to be. Michael looked up. "Man, Travis, we've got to do this. It's what we've been looking for."

The other guys raised their heads. "Yeah, all for one, remember?" said Ben.

"Yup," I replied, looking into their eager faces.

I was jealous of how this fraternity was so easily taking their attention away. Doing this together seemed like the only solution to prevent the fraternity from replacing the Smoking Guns. I only hoped that the fraternity members would not find out I was gay—at least not until after they had gotten to know me. Doubting their acceptance, I still had no choice.

"All for one," I said, scrawling down my info as Brad tucked away the others.

"Cheers, guys!" Jeff downed his beer. "You guys will hear from Brad by tomorrow. There will be no problem with any of you."

That night I was in such a macho world, such a straight world. Terrance chatted away with a buxom Japanese bombshell. Michael stood off to the side speaking with Brad and making gestures in our direction. James danced away like a complete fool. Ben sat next to me, contently bobbing his head to the jams. This is what the Smoking Guns wanted— fraternity life. For the rest of the night, I sat there convincing myself that I really wanted it too.

Waking up the next day, I looked forward to receiving a phone call. I had become okay with the idea of joining a fraternity and was ready to go whole hog. But as the day wore on, each of the Smoking Guns had called to tell me he got a bid. I became nervous. It had been three hours since Ben had called to tell me he got his bid. He was the last Smoking Gun except for me. Where was my phone call?

My phone finally sounded with an alarming ring. "Hi," I answered. My palms were getting sweaty.

"Hello, is this Mr. Travis Lin?" I could hear Brad's voice on the other end.

"Yes, it is." My temples pounded loudly.

"Thank you for your interest, but we are unable to offer you a bid." Silence. "Please try again next quarter." Brad was no longer the convincing salesman but rather an impersonal automated phone delivery message service.

"Click"—I heard the line go dead.

My face whitened as the blood drained away. Apparently I was not an ideal candidate. I asked myself, *Why not? Was I not cool enough? Was I not smart enough?* It just did not make sense. What was all that "open-minded diversity" junk that Brad had talked about? What was with Jeff winking at us and telling us the applications were merely a formality? He said there was nothing to worry about.

Three stories above the bustle of the students outside, I sat on my bed in my UCLA dorm room. The sun was beginning to set outside, casting long shadows on the cream-colored walls. As I stared at my wooden picture frames, the photos of the Smoking Guns reminded me of our camping trip at Big Bear, Michael's surprise birthday party, and a summer road trip to San Francisco to visit Terrance. How could something like this split us up? How come I didn't make the cut? I was mortified that after all this, I was somehow not good enough to belong. I stared at my reflection in the mirror next to my window. What was wrong with me?

I was lost in a daze when a sudden knock at the door startled me. Michael was standing there with his ungelled hair falling over part of his face.

"Man, I'm sorry," he said, half biting his lip.

Terrance was standing behind Michael with his back against the corridor wall. He stared up at the ceiling and said, "Yo, this is so not fair."

James kept his hands in his pockets and slumped his muscular shoulders as he kicked at the carpet. "I thought Jeff and Brad had our backs. I don't see why…" he said, trailing off.

Clearing my throat, I tried to hold back tears.

"It's okay. Congrats, you guys," I managed.

Faking my best smile and even a slight laugh, I walked back into my room. I sat on my bed as the guys filed in. "You guys should totally do it," I said, as convincingly as possible.

Terrance sat on the bed across from me and said, "But you see…" Then he stopped.

Michael pulled up a chair and continued, "It's because they heard you're gay."

The blood rushed into my face in horrified embarrassment. I could not believe what I was hearing. Who told the fraternity I was gay? I could not imagine anything worse. Just as I had expected, the fraternity would not be accepting of diversity when it came to gays.

"See, I talked to Brad a lot. I asked him how we all stood. But when you came up, Brad said you were iffy. Some UCLA girl that went to your high school pointed you out at the party that night. She told Brad you were gay," explained Michael.

"But I thought Brad said they were open-minded." I was visibly upset, immediately remembering those high school friends of mine. "Why were they spreading my business around?" I wondered.

"Yeah, that's what I don't get," said James. He took a seat on the ground.

"I thought you only told us," Terrance said, looking out my window.

"Plus you're not even sure. I think you're just confused anyway," said Michael, staring straight at me. I could not believe what he was saying. I thought, *Are you kidding? Just confused?*

Michael looked stern. "I mean, I haven't really ever seen you do anything, and you don't seem gay anyway. So I told him that it wasn't true. The girl got it wrong. I defended you, man!" he said, raising his voice. "I told him that she was starting some rumor, and that we were your real friends. You're not gay."

A smile crossed Michael's face. "Brad said if it was really a rumor, then all four of us could vouch for you next year. We can extend you a bid then."

I glared in response to his smile. I could not believe that he told Brad I wasn't gay and that he acted like that was acceptable. This fraternity had discriminated against a fellow Smoking Gun, and nobody seemed to care.

"So if you 'straighten up,' I think it'll work." The confidence that had once made Michael appealing now made him arrogant. "You know, get a girlfriend, hang with the frat guys, and of course just be one of us."

The proposal was clear: Become straight and become one of them. The guys left my room, and all that remained of the Smoking Guns was me. I had truly bonded with these guys. I had found my place with them. I thought I could be myself when I was with them. The fraternity was tearing it all apart, and now I was forced to choose between being gay and being a Smoking Gun.

Suddenly what Steven had said that first day of orientation—"Just be yourself"—no longer mattered. I don't know why, exactly, but I thought that if I could successfully change my sexuality, I could make the Smoking Guns and my parents proud. I was determined to make the change.

The following two quarters of that year were like an extended shower, cleansing myself of any outward gayness. I figured that the process would hurt me a lot less if I did my best not to think of Steven's words, "Just be yourself." I justified my actions by thinking that what worked for Steven may not necessarily work for me.

My first step was to disown any of the gay friends I had met at UCLA. I deleted their cell phone numbers and online screen names. I shrugged off accidental run-ins with past gay friends as mistaken identity. Secondly, I needed an alibi and an unknowing accomplice: a girlfriend. Terrence was on the move and set me up with a girl named Angie. She was shorter than me, with shiny black hair and a small, perfectly curved smile. As a new transfer, she was not familiar with any of my history and never directed any questions my way. We would hold hands as I walked her home each night. It was all perfect and innocent.

Every week I continued to be part of the Smoking Guns crew. They embraced the changes in my life feverishly. We would often gather in my room to shoot the breeze.

"Hey have you met Terrance's newest girl, Sophia? She's a riot. She drives him around in her spanking BMW," said James, snickering at the thought of Terrance's chauffeur.

"Ha ha, very funny, man! So Travis, how is Angie? I hear she's a hell of a cook." Terrance smiled, knowing full well Angie and I had been official for over two months.

I replied, "Yeah, I've been eating over there almost every night this week." It was true. Having dinner with her was fun, and she asked only that I wash the dishes.

"No wonder you never come to the Midnight Runs! You're always full," said Michael, smiling slyly. The room burst into laughter. The guys seemed to be truly happy for me. I had become straight as an arrow in their minds. They constantly reassured me that I would be a sure bet for the fraternity. However, the delicate walls I erected were cracking. I was slowly losing at my attempt to be heterosexual. It seemed the happier the Smoking Guns were, the less happy I was. I became more isolated and depressed. In order to be accepted, I had hollowed out my spirit. I began blaming the Smoking Guns for my unhappiness and used them as scapegoats for my self-hatred and anger. Everything was falling apart around me. I was a failure.

Soon enough I began avoiding the Smoking Guns. I lied and said I was busy whenever they wanted to come over to hang out. I deliberately ignored their calls on my cell phone. I snapped at everyone I ran into.

My girlfriend, Angie, was an innocent bystander who did not under-stand why I was no longer the same. "What's wrong?" she asked one night. "I don't get it. Did I do something?" She began crying. I just shrugged my shoulders, standing there fuming while she bawled her eyes out. "I think we need a break," she finally said. I nodded in agreement.

When Angie shut the door that night, I realized that I could no longer live this lie. Steven's words came back tenfold, yelling, "Just be yourself!" I had been hetero long enough—I was through.

A larger battle still remained with the Smoking Guns. It was a year later and their master plan to get me into their fraternity was coming to fruition. Michael, Terrance, Ben, and James had successfully negotiated a bid for me. The Smoking Guns came to my room to tell me the news. Michael was leaning against my desk congratulating me on my bid. A beaming Terrance had his arms folded across his chest and nodded along with Michael. James punched Ben playfully at the prospect of the Smoking Guns being all for one together again. Instead of sulking on my bed, I stood up, straightening out my back.

"Thanks, you guys. I mean really, for everything that you did." I glanced over at Terrance. "You know, this year has been crazy. We all dated, and we were all still friends." I turned and looked Michael straight in his eye. "But you know, lately…" I paused.

I was headed down a road that would put an end to the Smoking Guns. To accept my bid, I had to be straight. Pretending was not going to work, and if we were truly "all for one," they should be okay with me being who I am. It was not "all for the straight ones."

"Lately, that just isn't me." I shook my head. "I can't try to be what I'm not, to you or to the fraternity." I stood firm. "I'm still gay."

"Man…" Michael said, pursing his lips. He was getting agitated. "You know that if you want to do the fraternity, they expect the straight you." His voice was harsh. "You can't even try? How can you do this to me?"

"Hey, I didn't ask you to talk to the fraternity," I said, defending myself.

Michael pounded his hand against my desk and glared at me. "After all that talk with Brad? Man, that's too bad."

"Look, I'm sorry, Mike, but I can't go back in the closet," I said, stronger than ever. I could not let his anger affect me. He would not make me buckle this time.

"Hey, Travis." Terrance's voice was calm, and his eyes were sincere. "You know, I really want to do this. And if it's going to be weird, well, I don't know." He motioned to Ben. "Ben and I were just talking about how much we wanted to do this as a group, the Smoking Guns. But if you can't try…"

Ben pulled his Oakland A's cap down over his face. "All for one, Travis." He shook his head.

"Man, that's too bad, Travis." Michael had relaxed but his voice was bitter. "I gave Brad my word that you were not gay. We all gave them our word. And we can't have that."

Michael turned his back to me and yanked my door open, slamming it as he left.

Terrance stood up and patted me on the back. "We did give them our word. I'm sorry, man." He turned around to follow Michael outside.

I looked to James, who had been silent, and said, "I can't do that. They're asking me to be someone I'm not." My voice was steady.

In his light tone that was now oddly appropriate, James flashed a small smile. "I know. I guess I just thought it would be different, you know." I nodded my head.

Ben was sitting next to James, his expression was hidden in the dark shadow of his baseball cap. His lips were pursed in a pout. Ben got up and shook his head again.

"All for one, huh? Laters," he said as he left.

James placed his hand on my shoulder. "It'll be okay, Travis. They just need some time. What about you? You okay?"

I nodded. The Smoking Guns had stood where they needed to be, and it was over.

"I'll be just great," I replied.

James smiled again and winked. "I'll see you around, Travis."

With no regrets, I gained more confidence that day than ever. The Smoking Guns had ended, but my life was beginning.

As that quarter passed, the Smoking Guns "crossed" and became full members of the Asian-American fraternity. Terrance had his girls. Ben had his brothers. Michael had his role as ringleader expanded as a member of the Asian Greek Council. James ended up quitting shortly thereafter. The diversity they had mentioned pertained only to what the fraternity found comfortable. The flashing word BROTHERHOOD on the screen at the fraternity rush event was an illusion. The fraternity had no clue about the meaning of brotherhood. The Smoking Guns were not what I had thought them to be either. I had finally learned my lesson: I just had to be myself. That meant moving on to live my life openly gay—my way.

Lifestyles of the Gay and Fraternal

by Josh Ney, University of Minnesota, Minneapolis

Minnesota has a reputation for being a barren wasteland of ice and snow. There are some days, weeks, even months when the wind causes little ice crystals to form around the edges of your mouth. Late September was no different. I was making my way from the dollar-an-hour parking garage on one side of the Mississippi River to the Student Memorial Union on the other side, where I was to attend my first-ever Greek rush event. These Greeks were different, however, from any other fraternity on campus. These brothers were openly gay and part of the largest chapter of Delta Lambda Phi, the oldest national gay and progressive fraternity in the country.

As I walked onto the patio of the student center that overlooked the longest river in the country, a college man approached me from a crowd of other men. I assumed I was in the right place.

"You were on the front page of the *Daily* today, weren't you?" he asked, extending his arm for a handshake. He was slightly overweight and decadently dressed in what resembled the D&G fall 2003 line.

"Yeah, I guess I was," I replied, shaking his chubby hand and chuck-ling under my breath.

"It was a fabulous picture," he said. His face, perfect for drag, opened up into a blinding white smile. "I'm Merrick, the president of the frat. Welcome, and nice to meet you."

With his handshake and smile, any fear I'd had was suddenly gone. His calming spirit made the slight tremble in my right leg cease. He was the first real gay man I had met since returning from my stay in Rome.

"Thanks. I'm Josh, nice to meet you too," I said.

"Why were you in the paper, though? The caption was pretty lame and didn't say what it was all about," he asked curiously.

"Oh, I went to the GLBT orientation last week and they were like, 'Can we take your picture?' So I said okay, and there I am. I totally outed myself to the entire campus."

"That's brave," Merrick said, doing what could only be described as a ballet move to reach the long, cafeteria-style table and grab a Twinkie.

Yeah, brave or stupid, I thought. Less than one week on campus as a new transfer student and I was on the front page of the newspaper proudly proclaiming that I like boys. I doubted my mother would be pleased to hear the news.

"You need to fill out one of these," Merrick said, handing me what looked like an application to work at the White House.

I took out a pen from my handy, totally fashionable khaki corduroy mail carrier bag, and went to work. The application gave me a bit of a shock when I got to the question, "What does brotherhood mean to you?" Brotherhood. I had no idea what that word meant to me. My goal was to join the "gay fraternity" and avoid the whole stigma of homopho-bia in traditional straight fraternities.

Pondering the question, I was stumped. I simply wanted to meet other men like me. Being an only child, I wrote some bland answer: "Brotherhood means being supportive of others." The entire application left a bad taste in my mouth. I was the first prospective member to show up to the rush kickoff barbecue. All I wanted to do was meet the broth-ers and get some soda. Instead, I felt like I was at the first day of class writing "I feel" statements telling the teacher who I am and what I want from life.

To make matters worse, I felt like dirty men at the bar were ogling me. Brothers would stare in my direction as I filled out the endless application.

Other prospective members had begun to show up. We were all in one area sitting next to each other as we applied ourselves to the arduous task.

"I take it you're not a brother either," said the boy of obviously Norwegian heritage sitting next to me.

My slight Minnesotan *Fargo*-esque accent got the best of me as I replied. "Yeah, ya know, I'm not. I'm Josh, by the way. Ya know, I'm sure kind of nervous about this here whole rush thing."

"Yeah, me too. I have no idea why I came here. I didn't even plan on coming tonight. I guess I was just bored. My name's Ben."

Ben and I continued our quest to fill out the application. Gradually, guys who I assumed to be brothers came through the double-paned glass doors. I had never realized how many different types of gay men there could be. They were chic, of course, but surprisingly I found none of them to be all that attractive. The whole image of what fraternity men should look like did not fit these men. They were not tall, blond, buff, and tanned. I had imagined Adonis himself, a spectacle of tasty eye candy. I did not know whether to thank a higher being that the brothers were not perfectly built or to cry my little eyes out because I could not imagine dating any of them. It was a conundrum.

The night seemed to drag on and on, with more and more people arriving. Many of us had the look of deer trapped in headlights. We were frightened after the painstaking torture of the application. The social gathering was quite large, and the focus was on the rushees. A brother would stop by the table of novice wannabe fraternity members, say a few words, and then toddle off to find another brother. There was not a better word than *awkward* to describe the situation. Over the crowd we heard a booming voice coming to rescue us.

"We're going to the bar—who wants to come with?" shouted Clay, the resident pledge educator, standing atop a newly constructed art deco-meets-postmodern fountain.

Eager to go to my first gay bar, I went along. We went to the only non-smoking bar in the tri-state area, Jet Set. The bar tried hard to be a New York City-style trendy upscale joint. The attitudes of the brothers seemed to have changed between the rush barbecue and the bar. We were no longer rushee to brother; we were gay guy to gay guy.

We were all enjoying the bar and doing our best to mingle when Andy, the brotherhood director and resident Abercrombie & Fitch boy, meandered by, sipping his chocolate martini.

"One thing you little rushees should know about is the hands-off policy. No kissing, no dating, no sex, nothing of the sexual nature can go on between you, the other rushees, and the brothers as long as you are a rushee, or especially a pledge." He took another long sip, never taking a breath, and continued, "Although it's not like guys haven't broken the policy before."

My thought about the fraternity being nothing but one big booty call after another was going down the drain. These guys were about sex, yes, but not with each other. The stereotype of a gay fraternity that I had been battling in my mind was wrong. I had fallen into the trap of thinking, like the homophobes, that all gay men do when they get together is have wild sex. I was young, naive, and stupid, and I still had a lot to learn about these guys and what their fraternity was all about.

Right before our third rush event, I met Will. He had not attended the first or second event, which was a superlame pizza party. The fraternity was meeting for the third rush social at the Queer Student Center. Then we would go together to one of the brothers' houses for a Mexico theme party. Will was sitting in his light blue track suit with his back against a white support column. Immediately our eyes met. He smiled, and I extended my hand. There was something about Will—he seemed to have an old soul, and it was as if he and I had known each other in a previous life. He was tall, slender but defined, and tanned; he had sandy blond hair. He was by far the most attractive of the potential pledges in the fraternity.

"I'm Will," he said. His feminine tone was a shocking contrast to his rugged demeanor.

"Nice to meet you, Will. I'm Josh. I haven't seen you at other events before. Is this your first one?"

"Yeah, I've been pretty busy with school. I just thought I would come and see what this gay frat thing is all about," he said as we were being herded like cattle down the staircase to the cars that would take us to "Mexico."

The party was at Andy's home in the most suburban part of downtown Minneapolis. It was a charming little cottage, and I was surprised to see a rainbow flag flying in the front yard. Lining the sidewalk there were paper sandwich bags with votive candles lighting the path, which led to the front porch, where a large, lonely cactus sat by the door.

Unlike at the other parties, the concept of the fraternity was beginning to sink in. The food was of mediocre Taco Bell quality and the party was nonalcoholic, of course, but what made the gathering fun was the sense of belonging. Maybe this was the definition of brotherhood. Lying on a beanbag chair, listening to Gloria Estefan, and making small talk, I felt like I was at home. Rolf, an exchange student from Hanover, was among the many men I became close to. All the brothers were unique and had something different to offer the fraternity. Hearing Rolf recount his stories about his life in Germany was particularly fascinating.

"I was standing on the Berlin Wall when it came down," he said, as Ben, Will, and I listened as if we were at first-grade story time. "My mom took us there because she wanted us to see history happening. I thought it was cool that I could stand on the wall and my mom wasn't yelling at me to get off."

We all sat around chatting, eating tacos, and listening to really bad Mexican guitar-playing until about 10 P.M. The rush party was officially declared over, and the alcohol came out. A few of us left after a cocktail or two to head off to the bars. It was, after all, a Friday evening.

Several of the brothers, including me, went to a bar in Minneapolis called the Saloon. One long room separated by a divider allowed people to walk in a circle like horses on a carousel. That was really the only thing to do there besides drink and be gawked at by men old enough to be your father. The night was relatively boring until one of the brothers, Clay, got crazy drunk. He was the skinny pretty boy of the fraternity who always looked as if he bought all his clothes in the kids' section of Sears, right down to his Power Ranger "Underoos." Coincidently, Clay was also an Italian major like me.

Shirtless, dancing on the pool table, Clay, our pledge educator, had his pants halfway down his thighs, exposing his bright green thong. I hated watching this and imagined he would be mortified in the morning at his drunken escapade. Clay's behavior was my first clue that he was not the type of brother I wanted to be. It was the first night of many that I would wonder what brotherhood was all about. I still didn't have a good answer.

Something that was becoming more concrete was my feeling for Will. He was everything that I was looking for in a guy. Popular, funny, older than I was, he had seen the world and knew what he wanted from life. We were also spending a lot of time together outside of fraternity gatherings, becoming closer than we had with any of the other brothers.

"You are so a bottom," Will said one morning over runny eggs and soggy toast in a local restaurant.

"What are you talking about? What does that mean?" I said, the novice gay boy.

"Bottoms...you know...they're the submissive guy in the relationship..." He made a gesture resembling the letter O.

"Oh, I get it! So then, a top, is someone who..." I trailed off as I realized my voice had become loud in the confines of the restaurant.

"Yep, exactly."

"So what are you? I mean, can I ask that?" I was curious.

"Honey, I am a big ol' bottom," Will said.

Wow! I never would have thought gay sex could be so confusing. Not only did I have to find out who was gay and who was straight, I also had to figure out what position he favored in bed. Will showed how important this distinction was whenever I would say, "Oh, he's cute." Knocking the guy down to size, Will would come back with the line, "Oh, he's definitely a bottom." I learned a lot from Will about gay subculture.

Regardless of our sexual position preferences, my feelings for Will were becoming more than "just friends." I was well aware of the hands-off policy, but without any sex, my relationship with Will had become much closer than I expected. Was this brotherhood or something else? The brothers said that feelings of interest "like that" would change over time. They always said, "You'll see your pledge brothers in a different light after all the time you spend together. That's why the hands-off policy exists. Your pledge brothers will become so close that it will feel like sleeping with your real brother. How gross is that?"

Such analogies did not help matters, really. Will and I were not looking to have sex, but I did feel a deep sense of connection. He was teaching me the ropes of being gay—like an older brother. Maybe this was brotherhood. We were kindred spirits, and the fraternity had brought us together. Maybe brotherhood was a prerequisite to an intimate relationship. Being a brother meant close friendships without sex. I could handle that, but I doubted if it made sense if two gay men seriously fell in love. I guess the hands-off policy was more of a precaution to shield brothers—a "thou shalt not love another fraternity brother" commandment.

A week later Will, Rolf, Ben, and I skipped our university classes and headed off to a much needed day of beauty and shopping at the Mall of America, which gay men in Minnesota lovingly refer to as the MOA. Pledge educator Clay had been pestering us as usual with fraternity stuff and we needed a break.

All of us needed some winter clothing. I managed to make one of my largest impulse buys and shell out 120 bucks for a supercute pair of Diesel jeans. Will had scheduled a manicure and pedicure and convinced me to do the same. The pedicure was an experience in itself. Too much pampering and the pain around my cuticles made me never want to have that done again. Will was turning me into the true gay boy I was born to be. He was in every sense of the word a brother. Besides, he could not let me go out on my first date in six months with unpolished fingernails.

"You should never put out on the first date. Tease him a little," Will said to me over the phone as I was getting ready for my date with a guy I had met at the Saloon.

"Lord, like I would do that," I replied in self-defense.

"You can never be too careful. I think you have the makings of a true slut, Josh, but I say that with respect," he said, not missing a beat.

"What does that mean?" I asked. His comment stopped me dead in my tracks, my Gap polo clutched in my hand.

"It means that you have not come out of your shell totally. You're still developing your gay identity, and as soon as that happens—all I am saying is that those boys had better watch out," Will said with a laugh.

My evolution from naive just-out-of-the-closet queer was progressing at roadrunner speed. Will was showing me "the way to be gay." He helped me navigate the ins and outs of dating, right down to whether or not to have sex. This was truly brotherhood. It was deeper than friendship, more connected than a mere sex act. All this was happening because of that one blustery September evening when I made the decision to rush the only gay fraternity on campus. My concept of brotherhood was growing stronger. I had learned a lot about who I am and what it meant to be gay.

I guess it would not be a gay fraternity without a little drama along the way. Thursday nights were the night to head to the Saloon. People 18 and over are admitted, the bartenders are hot, and the clientele is a bit more trashy than usual. There is never a quiet Thursday night there—someone always seemed to be stewing in drama. One Thursday night a couple of weeks before initiation, Drama had set her sights on me.

Lou, an alumnus-to-be brother, asked me out on the dance floor. "Are you and Will sleeping together?"

"What did you say?" I said, the music drowning out every syllable.

"*Are you and will sleeping together?*" he yelled, and that time I heard it crystal clear.

"Are you psycho? He is one of my best friends, my brother," I said, ceasing all effort to groove. "Who said that?" Had the lighting not been dim, the red of my face would have shown my mounting anger.

"Some of the brothers, and a few of the alumni," he said.

"Why would they be saying that, Lou?" I asked, pulling him off the dance floor by his lime-green tank top.

"Well, you two have been spending a lot of time outside the frat, and a lot of the time you guys are alone. People talk," he said. I was furious that these rumors would spread without anyone ever having the balls to ask me to my face. Was this what brotherhood was all about—lying behind each other's backs?

I yelled back to Lou, "Well, then maybe I don't want to be a part of this fraternity anymore. If people are so shallow and lame not to even confront me about it, then I need to rethink my pledging." Upset, I drank from my Long Island iced tea.

"Don't say that. Just ignore them. Maybe watch yourself around Will," he slurred.

Downing my Long Island, I went back to join Will on the dance floor. Not only was I angry that the brothers would say that behind my back, but I also had a boyfriend. What if he heard this? All the while, the gay boys in the club were bumping and grinding to a remix of "All the Things She Said." Will and I left at some ungodly hour in the morning. I told him how the brothers had speculated about us and how outraged I felt at the whole thing. Will in his wisdom told me that I should forget about it, let it go. He always knew when to choose his battles, and I took his advice to heart even though I was pissed off.

Initiation into the fraternity was around the corner. I had calmed down and realized that Will was completely right that I shouldn't let rumors eat away at me. The fraternity and my pledge brothers meant way too much to me. Our bond had grown strong. The specific events of initiation, like in any fraternity, are secret rituals. The goal of the initiation was to strengthen the bond of brotherhood. One can classify what we had to go through as an act of tolerance. We were together for three entire days, and when I say together, I mean *together*: I was always within eyesight of my pledge brothers, and there was no escaping the fraternity. It was almost like we were prisoners working on a chain gang and being watched by guards.

The final initiation ceremony took place on another frigid Minnesota night similar to the one when I first met my pledge brothers and the others in the fraternity. The awkwardness I felt that first night was gone. We had become brothers who cared for each other as men, not just as gay guys. The fraternity had allowed each of us to bond in our own way. We all took hands. The complete circle represented the unbroken bond that we all had for one another, ready to be admitted into the fellowship of the fraternity.

Standing there and looking around after the sacred fraternity ritual, I saw my brothers as more than friends. We were family, and just like family we had our ups and downs. Across the way I saw Will, who would always be a wonderful friend and brother, nothing more and certainly nothing less. Even Clay, who had annoyed many of us as pledge educator, was not the jerk I thought him to be. I could see that he was now an integral part of the brotherhood. Each of the brothers contributed something unique to the bond that held us together.

In the end, the brothers of Delta Lambda Phi fraternity were united by two different things: the fact that we were all gay and the fraternal brotherhood. This double bond was stronger than straight fraternities could ever imagine. We were now and forever known to the world as brothers. Without any doubt I had the answer to the question, "What does brotherhood mean to you?"

BROTHERHOOD, TO ME, MEANS HAVING A SENSE OF BELONGING AND ACCEPTANCE IN THE FACE OF DIFFERENCE. IT IS NOT SOMETHING THAT CAN BE BROKEN BY PROBLEMS OR HATRED. BROTHERHOOD ENDURES FOR A LIFETIME.

Ordinarily Not Gay

by Eric B. Asselstine, University of North Dakota, Grand Forks

"I am a gay man."

A sudden chill ran down my spine and I broke into a trembling sweat as I pronounced those five simple words aloud for the first time.

I scurried around my residence hall room, muttering to myself, "Could anyone have heard what I just said? Oh, my God, I am going to lose every single friend I ever had. And my family—shit, they'll write me out of their lives."

I decided not to tell anyone. I had to shove my sexuality deep into my ironclad closet for just another month, until I would be in my own apartment, starting anew. It was only a matter of time then before my safely guarded secret would come out.

That summer I became a recluse, rarely leaving my room, not answering my calls. There I was, the California kid transplanted to the desolate Midwest, taking summer classes at the University of North Dakota. More than ever I felt alone, isolated, and miserable with each passing day. The fact of my sexuality clawed at my soul.

The only solace I found that summer was a crush. I fell hard for this man from Hawaii who was the resident assistant on my dorm floor. His name was Christian. He embodied everything I desired in a man: He was smart, directed, focused, and easy on the eyes. Christian was a pleasant distraction and helped me to let loose and relax. Every chance we got, we poked fun at each other. We would go out and party together. No matter what we did together, I was smitten in his company. He would drag me out of my dorm room, out of the depression of my closet. The escape seemed easy with him, and my sexuality did not seem to matter as much.

In late July, Christian decided to leave campus and spend the remaining weeks of summer back home with his family. I was devastated. The thought of him leaving me hit hard. His departure would mean the torture of my closet would return in all its fury.

That night I went to almost every local bar. I drank gallons of vodka-and-cranberry cocktails. Naively I figured the liquor would take the pain away. Christian's presence had eased the agony of my mental state, and with him gone I was alone again. I drank to escape that reality.

Walking back to my room that night, I stumbled up the stairs, hit my head on the banister, and dropped to the floor at my door.

"Are you okay, Eric?" a female voice said softly. It was the fifth-floor resident assistant making her final rounds for the night. She repeated, "Are you okay?"

Between snivels, I rambled unintelligibly. She helped me to my feet and had me open my door. It was obvious I was drunk. I sat down on the edge of my bed, the room spinning. She sat beside me, and then we lay down together on the bed. The thought that I had a woman in my bed startled me.

I kept mumbling until she patted my head lovingly and said, "Eric, you know it will be okay. I think you're cute, and I have always thought that about you."

With those words I was shocked back to sobriety. I stuttered, "Uh, uh," and sat up abruptly. "I'm not ready for more than friends," I said. Then in a tone of frustration, I blurted, "I miss Christian!" Tears ran down my face.

She sat up and glared at me. "Him? You miss him that much?" she asked. The alcohol amplified her voice. She seemed to be yelling in my ear. "You know he's gay, don't you?" She said, as if I would be repulsed. On one hand, I was pissed off that she thought that would somehow change my mind. On the other hand, I was thrilled to know Christian was gay.

"No, I did not know he's gay," I flared back drunkenly. "But you don't know the truth. I'm gay," I said, my words slurring together.

She grinned and continued talking, but my attention drifted in and out. She then patted me on the head and left my room. I passed out on my bed. She had not believed a word I had said that night.

No doubt I had opened the way for rumors and gossip with my drunken admission that night. I couldn't hide in my dorm room or anywhere else. With a horrific hangover, I concluded that I should tell someone I was gay—it was time. I promised myself I would come out to at least one person each day. Telling one friend at a time, then moving on to my family, I kept that promise. I was amazed, stunned, shocked, and so overwhelmingly pleased that almost everyone I told not only didn't care, they supported me and applauded my bravery. Finally I had put my demons to rest, leaving the closet to my clothes.

My sophomore year was a new awakening—I was out and proud to be gay. That year I spent an increasing amount of time at the Delta Tau Delta fraternity house. Some might consider that to be odd company for a gay man, but I had become friends with several men in the fraternity the previous year. Never did I consider myself a fraternity type of guy, though.

If they hadn't figured it out already, I told them one by one that I was gay. My Delta Tau Delta friends understood that I was the same person they had befriended the year before. The fraternity men were not really concerned about my sexuality. They knew I didn't hang around the fraternity to cruise or scope guys.

The brothers were incredibly interested in my life as a gay man, especially in North Dakota, and they asked lots of questions. The fraternity brothers were amazed that I was gay because I seemed so ordinary. I heard three questions again and again: "Dude, how do you know that you're gay?" "You're so normal—you can't be gay, can you?" "You're not a flamer. How can you be gay?" It provided for much fodder for jokes and the understanding that gay people transcend stereotypes.

Delta Tau Delta fraternity became a safe haven for me and an opportunity to develop close friendships based on truth and honesty. The majority of the brothers were highly academically oriented, laid-back, and successful as leaders on campus. The recurring joke was that the fraternity needed a gay brother to help the other brothers spruce up their wardrobes. The majority of the fraternity brothers were already rather snappy dressers, however. While I liked the idea of being in Delta Tau Delta, I assumed that being gay would be an obstacle in the Greek world. I was just pleased these men were my friends. It made a huge difference in my coming-out process.

The first Delta Tau Delta party of the spring semester took place in February. There were several hundred people there. A mix of guys and girls and a lot of freshmen showed up to check out the fraternity house. I partied with the brothers late into the night and ended up falling asleep on the basement couch. The next morning I woke up to the clank of beer bottles. Opening my eyes wearily, I saw the fraternity president, Steve, throwing cans and other party leftovers into the trash can. I yawned and asked him wearily, "Do you need any help?"

He chuckled and said, "Naw. You look like you need more sleep."

Steve was very down-to-earth, a no-B.S. kind of guy. Since he was the only one cleaning up the place after the party, I got up off the couch to pitch in. As I staggered around picking up bottles and cups, Steve thanked me profusely. My hangover kept me from saying much, but I was glad to help out. After finishing up I headed back to my apartment, a place where I began spending less and less time.

A week later one of my best friends, Delta Tau Delta brother Pete, visited my apartment to hang out and drink a few beers. Pete was straight as an arrow, a skinny kid from a small town in North Dakota. We had met my freshman year and become pretty accomplished drinking buddies, so by the time I came out he was able to look past my homosexuality. Pete had joined Delta Tau Delta the previous semester. Some might call Pete a wannabe redneck, as he claimed to hate gays. Nevertheless he had stuck by my side through my entire coming-out experience.

Sitting in my apartment drinking a cold beer, Pete popped the question. "Eric, would you ever consider joining Delt?"

Conflicting thoughts flooded my head. I worried the beer had got to him already. I replied, "Don't you realize I'm gay?" I paused. "Don't you think that could be a problem for the fraternity, for the brothers?"

Pete sat quietly and took another swallow of his beer, and the conversation drifted away from the question. I never thought about it again. Pete was such a great friend, and we went about our evening of drinking, watching television, and doing what college guys do late into the night.

Later that month, the phone rang at my apartment about 9 o'clock on a Sunday night. Pete was calling me from the fraternity house. "Hey, man, can you drop by the fraternity tonight?" he asked. "Some of the guys have a girl problem."

I laughed and said, "Oh, yeah! As if I can help you guys out with that."

Pete laughed too and pleaded for me to please show up.

Arriving at the Delta Tau Delta fraternity house about 9:30, I was told that the fraternity chapter meeting was running behind and to stick around because some of the brothers really needed to talk to me. Suddenly, I began to worry about all the alcohol I must have consumed at the last Delt party. I must have caused a scene that night. Crap!

Forty-five minutes passed, and there wasn't a person around. I never realized how quiet that house was. The only thing I could hear were hollow voices coming from the brothers in the meeting hall. *What could I have done wrong?* I asked myself.

Fifteen minutes later, Pete appeared in the doorway. He told me the meeting was still going on. I was getting pissed off at having to come over and simply wait. Pete said he understood and wanted to say more, but he begged me to wait. What needed to be talked about was very important.

Finally the meeting broke. The guys were hooting, hollering, and high-fiving each other, some making plans to go out that night. As they passed by, the brothers greeted me with a punch on the arm. Steve, the fraternity president, along with Pete and brothers Matt and Andy, also very good friends of mine, quietly asked me to come into the meeting room. Steve shut the door behind me. Pete's expression was blank. Andy and Matt were staring at me. Steve pulled a white envelope from his blazer pocket and handed it to me. A smile broke across his face.

"Will you accept this invitation to be a brother of Delta Tau Delta fraternity?"

Whoa! Had I heard him correctly? I looked at Steve in disbelief, opening the envelope. I did not know what to say. I had never seen myself as a fraternity man.

All four of them stood there grinning and waiting for my reply.

I said the first thing that came to my mind, "Did you guys discuss that fact that I'm openly gay, and what that might do to the fraternity's reputation on campus?"

All four responded in unison with a booming "Yes!" It was obvious that the lengthy meeting had been about that very matter.

I took a deep breath and answered, "Yes, I accept."

Pete came over and gave me a hug and a big pat on the back. All of the brothers offered me congratulations that night. I could not believe it had happened. These straight fraternity men thought I had what it took to be a brother, to be part of Delta Tau Delta.

By the end of February I was almost living at the fraternity house. The fraternity had become my home, my family. I was called the "drifter," sleeping on a couch or wherever. It did not matter to me: Acceptance was all around me and I felt privileged to be a part of the fraternity.

April rolled around, and I was a couple of weeks away from becoming an active brother in the fraternity when another brother decided to move out of the house, leaving an opening in the room with Steve. He asked me to move into his room. Steve was an awesome brother, but I wanted to make sure he was comfortable with sleeping in the same room with a gay person.

I sat down with Steve that night and asked, "Are you sure you're okay with having a gay man as a roommate? Some people may think you're gay. You could be labeled a closet queer."

He quickly responded, "Fuck 'em if they do. You're my friend, my brother." And the discussion was over. His decision was final, and I was his new roommate.

Moving into the fraternity house, I was always aware of the potential to make other brothers uncomfortable because of my sexuality. The showers were a definite concern, being nude with a bunch of guys lathering up. Only two shower stalls in each bathroom made showering exceedingly difficult for thirty-four guys getting ready for class in the morning. To help alleviate any of their fears, I always made it perfectly clear that I was not interested sexually in any brother. All the brothers claimed to understand that and not care, but some of the brothers asked if I found any of the men in the house good-looking. Always honest with a brother, I said yes, but then explained that I respected each brother and our brotherhood. Never would I do anything to damage the trust and the bond between us. I had a few incidents of walking in on another brother in the buff. We survived it, and often the brother managed better than me not to become flustered.

Brotherhood never let me down at Delta Tau Delta. Many nights the brothers would have long discussions about what being gay was like. The subject seemed to be on the minds of a lot of my brothers. The questions ranged from issues of whether being gay was a choice, whether I could change to be straight, to my favorite: "Boobs do nothing for you?"

The questions were harmless and often amusing. I responded with honesty and candor, and watching their faces was enlightening. It was also obvious that this was their way to bond and learn to be more progressive and sensitive to my being gay. Brotherhood is about looking after one another and caring for one another as your own blood brother. These discussions strengthened that fraternal idea of the meaning of brotherhood and allowed me to share openly and honestly with my brothers. Never did my brothers fail to respond with extreme care and love.

Word had been spread around campus that Delta Tau Delta had a gay brother who lived in the fraternity house. Increasingly I became known as the gay Delt, getting odd glances and stares from other frat men. For all I knew, they could have wanted to either kick my butt or take me out on a date. Either way I had Delta Tau Delta brothers backing me up. Ryan was such a brother. Whenever he heard anything even remotely anti-gay—a joke or a slur—he would stand up for me. Ryan was intimidating and *huge*—6 foot 6 with an impressively muscular torso and athletic build; he was an all-American shot-putter on the university track team. Ryan was my guardian. He would always say to me, "If anybody fucks with you, let me know, I'll take 'em down." A mere look from Ryan was enough to strike fear into the hearts of others.

The time had come. I was initiated into Delta Tau Delta fraternity on April 20, 2001. The initiation ritual was otherworldly, impressive, and almost magical. My fraternity brothers never wanted me to be anything other than who I am. My gay identity never meant I had to hide from fraternity life. I had come a long way thanks to the brotherhood of Delta Tau Delta.

Of course, some of the other fraternities on campus continued spreading rumors. Some said that Delt was the "gay house on campus." It never seemed to bother my brothers very much, but I was on constant alert to make sure I was not exuding "gay." At least one rushee was fooled that year: "I heard that you have a gay brother who lives in the house," he said. "Is that true?"

"Yes, it is true," I responded.

Later that year he joined the fraternity and found out that I was the gay brother he had heard about. The reason he had asked was that he wanted to find a fraternity where he could come out too. I was glad he had discovered Delta Tau Delta.

Acceptance is what we all want. Brotherhood granted me that acceptance and changed my life. Together we were men who cared for and loved one another. The promise of a fraternity for life remains strong with me today. That type of friendship can never be broken by homophobia.

Spaghetti Dinners

by Christopher N. Ho, University of Nevada, Las Vegas

"Hi, my name is Chris."

I could say nothing else to him. Drew was the most beautiful man I had ever seen in my life. He had eyes that sparkled like two emeralds cut by God himself and placed in an angel, and a smile that could melt an iceberg. I was transfixed by this vision of beauty. "Hi, my name is Chris." I tried my best to maintain my composure, but my tanned face blushing red was giving me away.

"Nice to meet you. My name is Drew," he said. Even his voice was angelic. I was hooked the moment his lips moved.

"What university do you go to?" I asked.

"Northwest Missouri State," he replied. Our eyes were locked on each other's as we stood at the bottom of the staircase where we met for the first time. Both of us were attending LeaderShape, a personal empowerment conference for college student leaders. Our outstretched hands locked in a tight grip, not letting go.

The University of Nevada, Las Vegas, had sent me to the LeaderShape conference to prepare for my position within the Leadership Advisory Board, a program that manages and maintains leadership activities throughout the campus. LeaderShape would last a grueling nine days in a serene wooded area of Champaign, Ill. Alpha Tau Omega fraternity had developed the conference program in the mid 1980s to help strengthen the leadership abilities of fraternities and sororities. While I was not a Greek leader, most of the attendees from across the country were fraternity members, including Drew.

Shaking Drew's hand and feeling his returned gaze felt good. My gut told me that he might be gay. Our connection was intense and was definitely mutual. But because Drew was a fraternity guy, I thought for sure I was wrong. Gays are not in fraternities; at least there are no gay men who are comfortable being out in a fraternity—my own campus experience would attest to that. The Greek world and the gay world just did not mix.

Over the next nine days my friendship with Drew began to blossom into a sense of trust and understanding. While he remained beautiful in my eyes, our connection became much deeper, beyond physical attraction. A few days into the conference Drew confided that he was indeed gay. I could not believe it. He had not come out to his fraternity and had debated whether he felt comfortable doing so. Drew was out only to a couple of his friends. Unlike me, Drew was not out to his family. I could tell the issue of coming out was weighing heavily on his mind. I wanted to be there for him, and we talked many nights about his fears and loneliness.

The final day of LeaderShape had arrived. We were pumped with excitement knowing that as leaders we could create a vision of positive change for our campuses. But Drew was not sure of his next step. Drew and I sat together that day and talked about what was going to happen when he returned home to Missouri. Looking lost, his eyes red and puffy from the hours of crying, he said, "What do I do now? I want to tell my fraternity about me. But I'm afraid of what they are going to think and do."

I understood his dilemma, having come out to my family and friends over the years. I desperately wanted to support Drew on his coming-out journey.

"You will know when it's the right time. The words will come to you." I looked away as a tear ran down his cheek. "I'll always be just a phone call away if you need to talk to someone." I took his hand in mine, softly caressing it. "Drew, you are a wonderful person with a lot to give the fraternity. They would be foolish to not want you as a brother. All your skills and attributes won't be forgotten just because you're gay." He slowly began to stop crying. "Do what is in your heart and know that I will always love you as a brother, no matter what," I said, letting go of his hand and smiling.

Our long conversation at LeaderShape gave Drew the necessary courage. He wanted to go back and tell his fraternity brothers that he was gay. LeaderShape had taught us to create a vision for positive change. We were both committed to leadership involvement and finding ways to have an impact on our campuses. At that moment, as I sat there with Drew, my vision became crystal clear. I was determined to do everything I could to be an out fraternity man on my campus. I figured that being part of the Greek system was the only way to effect change and help other men like Drew. The strength I saw in Drew's eyes gave me the passion to make a difference. Both of us shared the vision to make the Greek system a more welcoming place for gay brothers.

Returning to UNLV was refreshing. I was full of vigor and ready to tackle the challenges ahead of me. The idea of joining a fraternity grew stronger. I was eagerly attracted to the idea of brotherhood. I was an only child and felt the lack of siblings. I thought the fraternity might fill this void with an unbreakable bond lasting the rest of my life.

Since 2001, when I entered UNLV, I had been very involved as a leader and was well-respected among fellow student leaders. I figured I would be a hot commodity for any fraternity. I had done a lot on campus, such as being orientation leader for new student orientation and being a student ambassador to the president of the university. Plus I had many great relationships with administrators and staff. My reasons for rushing a fraternity could not be discounted as résumé-building. But I did hope a fraternity would value my leadership qualifications.

Rush started right away, the first week of the fall semester. Pi Kappa Alpha fraternity, referred to as "Pike," stood out immediately as my top choice. Two of the brothers, Paul and Sean, had been friends of mine from new student orientation. Both men knew I was gay and had no problem with it. One would never guess that Paul was even in a fraternity, much less the president of one. Paul was the type of guy who could be on the cover of *Teen Beat*—short, quiet, and innocent-looking with a face to melt any heart. Sean was the complete opposite—tall, stocky, but a total teddy bear. I'd never want to be on his "bad" list. Joining their fraternity would be an honor. They were equally excited that I wanted to join, and they encouraged me.

The Pikes were known on campus as jocks, academics, and leaders. Looking over the materials at the Pi Kappa Alpha table during Greek rush, I thought the brotherhood seemed diverse, and the brothers seemed to offer various skills and involvement on campus. Steve was the first person I met when I approached the table.

"How's it going? My name is Steve. I'm the rush chair for Pi Kappa Alpha," he said excitedly. Steve was a short, hyperactive Asian guy whose personality was infectious. He smiled and greeted everyone who walked by. After talking with Steve and spending time at the rush table, I had no doubt that I wanted to join Pike. "You should come to our party at the house," he said, handing me an invite. He was even more excited than before.

The Pikes seemed to be a perfect fit. I felt like I had something to offer them, and their brotherhood seemed to be the "real thing."

Walking through the wooden back gate and entering the backyard of the fraternity later that evening, I could hear the sounds of the partygoers enjoying the rush party. Grabbing a red plastic cup of soda, I walked toward the lighted pool. It was of normal size, shaped like a squeezed hard-boiled egg. I looked longingly at the pool.

"Hey, dude, what's going on?" The guy introduced himself as Kirk, another prospective member. He was handsome, with golden hair. Kirk asked, "Are you a brother?" I was enthralled. He thought I was already a brother. I must fit in with the fraternity.

"Actually, I'm a prospective like you," I said. He seemed glad. We started talking and walked around together for most of the party.

Kirk and I met many of the brothers. They would come up and introduce themselves and were very genuine, wanting to learn more about us. The party wound down and I approached Steve, who had invited me. I thanked him for the opportunity to meet more of the fraternity brothers.

Steve laughed and said, "You have a lot to offer to this fraternity. We'd like to see you around some more. Why don't you come out to Hooters with us tomorrow night?"

I paused, thinking, *Hooters.* So maybe they didn't know I was gay. Paul and Sean may not have told the fraternity. I didn't mind—it was probably a good thing so the brothers could know me first without the GAY stamp on my forehead.

"Sure. I can't wait," I said. I was totally looking forward to hanging out with these guys and getting to know them more.

The next night was the Hooters party. I arrived about 20 minutes early to make sure I had ample time to meet everyone. Walking through the large wooden doors inlaid with the Hooters logo, I entered the world of every straight man's fantasy—women in short, tight orange shorts and clingy white T-shirts showing off a nice rack, plus beer and food. I saw all the fraternity guys enjoying the food and "perky" service on the back patio. I couldn't help but feel as though I were in a bad episode of *The Twilight Zone* where everyone fits in and you are the odd man out.

Over and over again I reminded myself that it was going to be all right. I had nothing to fear. Like I had told Drew, "You're a wonderful person with a lot to give to the fraternity. They would be foolish to not want you as a brother. All the skills and attributes you possess will not be forgotten just because you're gay." I wanted to believe it now more than ever.

Steve was always extremely hospitable and greeted me with open arms. "Chris, I'm glad you could make the party," he said, and he began introducing me to brothers I had not met before. One of the brothers asked me, "Do you have a girlfriend?" My first reaction was to tell him, "No, I don't have a boyfriend either," but instead I quickly said, "No."

Luckily, Kirk was there. "What do you think of everything so far?" I asked him after refilling my drink and grabbing a plate of wings. He stopped to eye a couple of girls who were laughing out on the porch.

"It's interesting—there are so many hot girls, I have no idea what to do with myself," he said with a broad, corny smile.

The evening finally came to an end. When I said goodbye to Steve he handed me another invitation. This time the invite was to attend their preference dinner, which is reserved for those prospective members who are highly likely to receive a bid to join the fraternity. Wow. I was on my way to get a bid. The dinner was the final step.

I was overjoyed as I read, "The brothers of the Pi Kappa Alpha fraternity would like to see you at our dinner at the Old Spaghetti Factory behind the Galleria…" I must have made a great impression if I made it this far. Little did I know the extent of the impression I had made on the brothers.

The next day the phone rang. I almost dropped it when I heard Paul's voice. "Chris, how's it going?" he said.

"I'm doing rather well; I'm really looking forward to tonight's dinner." I said. That was an understatement, as I had spent two hours trying on outfits in preparation.

"I'm actually calling about the dinner," Paul said. "I'm on the freeway right now, but I would really like to talk to you about something." The tone of his voice gave me a sick feeling in the pit of my stomach.

Panic-stricken, I stuttered, "What do you want to talk about?"

"I can't really talk right now. I'm on the freeway and my girlfriend is with me," Paul responded.

There was the clincher: "I can't, my girlfriend is in the car." I knew something was wrong. Paul said he would tell me later at the dinner. Not knowing what he wanted to talk about was the worst feeling in world. Only one thought was in my head: *There is no way we are going to let a faggot into this fraternity.*

The fraternity dinner was at the back of the restaurant, where everything was set up as if royalty would be in attendance. Tables were adorned with beautiful red tablecloths and wildflowers as centerpieces. The lights were dimmed to an almost romantic mood level. These guys had totally outdone themselves with the spectacle.

One of the fraternity alums was the featured guest speaker for the occasion. He shared what the fraternity stood for and the values of brotherhood.

THE MEN OF PI KAPPA ALPHA ARE LEADERS AMONG MEN THROUGHOUT THE CAMPUS. WE STRIVE FOR EXCELLENCE IN ALL WE DO. WE PROVIDE OUTSTANDING SERVICE TO OUR COMMUNITY ON AND OFF CAMPUS. THE FRATERNITY UNDERSTANDS WHAT A TRUE LEADER IS, AND WE ALL POSSESS THE QUALITIES THAT MAKE US THE LEADERS OF TOMORROW.

He knew exactly what to say. His charismatic charm and delivery could sell ice to an Eskimo. All eyes were glued on him as he went on about the benefits of brotherhood in Pi Kappa Alpha.

The dinner was amazing: We had spaghetti with flavorful red marinara sauce and healthy chunks of ground beef, tossed green salad with ranch dressing, and vanilla ice cream for dessert. The food reinforced what the alumnus had to say about the style and class of the fraternity and how a Pike fraternity man was a "true gentleman." The food, the atmosphere, and the company were a memorable embodiment of what I hoped for from a brotherhood. I could be part of this fraternity and be proud to be a brother.

Paul and I never got the chance to talk that evening. I had hoped the issue, whatever it was, had magically disappeared. The next day in the early afternoon, however, I got a phone call from Paul. I had been thinking about how much fun I had had with all the brothers the night before.

"Chris…it's Paul from Pi Kappa Alpha," he said, sounding relaxed.

"Hey, how's it going?" My voice quavered.

"I've wanted to talk to you about the fraternity. I'm sorry we didn't have a chance to talk last night," he said. I braced myself. "Chris, you are a great guy with a lot to offer a fraternity in your leadership abilities and your charisma." Then came the dreaded words: "I believe that our fraternity is not yet ready for someone like you to join at this time." He paused.

I didn't know how to respond. I felt anger and frustration, hopelessness and failure. I asked the stupidest question: "So does this mean that I won't receive a bid from the fraternity on bid day?"

"That's right," he replied. "I did my best to make them understand about you, but they wouldn't listen to me. If I had it my way, there would not be an issue," he said.

After all the years I had been out to my friends and family, I never would have guessed I would experience such prejudice and bigotry first-hand. The Pi Kappa Alpha "true gentlemen" could not get past that I was gay. Everything else I had to offer didn't count.

I couldn't sleep that night thinking about the Pikes and wondering what I could have done differently. The only choice really was not to be gay. Not knowing where to turn, I decided to visit the Greek life advisor, Curt, whose responsibility was all the fraternities and sororities on campus. He knew of my interest to rush Pike and was genuinely concerned that I was now in his office.

"Curt, I don't want to get anyone into trouble, but I think there is something you need to know about," I said calmly, not crying. "I got a phone call from Paul last night telling me that I was not going to need to pick up a bid from Pike because they're not ready to have 'someone like me' in their fraternity."

"He actually told you this?" The look on his face was one of pure shock.

"Yes, Curt, that's what he told me on the phone last night." My emotions were getting the best of me.

Curt was obviously irritated by the news. He understood my position and agreed the Pikes' actions were not acceptable.

I had no idea what might happen to Pi Kappa Alpha fraternity. I wanted it to be over. I am not a vindictive person, but I wanted someone to tell the brothers that this was not appropriate behavior. They had actively rushed me and then decided that because I slept with guys and not girls I would not be good for the fraternity. I thought the brothers had gotten to know me better.

Never could I have imagined going through the whole ordeal again, but fate has a weird sense of humor. The following spring I was approached by my friend Kevin, a member of Phi Delta Theta fraternity. He had heard all about the Pike incident and made the comment that I would always have a home in Phi Delta Theta fraternity.

Phi Delta Theta was known as the fraternity with the most leaders. Kevin, a lanky white kid from Vegas, was not an exception: He was well respected on campus and a master of persuasion.

"Come on, Chris, you would be great as a brother in Phi Delta Theta," he said. He was positive that he could get me in as a pledge.

"You know what happened last time I tried," I said.

"But I have the ability to get you in. There are people who owe me favors," he said.

Did I really want Kevin to pull favors to get me a bid? Phi Delta Theta seemed like a wonderful choice. My leadership involvement might be more highly valued among an established group of campus leaders.

"All right. Let's see what happens," I said. I genuinely did want to be involved in a fraternity, and I didn't have much to lose.

The first Phi Delta Theta rush event was a barbecue in the campus amphitheater. I went and talked to the brothers I already knew. Kevin wasn't there; as usual he was off doing something for student government.

Word had spread quickly through the fraternities about the Pike controversy. I started to feel marked, like Hester Prynne from *The Scarlet Letter* but with three letters plastered across my chest: GAY. Everyone knew who I was, and I tried to rise above their stares and present my best image. It must have paid off because I received an invite to the Sword and Shield preference dinner.

The Phi Delta Theta dinner was oddly similar to the dinner with Pike.

The restaurant was a quaint Italian bistro with red and green picnic tables.

"Kevin, I don't know if I can do this. What if I have to go through the same thing I did last semester with Pike?"

"You're going to be fine, and I have everything under control. I've called in a favor. We should have no problem getting you in," he said.

Sitting down to dinner, I wondered how many of these guys were actually going to receive bids. Looking down the table, I came across a face that I had not seen in a long time: that of a guy named Scott. About two months earlier we had fooled around at his apartment. This was going to be interesting because Scott acted gayer then me, but nobody in the fraternity knew about him ahead of time.

Just like at the Pike dinner, I really enjoyed myself. I talked to a lot of the brothers and we all laughed. Spaghetti was the main course. Afterward Kevin told me that the fraternity would be meeting soon to discuss who was going to be offered bids, and he would call me with the news. Once again he assured me everything was going to be okay.

Later, the phone rang. I answered to hear Kevin yelling.

"Chris, this is really fucked up! The vote came down to one person. He told me he would vote for you. Fuck." Kevin had failed, and so had I. It was exactly like before. The hurt was in not understanding why my being gay would matter, but this time I didn't let my emotions get too overwhelmed by it all.

"What about Scott—did he get a bid?" I asked.

"Yes, he did. But why do you care?" Kevin asked.

"Well, I didn't tell you before, but Scott is also gay. He and I were intimate a while ago." Kevin immediately freaked out.

"What? You never told me that! Now, that is really some fucked-up shit."

"Would it have made any kind of difference if I had told you he was gay?" I asked, already knowing the answer.

Kevin was silent. I would have expected him to admit that knowing Scott was gay would have prevented him getting a bid too. "To tell you the truth," he said finally, "it probably wouldn't have made any difference. Scott acted straight. None of the brothers suspected he was gay. It probably wouldn't have mattered."

Did that mean that if I pretended to be straight, I would fit in? I was not going to change that to fit in with a bunch of fraternity guys.

Two of the largest fraternities on campus had rejected me for being gay. My commitment to Drew and our vision of change loomed over my head. I needed a pep talk. I called one of my friends, Karen, a sister in Sigma Kappa sorority and an influential leader in the Greek system. We had been close friends ever since new student orientation. She was aware of the Pike debacle, and I knew she would not readily pass judgment.

"Karen, I need someone to talk to right now. Phi Delt rejected offering me a bid too," I said.

"Why would they not want you in their fraternity?" She exclaimed, knowing the answer was simply homophobia. "Chris, will you do me one favor?" she said. "I know you have been through a lot, but the guys of Alpha Tau Omega are having their preference dinner tomorrow night. I think you should go over there and check them out. Please give them a chance."

Karen begged me to go, and she had never steered me in the wrong direction. I had no idea who these Alpha Tau Omega guys were and had never really met any of them.

Maybe it was some sort of omen, but the only idea I had of Alpha Tau Omega was from LeaderShape. They were the fraternity that founded the program, and LeaderShape was where my spark for fraternity life began. That was enough to give me an interest in the fraternity. I agreed reluctantly to give it one last try. Karen got very excited and said she would call Brian, the fraternity president, immediately.

Drizzling rain was coming down when I arrived at the Alpha Tau Omega fraternity house. There were cars parked all over the cul-de-sac, and a porch light illuminated the front entrance. I knocked on the door, which was opened by a short, round guy.

"You must be Chris. We've been expecting you. Come in and meet the brothers." He introduced himself as Brian, the president of the fraternity, and welcomed me into the house. With his demeanor, he commanded respect despite his stature.

When we approached the middle of the living room, Brian announced to the entire room, "This is Chris Ho. He is here to meet us, to learn about our fraternity, and to become a pledge. Let's show him how we do it here and welcome him to the fraternity."

The energy and mood of the fraternity was different from my two previous experiences. The open welcome was followed by handshakes and meaningful conversations.

We all sat down at the tables arranged in the living room, and dinner was served. The menu was, you guessed, spaghetti. I could not believe the irony.

Alpha Tau Omega fraternity was based on the principles of brotherhood, community service, and a relationship with Christ. As the night progressed I began to feel more comfortable, and the discussions seemed even more meaningful. These brothers seemed to know about my sexuality but did not care. Finally, I had found a fraternity where I could be accepted for who I was—I hoped I was right about that this time.

After the dinner, I was asked into Brian's room. Three of the brothers were sitting there. I took a seat in front of them.

"Chris, we called you in here to talk briefly about your joining this fraternity," Brian said. "We understand that you have gone through a lot in the past year and would like to know if you are still interested in fraternity life."

Then Kent, an older brother, said, "If you are interested, we would be more than happy to have you as a member of this fraternity."

"We believe that you would add a lot to the fraternity. Your difference will add strength to the brotherhood," Brian said.

After all I had been through, I could not believe what I was hearing. I nodded my head affirmatively.

"You can pick up your bid tomorrow, and if you choose to accept it, we'll see you tomorrow night," the third brother, Jaime, said with a grin on his face.

The next night I showed up to accept my bid to join Alpha Tau Omega. I was greeted warmly by a handful of the brothers. The sense of pride was the best feeling: These fraternity brothers knew I was gay and still accepted me into the brotherhood. Being openly gay and joining a fraternity was possible.

The rest, as they say, is history. I pledged Alpha Tau Omega and became a brother. The love and support I got from my brothers was wonderful. In the spring of 2004 at the UNLV Greek awards ceremony, I received the New Member of the Year honor in front of the entire Greek system. I have never been as proud of my accomplishments as I was on that day.

Alpha Tau Omega was the right fraternity for me. My vision to lead had been actualized. I was openly gay and a fraternity man, living my life without fear, side by side with my brothers. It took me three tries to finally crack the shell of the Greek system. But I did it—my determination held strong. My days at LeaderShape with Drew will always be the reason for my determination.

I have no regrets about my first two attempts to join a fraternity, and if I had to do it again, I would. But this time I would skip the spaghetti.

A Question of Love and Loyalty

Hide Away

by Chris Zacharda, Bucknell University, Lewisburg, Pa.

"I think yours is bigger than mine," Dan said, just barely audibly.

Even though I'd heard what he said, I asked nervously, "What are you talking about?"

Both of our hard-ons were visible through our sweatpants. We were lying in the dark on opposite couches facing each other, pretending to watch *Red Dawn* but really watching each other. I stood up, my legs shaking, and went over to his couch. He slid his sweatpants down around his knees and pulled me toward him. I felt like I was swimming. Everything was moving in slow motion. I had never done anything like this before. I had been waiting for this moment for years, but suddenly I was terrified. I was overwhelmed by the scent of Ivory soap as my face brushed against his flat stomach. I could feel an icy December draft blow through the living room.

"This is our little secret," he whispered. "Just our little secret. No one can ever know about this. Our little secret, our little secret," he mumbled over and over again. His whisper was just barely audible over the cold wind whipping outside against the windows.

When we were finished, he could see that I had been crying. "What's wrong with you?" he barked. He wouldn't look me in the eye.

All I could say was, "I don't know what's wrong with me. I don't understand what's happening." I couldn't stop shivering. More than anything, I thought, *I want him to tell me it will all be okay.*

"Well, I don't want to talk about it. And you can't tell anyone, Chris. Now get your stuff and I'll take you home." My excitement was now replaced with something darker—shame, regret, and dread. Even though I had had these desires for years, I always told myself that I could never be gay. Dan's response confirmed in my mind that what we had done was wrong. *Why was I so sick that I let this happen?* I asked myself repeatedly. I would have to live with this shameful secret all my life. And I dreaded that Dan would hate me because I was some sissy for crying. I just needed Dan to tell me everything was okay.

Dan and I repeated our sexual escapade again and again. Each time the sex was more intense and more laden with shame. He would often remind me that we were friends and no more. We fooled around together frequently for the rest of high school and even during parts of college. I still cried after sex. I thought Dan was the only person in the world who was like me. Nevertheless, he seemed fine after each sexual encounter, his perfect smile replaced by a stoic bravado that always pushed me away. He projected such intense shame and disgust for the sex that was part of our friendship that I grew to incorporate those feelings into who I was. He would yell, "We're not gay. We can never be like that. If anyone ever knew what we do, it would alienate them for sure. Is that what you want?"

The world around us in the late 1980s only reinforced what Dan told me. I kept my sexuality buried and felt so confused and lonely about being gay.

High school in blue-collar York, Pa., was a breeze. I was a big fish in a little pond, and few people would have suspected that the class president and swim team captain was secretly tortured by a shameful sexual relationship with a friend.

In the fall of 1989 I went to college at Bucknell University, a small private school in the middle of Pennsylvania. College meant that I would have to leave Dan and our sexual torment behind. As a result I felt more lost than ever.

The Bucknell campus felt like a J. Crew photo shoot: Many rich preppy kids went to Bucknell, and there were expensive cars everywhere. The campus seemed perfect—the people, the clothes, the cars, the buildings, the lawn. Of course, I did everything to hide my middle-class upbringing, pretending to be just like everybody else. Since I had been a competitive swimmer since age 5, the first students I met on campus were swimmers. While Bucknell was not necessarily a national powerhouse, I was nonetheless honored to have been recruited for Bucknell's NCAA Division I swim team. The competition on the team was fierce, with many top-ranked high-caliber swimmers. A few on the team had even made the trials for the Olympics. These men seemed huge compared to those from my high school swimming days. Everywhere I was surrounded by tall, muscular college athletes with perfectly smooth tan skin in tight Lycra Speedos. Desire churned within me as I trained beside them every day. I would not dare let my eyes linger or glance too longingly. The thought of being discovered as gay on campus paralyzed me. My sexual identity remained locked away despite the distractions. Instead I put all my energy into building my skills for the swim team—swimming harder than the guys who were much faster than me. As a result I landed the swim team number 2 butterfly position, which was pretty rare for a freshman. I had found peace under the water.

One Friday after swim practice our swim captain told all the team members that the coach wanted to meet us on Saturday night off campus at another swimmer's house. Most of the new swim team members were led to believe this was urgent and that somehow we had pissed off the coach. We were told to wear a dress jacket and a tie and, most important, be prompt.

When I arrived that Saturday, the coach was nowhere to be seen. I was overcome with dread. The swim team captain, with his wild black hair and giant, armor-like pecs, cocked his head and yelled, "Line up, losers. I don't want to hear a word from you faggots. Tonight you're going to prove you're a man." It was clear that this was our initiation.

Each of us was then blindfolded and led single file by the senior men into the damp, dreary basement of the house. It reeked of mold and piss. We were tightly assembled beside one another, and I felt the bodies of other freshman swimmers pressed against me. I was scared and yet turned on by the physical proximity. We were left there, herded like goats in the basement for what seemed like an hour, sweating profusely, with the senior members shouting insults at us the whole time. Then we each got slapped across the chest with a name tag—a nickname, mostly girls' names. I was Sheila. The captain commanded in his booming voice, "Don't let anyone take your name tag or we'll pummel your ass." They led us up the stairs into another room filled with the roar of guys chanting and yelling slurs. Dozens of hands punched and tore at my chest, trying to rip off my tag. We were drenched with beer and huddled closely together. Every time my name tag was removed from my chest, an upperclassman would yell at me to chug a beer. I repeatedly accepted the punishment. I knew I could drink a lot, and I thought that was sure to impress them. I was so eager to please that within minutes I had chugged six or seven beers. I was feeling quite drunk and was soaked in beer by the time the frenzy was over. My blindfold was slowly removed. There in front of me stood Eddie, a truly magnificent blond Adonis, smiling and cheering. He was the first to shake my hand and slap me on the back, yelling "Welcome, you're one of us!" The reassurance was a relief.

Eddie was a senior and captain of the water polo team. His team often trained with the swimmers. He always wore a blue baseball cap and a tight white ribbed T-shirt, showing off his massive biceps. I had never really spoken to Eddie before that night. A few times I caught him watching me at the gym. He would always smile when we made eye contact. I never thought anything of his occasional glances and always ignored his all-American good looks for obvious reasons—I could not risk getting caught.

That night of initiation, Eddie had mostly protected me from the other seniors who were barking orders and baptizing the new recruits with beer. Eddie made me feel safe that night. Other new members were not so fortunate. Eddie and I found ourselves separated from the pack, lingering in the backyard, more beers in hand.

"Why are you being so nice to me?" I asked.

He slowly shook his head, saying nothing, with a broad smirk across his face. "Are you wearing cologne?" he asked, leaning in and smelling my neck. My heart skipped a beat as I felt his cheek touch the collar of my shirt. "And why are you wearing an undershirt? Are you a Mormon or something?" He subtly unbuttoned the top button of my shirt. The ground beneath me tilted and I swayed a bit, catching my balance.

Emboldened by the beer and sensing an opportunity, I leaned in to him and grazed his thigh with my hand. Eddie grabbed my wrist, thrust his elbow against my chest, angrily bent my arm behind my back, and barked, "Don't ever do that again."

Terrified, I pleaded drunkenly, "Why not?"

Eddie responded with, "If you ever do that again, I'll do this," and smashed his knee into my crotch. He shoved me to the ground and walked away. My heart stopped; my secret was out. Lying in a ball on the ground, I waited until Eddie had left, and despite the pain I ran back toward campus. My head was swimming from the humiliation and the beer. I was crying once again in shame as sweat streamed down my face and further soaked my beer-drenched sports coat. By the time I got back to my dorm I was out of breath and shameful tears had dried on my cheeks.

That next week I avoided Eddie at practice and on campus every day. When I would see him unexpectedly I would panic and leave. I could only imagine him bragging to the whole swim team about how the faggot had made a pass at him and how he threw the fag to the ground. I felt positive that Eddie had told everyone what happened, and I slowly withdrew and eventually quit the swim team. The loss was even deeper than I imagined. All I had ever known was in the pool. I did not know what to do with myself on campus. I was alone, starting over again.

With swimming cut from my life, I threw myself into partying and making out with girls to drown my shame. I desperately wanted to change who I was. I drifted from one hookup to the next, offering no explanation to the girls. It was a gimmick, my hopeful solution to convince my friends that I was indeed straight as an arrow.

Later that semester, for my 18th birthday, I went out with Julie, a popular member of the Kappa Alpha Theta sorority. She was a junior and an RA in another building. She had asked me to be her date to her sorority's fall formal event. The thing I remember most about Julie was her enormous breasts—even a closeted gay man could not forget them. All the guys on my floor would talk about how hot "they" were. Yes, guys would refer to the tits as an entity rather than to Julie. I went along with the breast banter to blend in. After all, those breasts were the perfect mask to solidify my manhood and growing reputation as a "pussy hound."

The night of her formal, Julie and I got drunk and hooked up, and I got to meet her breasts firsthand. I was also introduced to many upperclassmen from the campus fraternity, Sigma Alpha Epsilon. The SAE fraternity men struck me as a wild, fun, and eclectic group. Some, of course, were handsome J. Crew men while other brothers were rather plain. One in particular was short and funny, a riot at the party. The down-to-earth

SAE attitude was a stark contrast to the intimidation that was the norm on the swim team. That night each of them made me feel welcome, even though I wasn't a brother or even a fraternity member. The experience encouraged me to attend some parties at the SAE house and just hang out there. The sororities on campus had nothing but good things to say about SAE, and girls in general thought they were cool. While the SAE guys would go out of their way on campus to talk to me, other frat guys would go out of their way to appear "too cool for school," barely nodding at a freshman. By the end of the fall I was seriously interested in SAE, and I wanted to be part of the fraternity. It would not only be a great source of friendship but would offer another layer to my mask along with Julie's breasts. Nobody would ever think I was gay in a fraternity.

Bucknell had deferred fraternity rush, which means that all fraternities on campus wait until the spring to recruit new members. During the rush process I received several invitations to different fraternities. I was lucky to have found SAE. I was amazed at how comfortable I felt around these men. I figured that my sexuality would never be an issue because we seemed to have so much in common. The other fraternity houses tried hard to be hypermasculine, but with SAE there seemed to be all kinds of guys—jocks, dorks, studs, nerds, leaders, rich guys, guys on financial aid, and most important, likable guys. I knew I had to be a pledge of Sigma Alpha Epsilon.

By the end of the last night of rush, I received the news secretly. Some of the sophomore fraternity members eagerly whispered as I left the house, "Congratulations, Chris—you did it! Come tomorrow. You're going to be one of us." They even slipped me the pledge grip. I was not supposed to know that I had even received an invitation to join the fraternity until the next morning. I felt proud and relieved. Nonetheless, a tiny voice in my head said, *Don't get your hopes up just yet; something could go wrong.*

I heard footsteps running down the hall of my dorm at 5 o'clock in the morning. Even the slightest noise always woke me up. I leapt across the room, finding an envelope with my name on the floor under the door. I tore open the envelope and yelled aloud, "I'm in!" The fraternity letter extending me a bid instantly made me feel the power of acceptance. This was the beginning of a time that would change my life. I would never be alone. My sexuality was a distant memory, locked away.

All the fraternity pledges scattered to the fraternity houses at noon for bid day. It was cold, with snow on the ground, but that didn't matter. Each of us declared our acceptance by running madly onto the SAE porch. Seventy SAE men welcomed us with crazy hollering. As I got onto the porch, two guys were fighting over who got to give me the SAE letters. I put on my new SAE T-shirt and a roar of cheers erupted from the front porch. The cheering was almost deafening. I could not hear anything that was being said to me, but I smiled and enthusiastically nodded my head. A few brothers handed me beer, but nobody ever forced me to drink or tried to douse me with alcohol. The awful memory of the swim team initiation dissipated. I felt as if I was coming home, and I knew that I had found my place on campus.

On that snowy day in February our pledgeship had officially started, with 23 new members for the pledge class of 1990. All the pledges seemed to have an instant bond as we were introduced to the SAE fraternity officers, many of whom I had already met and hung out with. Rich, the rush chair, was the hero of the hour. He had recruited one of the biggest pledge classes SAE had ever had, far bigger than our rivals'. Standing on the window ledge of the chapter room, surrounded by dozens of brothers cheering him on, he seemed larger than life. His face, red from yelling and drinking, was inherently kind, and he wore a big goofy drunken grin. "Let me be the first to welcome you to SAE. We are so stoked to have taken the best pledge class on campus!" The room erupted in yelling and the brothers pounded on the floor. He continued, "You're about to start the best years of your life, and we're glad you picked SAE." I would come to learn that his words could not have been truer: Rich and the fraternity would change my life forever.

The pledge process was designed to teach us how to be "true gentlemen," the motto of SAE. This included learning to treat people with compassion and understanding, and the value of expending blood, sweat, and tears to help a fellow man. We would spend countless hours learning all about one another, bonding, and proving ourselves in the eyes of the brotherhood. Not only was it important to prove ourselves worthy of being initiated into SAE, we also had to learn to appreciate those older brothers who were already in the fraternity. I was determined to be the best SAE pledge, even saying once to Rich, after several beers, "One day I'm going to be SAE president." I later laughed at my drunken optimism and thought, *A gay fraternity president…yeah, that would never happen, even if I am closeted.* The fraternity kept me so busy that my sexuality was sidelined. Instead, I was focused on SAE.

One of the first aspects of pledging was our "Senior Pop." Each of the pledges was given a senior college fraternity brother who would share the values of the fraternity and be a close mentor to the pledge. Since our pledge class was larger than the senior class of fraternity men, some of the pledges with last names near the end of the alphabet were matched up with a few junior classmen in the fraternity. Thanks to the letter *z* and a lucky draw of fortune, I was matched with Rich. I was now able to study Rich and get to know him better as a brother and as my new Pop. A handsome Irishman, Rich had the most beautiful green eyes I had ever seen. He was about my height and typically wore an SAE hat over his messy brown hair. Rich was always the first man in the fraternity to start the party. I could usually find him at the house, hanging out in the TV room with a beer in hand.

Senior Pop Week started and I could not wait to spend time with Rich. He took me to dinner off campus, where we talked about everything from Irish families to our favorite beers. Rich would frequently introduce me to all the pretty Alpha Chi Omega girls who were his friends. Whether it was playing a drinking game, studying for a test in biology, or sharing his fraternity experience, Rich was always there for me. He was a great fraternity mentor—smart, humorous, respected, and very cute. Needless to say, I was smitten with Rich, and I wanted to be just like him.

The last night of Senior Pop Week we had the official Pop & Son Throw-Pong Tourney, a drinking game about throwing a Ping-Pong ball across a table into your opponent's cup. If your team gets a Ping-Pong ball in the cup, you score and the opponent has to drink a beer. I learned quickly that I was rather good at bouncing Ping-Pong balls, and to my surprise Rich held the fraternity title of Throw-Pong Master. Being on the same Pop & Son team, Rich and I cruised to victory in the preliminary rounds. To keep the competitive spirit alive, we each made sure to drink a few beers before winning another match. Rich made me feel like a total stud because we won Throw-Pong. While we waited for the next Throw-Pong match, Rich introduced me to the Alpha Chi girls who had raided our Pop & Son party. They fawned over Rich, hugging and kissing him, telling me how lucky I was to have Rich as my Senior Pop. This made me admire him even more. Awkward, familiar feelings began surfacing as I watched Rich with these girls. I wanted to be the one who was bragging about how great Rich was. I wanted to be the one he was hugging. I wanted to be the one kissing him.

The party grew more crowded as Rich and I continued entertaining the Alpha Chi sorority girls. He and I were smashed together in one corner of the room. Rich gradually slipped his arm around my shoulder, drinking and singing fraternity songs with the rest of the crowd. Eventually he slipped his arm around my waist, screaming to some Alpha Chi girls who had just walked in, "Hey! This is Chris, my new Senior Son. He's the coolest pledge we've got!" I laughed, tugging at his shoulder. I joined in the singing and tightly wrapped my arm around his waist. The crowd soon shifted, tearing us apart as we were singing. Moments later, Rich had disappeared.

I looked all around for Rich. Our turn to compete in the Throw-Pong finals was coming up, and he was nowhere to be found. I ran up to Rich's room to see if he was there and found him passed out on his bed. I knelt down to his mattress on the floor and shook him awake. Rich opened his big green eyes, leaned forward, and kissed me full on the mouth. He pulled back, his eyes looking directly into mine with a devilish twinkle. I was floored, stunned. I had never kissed another guy on the lips before, not even Dan. For Dan, kissing on the lips was too personal and conjured up images of faggots—men pretending to be women. With Rich, in that moment, I felt only exhilaration. The noise from the party downstairs faded away. I was acutely aware of everything in front of me, all of my senses tingling. The smell of a candle burning next to the bed was as sweet as honey. I could see the flicker in his eyes as he stared up at me. I could feel the softness of his flannel sheets against my hand as I leaned against the bed. My face burning red-hot, I asked, "Do you know who I am?" I braced myself for anything, hoping that he knew it was me.

He slowly lowered his eyelids as a drunken smile swept across his face. Looking up at me, he said, "Yes. It's Chris." My heart leapt.

Rich leaned up and kissed me again. My body was shaking, my heart pounding. We kissed longer and harder the second time. I leaned into him as he wrapped one arm around my back, pulling me closer to him. I could taste sweetness in his mouth, perhaps from the beer. A million thoughts swam in my head—*This is the coolest thing ever…I'm kissing another man, and I'm loving it…If time would stop, I'd be happy in this moment forever…God, he tastes so good.* In that instant, I knew what love felt like.

I heard footsteps coming up the stairs toward Rich's room. I stood up quickly, regained my composure, and moved toward the door just as a sorority girl opened it. She was startled by my presence, and I was afraid that she had seen or sensed something odd. I acted casual, not wanting to draw unwanted speculation, even though I was shaking and my face still burned red-hot from the second kiss. Rich was completely passed out now. Both of us left him alone to sleep. I did not see Rich again for the rest of the night, though his kiss lingered in my mind.

I woke up the next morning feeling completely alive. I was high on love. Still, I was clueless as to what to do when I next saw Rich. I only knew that I had to get back to the fraternity house and find Rich. When I saw him, I could not read his behavior. He acted like nothing had happened. His smile was nice enough but certainly held no indication that his world had changed last night like mine had. I had successfully pushed my sexuality to the back of my closet, but Rich had ripped the door open. I had to find out if last night meant anything to him, even if it meant risking him finding out about me.

That night Rich and I made the round of parties, business as usual with the fraternity brothers. As the night went on other brothers peeled off, leaving just the two of us together, alone again. We ended up back at the scene of the previous night's kiss, which was still weighing heavily on my mind. We threw our coats on the floor; both of us were wearing sweaters for the cold March night. We kept drinking and laughing, sitting next to each other on the couch and listening to Paula Abdul. We talked a lot about our families, especially the tense relationship we both had with our fathers. But there was still no kissing. I thought repeatedly, *Does he regret last night?* I was tormented and afraid that if I made a move to get closer, Rich would hurt me, and I would relive my experience the night of the swim team initiation with Eddie.

It had gotten late, and sunrise was looming. We had had a few more beers and talked a lot about high school. Still, nothing was happening; maybe it was my turn to make the moves. I knew my time to find out was limited. I got up and took my empty bottle to the kitchen. When I came back Rich had lit a candle and turned off one of the lights. I sat next to him on the couch, this time much closer, my leg pressing up against his. He put his arm around the back of the couch, opening his body to me. I slowly leaned in to him, as if to rest against his shoulder, quickly looking into his deep green eyes. His lips grazed my neck. The touch sent shivers through my body. He pulled me closer and his lips met mine. We kissed long and hard. I wanted to push my body right through his skin, melting into his chest. My body went limp in his arms. Each kiss washed away more tension and fixed me in the moment.

We broke apart and Rich looked at me, startled. "Why are you crying?" he asked, holding me gently. His handsome face was now full of concern.

I replied bewildered, "I don't know." I was so happy and emotionally exhausted that I had not even noticed the tears. I did not feel the shame that had dominated my sexual encounters with Dan. I knew these feelings were mutual and much deeper with Rich. We had a common bond of brotherhood. These tears were different from the ones I had cried with Dan. But still I was afraid. As if Rich sensed my turmoil, he pulled my head up and whispered softly in my ear, "I love you, buddy." I lay beside him, finally at peace, and I knew it would be okay.

As the sun rose that next morning, Rich and I spent hours lying on the couch, talking and kissing, arms and legs entwined. Both of us were still fully dressed and eager to talk about our sexuality and attraction to other men. I found out that Rich also had a guy who would make him feel ashamed after they had sex. After years of shame, we felt only love when we kissed. We were both amazed at how natural it felt to kiss.

Rich and I spent many long nights that stretched into early mornings lying in bed together. We gradually explored one another and slowly, comfortably got into sex. I always felt trust, security, and a deep, unquestioned bond with him. Falling in love with a brother seemed like the most natural thing to do. Sharing some of the fraternity rituals with someone you love physically and emotionally can be an amazing experience, enhancing their fraternal meaning by looking at the rituals through a lens of love. The loyalty that SAE instilled in fraternity men complemented how Rich protected me and allowed our love to grow stronger. His devotion was what the SAE founding fathers had envisioned—minus the sex, of course. I knew Rich believed in many of the same fraternity values I had come to treasure, and he believed in me. His compassion gave me the personal confidence to find love for who I am within myself.

The sexual episodes with Rich became more intense, as did the bond between us. One particularly amazing night happened on the banks of the Susquehanna River, which runs near the campus. Rich wanted to show me a favorite resting spot. It was a strangely warm night in mid spring, and it was so dark that we stumbled with nearly every step. The occasional sound of snapping twigs broke the silence. We emerged from the trees onto the riverbank. The only sound was the water flowing lazily. Hand in hand, we walked to the water's edge. Then, breathing in unison, we turned to face each other and started gently kissing. Rich pushed me against a nearby tree, pressing his body hard against mine. Slow kisses quickly became a blur of sex, tearing off each other's clothes, rolling naked on wet leaves. Our bodies arched to meet waiting lips. As we lay ravaging each other, a sudden storm showered us with rain. A cloud of fog engulfed our bodies as the cold rain shower splashed against the heat of our bodies. At that moment, I was pure orgasm.

Rich always had a way with romance. Anywhere we could look and find the constellation Orion in the night sky made us feel safe together. I thrived on the love and acceptance I got from him. He would call me his "Greek God" and would repeatedly tell me how hot it was to be "enraptured by my hard, muscular swimmer's body." Rich made me feel good inside. Our only fear was that the fraternity would find out that we were gay and having sex. As a consequence, we both dated women as a cover. It was like living the double life of a superhero: mild-mannered straight fraternity guy by day and a hormone-driven gay boy by night. During the spring fraternity formal, Rich and I took female dates to support our masked identities. We obligingly messed around with our female dates in public, kissing and making out for all the brothers to see. I was jealous seeing someone else kissing Rich even though I knew she meant nothing to him. Either way, our secret identities were still intact and the brothers were oblivious to our masquerade.

That summer of 1990, Rich had an internship in Rochester, N.Y., and I went back home for my job as a lifeguard. We wrote each other every week and even spoke on the phone once in a while. The conversations were awkward, with us whispering into the phone so as not to arouse the suspicion of our families. We made grand plans to see each other later in the summer, perhaps sneaking off to my grandfather's house on the banks of the Delaware River near the Pocono Mountains of Pennsylvania. We talked about how much we missed each other and counted down the days until school started again. And we always said, "I love you."

One night that summer, just a week or so before we were to go back to school, I discovered a song by Erasure called "Hideaway." The lyrics tell the story of a boy who decides that it's okay to tell your parents that you're gay, even if the choice means alienation. That was a revelation to me.

I wanted to be that boy. I could not wait to share the song with Rich. Music always played a vital role in our relationship, and we would frequently make mix tapes for each other. Rich received the Erasure mix tape in the mail along with my letter telling him about the message of the "Hideaway" song. His response was not what I had hoped for. Part of his letter read, "You don't want to be that boy. How could you hurt your family and friends like that? It's better to keep it all a secret..." Not only did Rich hate the "Hideaway" song, he went on to write that we could not continue down our path, for fear of not being able to turn back.

I was crushed. It was like a switch had been turned off in Rich. One minute he loved me; the next minute he was pushing me away. The only person I had ever really loved was telling me it was over. Feelings of shame again consumed me. I felt like I had done something wrong. I knew Rich loved me and I loved him. *Our love is real. What could be shameful about this?* I would ask myself over and over again.

Rich and I both lived in the fraternity house that year. Each day was a tug-of-war, careening between love and anger. Rich would acknowledge me only when he was drunk. He would call my room, let the phone ring once, and hang up. That lone ring was my cue to walk down to his room and service him. Sometimes I would storm out of his room in anger, knowing that he just wanted sex. Other times Rich would caress me and purr in my ear, telling me he had always loved me. The pain he inflicted was so cruel. Gradually, I began to see our relationship for what it had become—sex.

Rich graduated from Bucknell that spring. The emotional toll ended as our sexual relationship gradually faded away. I was ready to move on when I realized on graduation day that I was proud of Rich, but I was not sad to see him leave. And with some distance, we were able to begin a new phase of our relationship—friendship. Rich and I learned that through our love and our brotherhood, we forged a bond that could never be broken. Unlike many college men, we were lucky to have had each other to process our internalized homophobia, explore our sexuality safely, and as a result become stronger, better men than we were before.

The following year, I was elected president of the fraternity. Yes, it did happen—a closeted gay fraternity president. I think it happens more often than not, actually. The fraternity kept me so busy that year I did not have time to grapple with my sexuality. Instead, my entire focus was on SAE, and I flourished as a leader. With strong leadership comes self-confidence, and the brotherhood gave me plenty of that. I was proud to be their leader.

My fellow SAE brothers never found out about Rich and me. The brotherhood love we had shared remained a secret. Like Rich, I concluded it was best to remain in the closet during college. I was not ready. Nevertheless, the fraternity and Rich taught me a valuable lesson: to love without shame, a lesson that many gay men have to learn sometime in their lives. Eventually, after leaving college, I was able to come out and love myself for being gay. I credit SAE, the brothers, and our fraternal values for the strength to eventually come out to my parents and friends. SAE taught me that loyalty breeds trust, that discipline breeds success, and that goodwill breeds humanity. I chose to trust the brotherhood and return the favor by coming out to my SAE brothers. The men believed in me and gave me what I needed and desired—acceptance. No longer do I need to be afraid and hide.

Lovers to Brothers

by "Michael Goldberg" and "Alan Marshall," the South

My lover and I reflect on our more than 20 years of experience in the fraternity world and can only think of one statement: "Never say never." We are both professors in the same academic department on a campus nestled in a valley surrounded by beautiful mountains, rivers, and spacious parks. The university is home to an active Greek community. The students on campus look like they stepped out of an Abercrombie & Fitch catalog. As would be expected in a Southern town, people are friendly and life progresses at an unhurried, comfortable pace. In our separate voices of Michael and Alan, the unlikely story of our brotherhood begins.

MICHAEL: EXPOSED TO THE HOG

"The what?" I asked.

"The Hog! Come on, you never heard of the Hog?" one brother responded.

"Sorry," I smiled.

Silly me, I thought. The Hog must be part of some secret ritual I missed during initiation into the fraternity. Well, I soon learned that the Hog was a ritual, all right, but not a secret one. Every fraternity brother and most of the campus student population knew of or had witnessed the Hog at some point during their academic tenure. The Hog was, shall we say, a rather large appendage of the fraternity president. He provided the apt moniker himself, referring not only to its size but also to his reputation as a sexual pig. "You'd do the wind if it was blowing in the right direction," I told him. He gleefully agreed. The Hog was displayed at pretty much every evening social event. That was my first exposure, so to speak, to the fraternity. I thought, *God, I'm going to love my position as faculty advisor.*

ALAN: SUPER BOWL SUNDAY AT THE FRATERNITY HOUSE

I don't remember the teams that were playing in the Super Bowl that year. I do remember the commercial featuring former presidential nominee Bob Dole. The commercials seemed more important not only to me but also to the group of men and their dates sitting and watching the game. I was at the fraternity house with my partner, Michael, who was also the chapter advisor. We were both sipping whiskey sours and enjoying the ritual that was playing out in living rooms across the country—compulsory viewing of the Super Bowl.

As a new set of advertisements came on the screen, the fraternity president yelled, "Commercials!" quickly followed by a chorus of "shh" as 20 college men leaned forward in their seats to watch. You could have heard a pin drop. When the game came back on, everyone leaned back and relaxed.

On the six-foot couch opposite my chair, two guys were sitting right next to each other, practically on top of each other, and there was nobody else on the couch. I was confused and thought, *Why didn't they separate themselves? There's plenty of room, and sitting so closely violates a major straight-guy norm.* This was odd behavior for fraternity men. Then one of them happened to spill his drink directly on the other's crotch. "Oh, here, let me get that," he said, dabbing the other man's crotch with a napkin. I made eye contact with Michael and shifted my eyes over to the couch to alert him to what was going on. He smiled and winked back.

Needing to stretch from sitting so long, I walked to the kitchen for a piece of pizza. In the 15 feet between my chair and the kitchen, I was stopped by three different brothers, each of whom wanted to make sure I was having a good time.

"Hey, Doc, enjoying the game?" one man said.

"Good to see you—glad you could make it," another one said.

"Professor! You doin' all right? Need anything?" the third man said.

Wait a minute, now. *This is odd,* I thought. *Here I am, an openly gay man, with my partner, at a fraternity party. And these fraternity men are treating me like an honored guest.* This was my first contact with the fraternity, but it would not be my last.

MICHAEL: THE CHAPTER ADVISOR INTERVIEW

In the fall of 1995 I was hired to teach criminal justice at a comprehensive university in the South. I was no stranger to teaching or to fraternal life: I had taught at three other campuses and I had been a fraternity chapter advisor at two of the three institutions. Still, I had the feeling that this one would be different.

My first week on campus, I introduced myself to the university's Greek life coordinator. I explained that I would be happy to assist in any way possible with supporting fraternities on campus. I described my past affiliations as a chapter advisor and having grown up in a fraternal household. My father was a Master Mason. Freemasonry is the largest and oldest worldwide fraternal organization, focusing on community service and protecting the less fortunate. I was also very active in DeMolay, an organization for young men ages 13-21, sponsored by the Masons. The coordinator told me about a new fraternity on campus that was seeking a chapter advisor. "Sounds like you'd be great for the position," he said. The fraternity was still a colony then, although the chapter has now grown to be one of the most active and acclaimed on campus.

No sooner had I returned to my new campus office than I received a call from a chapter member asking me to come by their fraternity house for an interview. *I need to be interviewed?* I thought. While I was a bit taken aback by the idea, I thought it would also provide me an opportunity to interview the men in the fraternity as well.

I had assumed that my background as a former police officer would probably be a plus during the interview. The men would probably want a faculty advisor who could keep them out of trouble. On the other hand, I did not know how my sexual orientation would play out. As a result, I never formally came out to the fraternity men during the interview. My sexual orientation was not a campus secret, however, and I had had many boyfriends prior to Alan, often parading them around campus. One of the fraternity brothers later told me that even Helen Keller would have known I was gay. "Plus, if one student on campus sees you at the gay bar, the news might as well be on the campus computer server," others told me.

Overall, I found the interview process to be a formality. I felt extremely comfortable with the brothers. They answered my questions and addressed my concerns, and I guess I did likewise. As it turned out, it was a perfect match.

ALAN: MY COLLEGE IMPRESSION OF FRATERNITY LIFE

About eight years before I met my boyfriend, Michael, I was beginning my undergraduate education at a midsize public university in the Midwest. I hit the ground running when I set foot on campus—good grades, a solid career plan to become a professor, and lots of involvement in student activities. In my first few weeks of class I received a call from my grandmother, whose advice I truly respect.

"Have you thought about joining a fraternity?" she inquired.

"A fraternity? Are you serious?" I scoffed at the notion. All I knew about fraternities came from the classic movie *Animal House*—and I didn't have any use for keggers and toga parties.

"You should think about it," she said. "It's something that will be with you for your entire life." My great-grandfather had been an active Mason and both my mother and grandmother had been in sororities. I thought about fraternity life and thought the idea might be fun, but I never seriously pursued rushing a fraternity. I agreed, though, that I would keep an open mind.

My opinion of Greek organizations soured when a fraternity pledge on campus died following a hazing incident at one of the fraternity houses. In addition, when I was on the campus judicial board, I heard a case about a theft involving fraternity members. Unfortunately, these events led me to believe that fraternities had little to offer beyond criminal activity. In my graduate studies I began to research crime on college campuses and grew tired of reading account after account of the relationship between fraternities and assorted acts of deviance among male peers.

"Me? A fraternity brother?" During my college days, the answer would have been a resounding, "I don't think so."

MICHAEL: THE INITIATION ("GIVE ME MY PIN, I'VE GOT A HOT DATE")

While I was chapter advisor to many Greek organizations, I was never initiated into a fraternity, mostly by my own choosing. This fraternity chapter was different, though. I was developing a very special bond with the fraternity men and I wanted to participate in all their activities, including traditional rituals and special ceremonies. Therefore, it was necessary for me to be formally initiated. In spite of my years of experience, I was still unsure precisely what "initiation" would entail. I think I allowed my imagination to get the best of me—too many porn videos of fraternity boys having wild sex. While that might happen, I certainly missed it. In reality the initiation ceremony was a beautiful and memorable experience.

The night of fraternity initiation was supposed to be a surprise and an honor. While I was certainly honored, I think the fraternity brothers were the ones who got the surprise. I received a phone call and the brothers instructed me to get dressed up and head to the chapter house for an "important event." The brothers were unaware that my lover at the time, Brian, was in town visiting from Washington, D.C. We were having a long-distance relationship, and I had promised him a special weekend. I told him I had to go to the fraternity house for a short time.

When I arrived I was escorted to the fraternity initiation ceremony, where I told the men that they really needed to rush things along. I said, "Hurry up and give me my pin. I have a hot man date waiting for me." After declaring me a brother and, of course, the chapter advisor, I promptly returned to Brian. The men fully understood, having seen me with a parade of hot boyfriends. After my hurried departure, the initiation process continued with the remaining initiates. As it turned out, I had unknowingly walked out before the conclusion of the ceremony, believing it to be over. Months later, I received the full initiation ceremony, thereby completing the requirements for brotherhood. The fraternal bond was forming.

ALAN: MEETING A LOVER AND A FRATERNITY MAN

When I was nearing the completion of my doctoral degree, I went to a criminal justice conference in New Orleans to network and find the perfect job. The night before I was scheduled to arrive, one of my friends from graduate school called excitedly: "Alan—great news! Our department is hiring a new faculty member, and you're perfect for it. I've set up an interview for you at the conference." It was a great interview, and I met Michael, a faculty member at the university. He was gay and single. The situation was ideal. I instantly felt that I would be comfortable with the position: It was a good school, the job was promising, and I would have a gay colleague and friend.

A few months later the academic dean called to offer me a faculty teaching position. I packed a moving van and headed South, excited to become a criminal justice faculty member. Michael and I began spending a lot of time together, both on and off campus. Michael was handsome and athletic, and I loved his unbridled optimism and his ability to make me laugh. Michael told me that he had noticed first my sparkling blue eyes and that he enjoyed my dry wit, intellect, and confidence. Our offices were across the hallway from each other, and before long we became lovers. Our relationship was strong, and the only thing that I came to resent about Michael was his involvement in the fraternity that he advised.

For me, the resentment was more than not knowing the secret handshakes and passwords—it was the idea that I could never share something that was so important in his life. One night about five years after his own initiation, Michael left for the fraternity house wearing a suit. "Where are you going all dressed up?" I asked.

"To a fraternity initiation," he replied.

"So, is it like in the videos?" I replied bitterly.

"I could tell you...but I'd have to kill you," he joked—at least I hoped it was a joke.

As he left I realized that I wanted to share in the brotherhood that Michael had with the fraternity. Watching him, I could see that Greek life was about more than the negative stereotypes I had from my college days. I was jealous that I had missed my opportunity to become involved.

MICHAEL: TWO-BEER QUEERS AND A NAZI

When I was going to college in the late 1970s, the rule of thumb was that the only difference between a straight guy and a gay guy was a six-pack of beer. Boy, have times changed.

I was at a fraternity party during the holiday season. In the living room of the fraternity house, several members were playing "beer pong." In the course of the game, not only did the Hog make a stunning presentation, but a 22-year-old brother also displayed his genitals. While not quite of Hog proportions, his penis was not too shabby. The 22-year-old then loudly announced to the crowd, "I'm a two-beer queer," and proceeded to dry-hump a brother next to him. Apparently this was such a common occurrence that I was the only person who paid attention. I wasn't sure if I was supposed to be an observer or a participant—regrettably I chose the role of the observer.

After a few hot flashes from my delightful observations, I was approached by one of the fraternity brothers who wished me "Merry Christmas." Before I could respond respectfully, the fraternity president screamed at the poor unsuspecting soul, "He's Jewish, you Nazi!" Publicly shamed, the brother apologized profusely. "Don't worry about it. I know what you meant. I get that all the time," I told him. "Happy holidays to you too."

I quickly learned from this glorious evening of sights and commentary that I was indeed accepted by these fraternity men. The brothers were comfortable around me, cared about me, and truly wanted my acceptance. I felt the same.

ALAN: THE CIRCLE OF BROTHERHOOD

It was a ruse. I had been distracted by a brother's date under the pretense that she had lost her keys and needed help looking for them. When I walked back into the banquet hall I found Michael dancing bare-chested, a big-ass grin on his face, dollar bills sticking out of his waistband, a gaggle of fraternity guys bumping and grinding against him. It made a burlesque show appear tame. My only disappointed thought was, *Why couldn't it have been me?*

Michael had always told me about the brotherhood experience at banquets, and he really wanted me to witness it firsthand. So, with his fraternity brothers' encouragement, Michael offered me an invitation to attend the banquet as his date for the evening.

For most of the banquet, I felt very welcomed by the brothers. Many of them came by our table to make sure that Michael and I were having a good time. They attempted numerous times to get Michael and me onto the dance floor and succeeded only after the DJ was able to locate a disco album and brush the dust off. At one point during the evening, a brother even approached Michael and I and said, "I really want to dump my date and hang out with you guys." While we were flattered, we thought it best that he return to his female companion to prevent a domestic situation.

There was only one point when I felt excluded: Michael with all his fraternity brothers, arms wrapped around each other, reciting the fraternity pledge and singing Billy Joel's "Piano Man." The female dates and I were huddled off in a corner watching. While the female dates were taking pictures and cheering on their boyfriends, I felt isolated and lonely. Toward the end of the evening, though, I began to think about what it would be like to be a part of the larger circle of brotherhood—part of this fraternity.

I had watched the Super Bowl with these guys. I had now attended a fraternity banquet as Michael's date. I had interacted with the fraternity on several other occasions and was always treated with great respect and acceptance by the brothers. Notions of homophobic Greeks that I had had up to this point were being dispelled. I had come to see the fraternity as a quality group of guys with strong bonds of enduring friendship. It was definitely more than just partying and social activities—the displays of brotherhood that I saw from the fraternity men were sincere, even touching. Still, I felt left out; something was missing.

MICHAEL: ANOTHER BROTHER, MY LOVER?

I have been serving for about nine years as chapter advisor for the fraternity. The fraternity men continue to come up with creative ways to impress and surprise me. A few weeks before the end of the semester, a few of the brothers approached me at my campus office. Smiling, the men proceeded to tell me that the fraternity voted to extend an invite to a new member at their last meeting. The new member was Alan. I was taken totally by surprise. The fraternity men have always been very accepting of me and have always welcomed Alan at any fraternity function, but I could not believe that they had taken it on themselves to open their brotherhood to my lover. Then one of the brothers shyly asked me, "Is that acceptable?" I wanted to hug each one of them right there on the spot. I was so amazed, impressed, and overcome with emotion. I told them that the idea was wonderful, but they would need to approach Alan and ask him if he wanted to be a fraternity brother.

The next day, the fraternity sent a rather nervous brother over to my office to ask me where Alan's office was. I pointed across the hall and he went cautiously over to knock on his door. I later discovered that his nervousness was not because he was approaching the gay lover, as I suspected. Instead the brothers were worried whether Alan would in fact want to become a member. Since our offices were so close, I could hear the conversation, and all I could do was smile in pride.

ALAN: FROM A LOVER TO A BROTHER

I was sitting with my feet up on my desk, leaning back in my chair, grading a mediocre paper. A student knocked on my door and I waved him in. I noticed he was wearing the letters of my lover Michael's fraternity.

"Umm…Dr. Marshall?" he said.

"Yeah, that's me," I replied, dropping my feet to the floor to greet him.

He identified himself as a member of the fraternity, and in a quiet, uncertain voice said, "At the last meeting, we voted to initiate you as a member of the fraternity."

I was temporarily speechless. I then smiled and said, "I'd be honored." I truly was honored, and I was moved that the fraternity, of their own volition and without Michael's knowledge, had seen the quality of character in me to want to make me a brother.

Without disclosing the ritual's secrets, I can say that the fraternity initiation that followed was emotionally powerful and meaningful to me. Right before the initiation I said to another brother, "I'm excited, and a little nervous, but in a good way." He responded, "I was excited too when I heard about you finally becoming a brother." That meant a lot, and it eased my nerves. Still today, I cannot find words to express my emotions when Michael, my lover and my partner for life, affixed the fraternity badge to my lapel. The men in the fraternity not only accepted us as lovers but now also gave us the bond of being brothers in their eyes.

Brotherhood embodies feelings that transcend a Super Bowl party or fraternity banquets. Those who have been initiated into a fraternity of true brotherhood know the feelings I had that night. True brotherhood is the sense of enduring friendship, the feeling of belonging and loyalty, and respect for the ritual itself. These are feelings I will never forget— feelings that make me proud to be a brother.

MICHAEL AND ALAN: THE BROTHERHOOD

Our story is about brotherhood. Fraternities are too often perceived as exclusionary or homophobic. As we have experienced it, this is not the case. Our fraternity has embraced diversity and views brothers as brothers. We support our chapter—our chapter supports us—and it's about a lot more than gay or straight. That's what brotherhood is all about.

Building a Bridge

by Stefan Dinescu, University of Connecticut, Storrs

My life needed a complete makeover. I didn't want to be closeted any-more. I wanted people to know me for who I really was. Connecticut was a fairly liberal state, so the transition was easier given all the media atten-tion given to gays. Plus, I never had a hard time fitting in and socializing with others. Being 6 foot 2 and relatively attractive, I was a natural social butterfly. Off I flew to the University of Connecticut in the fall of 2000 to begin life all over again.

Jay was my first introduction to fraternity life. He was a beautiful man, the boyfriend of a girl I knew well. We were going to the UConn soccer game together one night with a bunch of friends. I had never met Jay before. I opened the door to the common room of their residence hall suite and there he was. Jay could have easily been a Greek god from mythology: His suave, tousled blond hair, broad muscular shoulders, and flat stomach would make a sculpture anyone would worship. His smile was to die for, melting many hearts.

As I came into the room, Jay immediately got up from the couch. He gave me a vigorous handshake and in an eager voice said, "Hi, I'm Jay. You must be Stefan. I've heard so much about you."

Unlike my preconceived notions of fraternity men, Jay came off as genuine and without any air of superiority. His looks were an added bonus. Never would I have expected such a warm, pleasant welcome from a fraternity man to a freshman.

On the way to the soccer field and during the game, Jay and I spent the majority of the time talking to each other. Sitting on the soccer field bleachers, he would ask questions casually mixed with polite conversation. Jay was thoroughly a sweet guy who would do anything for anyone. I had quickly guessed his agenda, however: Not only was he interested in becoming friends, he was recruiting for his fraternity, Beta Theta Pi. The fraternity was fairly new on campus. Betas had a reputation for being highly selective and discreet with their recruiting. Due to negative perceptions of fraternities on campus, the Betas tried not to reveal up front that they were in a fraternity. They didn't hold open-invitation socials. The brothers sought out particular individuals one by one.

Jay had me intrigued by taking an interest in potentially recruiting an out gay man. I didn't flaunt my homosexuality, but I was not afraid to let it be known either. While Jay and I were talking, I would nudge my friends and shout out jokes like, "Look at number 45 out there, he is so fine." or "Damn, wouldn't it be great if there was a soccer rule that you had to play in just boxer briefs?" I was always the joker; it was natural for me to be an entertainer among my friends. That was my personality, and Jay certainly seemed amused, chuckling and laughing with all of us. Getting to know Jay felt good that night, considering the negative encounters I had had with straight men. Seldom did a straight guy take interest in getting to know me.

As I had been effeminate my entire life, most of my close friends had been female. Mostly I was a quiet and weak kid, and rarely did I defend myself when confronted by others. There were times after middle school gym classes that I was assaulted in the locker room. The older, often larger bullies would beat me up and do what they liked to sexually degrade me. Such acts were usually followed later in class or on the way home with insults, calling me "gay," "fag," or worse. The incessant hell growing up made me wary of straight males. I had determined they were my enemies and not to be trusted. College and fraternity life would challenge those fears, and it all started with Jay. We would get to know each other well over my first semester, and I would learn that Betas already had gay men in the fraternity. My guard came down ever so slowly.

Jay went to study abroad the following semester, but not before telling the rest of his brotherhood about me. He had passed along my contact information to the brothers, and shortly into the spring semester I received in the mail an invitation to a party on campus from Sebastian. He was the openly gay Beta whom Jay had told me about. Sebastian had invited my friends and me to attend a dance at his synagogue, the Hillel House.

The frigidly cold January evening was typical for that time of year in Connecticut. A few of my friends and I walked across campus to the street that had three churches and Hillel House, all side by side. Inside the disco lights zipped across the stained glass and the bass of the music thumped in the night. We paid the cover, dropped our coats on the couches, and headed for the dance floor. In the middle of the floor in a crowd of people, I spotted a gorgeous guy dancing with some friends. His commanding dance moves and his sheer confidence caught my full attention. One of my friends elbowed me and over the music said, "That's Sebastian right there, the one dancing. Isn't he hot?"

Oh, Sebastian was definitely hot, and he knew it. Watching him dance was mesmerizing. While he was a little on the short side, he made up for it with amazing chestnut brown eyes, a gorgeous ear-to-ear smile, and a sexy, muscular body that knew how to dance. I wanted to get to know him better. Sebastian had noticed us too. I hoped it wasn't my staring at him that gave me away. He came up, introduced himself, and started dancing beside me. He wanted to make sure we were dancing and having fun. Jay had told him all about me, and he was glad I had come.

Dancing with Sebastian in the Jewish religious center was surreal. There I was, dancing alone with another gay guy. The exchange of words seemed superfluous. We communicated more that night through our dance moves. It set the scene for much more I hoped would follow.

Sebastian and I became good friends, and in Jay's absence we started hanging out a lot, spending almost every day together. Things were beginning to heat up between us, but we wanted to get to know each other first.

One night Sebastian invited one of my friends and me to watch a movie in his room. By that point in the semester, quite a few weeks after we met, we had become close friends. I was totally enamored. When the movie was over he walked us outside to his dorm foyer to share a nightcap cigarette with us.

Just as we were about to leave, I blurted out, "Oh, my God, I totally forgot my keys in your room. Hold on, let me just run and grab them."

Now, seriously, I had not planned this. I honestly did forget my keys, but as the words left my lips I realized how my subconscious had taken the driver's seat.

Sebastian answered, "Wait, my door's locked. I'll go with you."

My friend, being a sharp woman and taking the apparent social cue, said, "You know what? I'm just going to run down to the dorm. I'm cold, and it's only a minute's walk."

Fantasies raced through my mind as I said goodbye to my friend. Sebastian was the perfect guy. When we walked back together to his room I fully intended to get my keys and leave despite my underlying interest in something more. I was afraid that acting on my attraction would ruin our friendship.

When we got back to the room, he said, "Why don't you take off your coat and stay a second? I want to show you some pictures." I happily obliged. He pulled out some photo albums and we sat down in the middle of the couch. He spread the photo album across our thighs, our legs touching from hip to knee.

Flipping page after page of pictures, Sebastian showed me photos from a camp for special needs children that he worked at the previous summer. He told me stories of all the funny things the kids would do. All this made me fall even harder for him. He showed me pictures of his travels and asked about mine.

It was getting late, and we had been talking and looking at his photo album for over two hours. Getting tired, I leaned against the left arm of the couch. My feet found themselves nestled under his thigh. I told him about growing up in Romania and what that had been like. Somewhere in the middle of my story, I noticed him looking directly into my eyes. My heart fluttered looking at his huge glossy brown eyes. He shook his head.

"What?" I asked.

"You are just too cute," he replied with a big smile. In one swift and gentle motion he crawled across my legs and leaned in to kiss me.

Fire. His kiss turned me into putty. It was the type of first kiss that makes you envision your entire future together. Sebastian lay on top of me, kissing me, his left hand under my head caressing the nape of my neck while he slowly massaged me from my arm down to my knee with his free hand. Each stroke was heaven. I hoped he would go farther—I was too timid to make any moves myself.

Suddenly, he broke the kiss. The romantic mood came to a screeching halt and he retreated to the other side of the couch, looking as if he was in some sort of pain.

"What's wrong?" I asked, bewildered.

"I can't do this," he said.

I sat back, confused.

"When I have a boyfriend and he walks in the room, I go up to him and kiss him hello. I couldn't do that comfortably in front of the Betas if we were dating," he said. He did not know how to act getting involved romantically with a potential future brother in the fraternity. I was terribly attracted to him and didn't care whether he was a Beta. The fraternity had nothing to do with me. But for him, it was different. He decided that the prospect of being future brothers meant that it could never go beyond that first kiss, and I did nothing to dissuade him. That night I walked home across campus, rejected and confused.

The Betas threw a party a few weeks later at one of the apartments where a few brothers lived off campus. For the first time I would meet all the Betas I had not met earlier through Jay. One brother said, "I heard so much about you and could not wait to meet you." Another brother introduced himself and said, "Hey, I heard about your moves at the Hillel dance!" All the Beta brothers welcomed me with open arms, much like Jay had done earlier in my first semester. Many of the brothers told me how they had hoped I would consider joining the fraternity.

Being at a party where guys were flirting with girls and people played beer games was an unusually "queer" experience, outside my usual element. I found the entire party to be hysterical. If I jokingly flirted with a fraternity brother in conversation, he would flirt back for the fun of it. When I danced at the party, the guys started catcalling and complimenting me on my moves. My sexuality did not matter at all. I was sure that being myself would make them reject me. Instead, being gay was the hottest thing. They could not get enough of Stefan: my wit, my dancing, and my flamboyant personality. The whole party felt like a funny sitcom.

I stepped outside for a smoke and Sebastian joined me. I was totally over what had happened in his dorm room weeks ago. I understood where he came from, and I had decided to respect his wishes and continue our friendship. Nevertheless, tonight's party with his fellow Beta brothers had made me curious about something else. Having been asked repeatedly by various brothers to consider joining the fraternity, one burning question remained.

"Why did you do it? Why did you join the fraternity?" I asked as I puffed on my cigarette. "What made you want to join a straight and stereotypically antigay organization like a fraternity?"

Sebastian was popular and had a lot of friends, so he definitely did not join because he was lonely. I could tell he was thinking about how to answer my question.

"I really don't need any more friends in my life. I have plenty," I said. He exhaled smoke to respond.

"It's not about having friends. It's about having family. The brothers have always been there for me when I needed them most, while some of my other friends haven't."

He went on, becoming noticeably emotional.

"When I lost some friends during 9/11 in New York, they were there for me. They consoled me when I cried and flipped out. They listened and gave advice. They are family to me, and I love them."

Wow! It was that simple, and yet I had not noticed. Beta Theta Pi fraternity brothers were a family. His words left a lasting impression on me. It really touched me that Beta meant so much to him as a gay man.

Still, I did not know how I would answer the question myself. My experience had been different my entire life, as I had been subjected to harsh, negative acts by heterosexual males. I had never reconciled my pain and anger toward those bullies who molested me in the boys' locker room in middle school. I never forgave those who chanted "Stefan's gay, Stefan's gay" in the cafeteria. Since then I had had mostly female friends and had been extremely wary of being too close to straight men. My fears had become deep scars.

Later that semester, Sebastian extended me a bid on behalf of the fraternity to join Beta Theta Pi. He was excited along with the brothers to have me as part of their family. Sebastian had also decided that our night together should be forgotten. He would much rather have a fraternity brother for life than a one-night stand that both of us would later regret.

That day with Sebastian I decided to accept the bid to join Beta Theta Pi. Accepting was not only about gaining a band of brothers. For me, it was also about bridging a chasm that was created years ago. Jay and the other straight brothers helped me to build a bridge of understanding.

The act of joining the fraternity was a reconciliation with my past, an attempt to heal the scars and end the loathing of the idea of male friendship. Beta Theta Pi helped remedy my damage by offering the fellowship of men—a brotherhood. The Betas were already a family, and the day I accepted my bid I became a part of their family too.

Brothers Now and Ever

by Jonathan Vogel, Bethany College, Bethany, W.Va.

In October 2003, I made a trip to the pastoral hills of West Virginia to catch up with some old friends. The Phi Chapter of Phi Kappa Tau was celebrating 80 years on Bethany College's campus, and in what has become a tradition, a hundred or more brothers from throughout the years visit Bethany every five years to revisit days gone by. The campus had changed with the times in many ways. Modern housing, so lacking years before, now dotted the landscape. Some fraternities and sororities that once were campus fixtures were no longer. One constant remained: The brotherhood of Phi Kappa Tau was just as diverse and accepting as ever.

In September 1991, I was a pudgy, insecure freshman with long floppy hair dyed one time too many, trying to leave behind me the four years of hell some call high school. It was a new start, a clean slate. No one knew about me or my life back in Washington, Pa., even though it was a mere 30 minutes away. Orientation weekend involved all the freshmen, who had the run of the campus, and a few early returning upperclassmen. My resident assistant, Dan, a lanky sophomore communications major, invited a few of us from the hall to his fraternity house, Phi Kappa Tau, which stood at the very top of New Parkinson Hill. "We're the only fraternity on the hill with all of the sororities," he said coyly, to make a visit more enticing.

That first night on campus I grew restless and decided to check out Phi Kappa Tau. I remember trekking up the steep, dilapidated path known as "Cardiac Walk" to the Phi Kappa Tau fraternity house and walking through the front door and up the steps into the second-floor lounge. There was a group of four people, two girls and two guys, smoking, drinking, playing cards, and having a good time. As the front door clattered shut behind me they looked up through the smoky haze and the conversation stopped.

"Hello," I said, and mentioned that Dan had suggested I come to hang out.

One of the brothers, a shaggy blond guy, removed a half-charred cigar stub from his mouth and looked me up and down. "What's your name?" he asked. Suddenly, I did not feel so sure about being there.

"Uh, I'm Jon."

There was a heavy pause as he and the others gave me the once-over, and then he spoke again. "Do you play cards?" he said.

"Uh, well, yeah—"

"Ever play euchre?" he interrupted.

Hesitating for a second, I wondered, *Am I going to be the butt of some idiot freshman joke here?* Then I answered warily, "No, what's that?"

The group was instantly all smiles again. The blond guy stuffed the cigar back in his mouth with a grin and said, "Well, you're gonna learn now. Come on over!"

I had a ball that night learning the nuances of euchre. The object is for you and your partner to take as many tricks as possible by calling a suit trump, using only the 9 through the ace. The jack of that suit is top trump and beats all. The knack is remembering that the jack of the same color is the second-highest trump. It took me a few rounds, but I ended up getting the gist of the game, and by night's end I was able to "euchre" my opponents by taking the majority of the five tricks or rounds when they called trump. Not only did I learn what has become my favorite card game, but Phi Kappa Tau also made a lasting first impression on me. These men did not know me from Adam, but they made me feel welcome. The experience made the start of my first semester that much better.

Freshman year at Bethany College seemed promising. I was pursuing my passion, theater. In addition, I was able to focus on a liberal arts education that my parents approved of. I felt like I was starting to make friends, but there was a huge problem brewing. Morlan Hall, our dorm, was not much for comfort; our accommodations were pastel-painted cinder-block rooms with stiff twin beds and not much else. The communal showers were either tepid cold or scalding hot. The heating was not much better, either frigid or saunalike, depending on the day. The guys on my dorm floor were just as unpredictably hot and cold. My initial acquaintances began to drift off into cliques. The less than desirable, like me, were seen as vulnerable and were open to abuse by the jocks. There was never any explanation why the dorm floor still functioned with high school mentality. Life there became a living hell for me since I was at the bottom of the male hierarchy and did not fit in.

The final straw was the day that Brian, Marco, and Menzo assaulted me. They were three of the brawny macho football players who were definitely the alpha-male control clique of the dorm. I had come back to the hall that afternoon after class, exhausted. All three of the guys were there loitering in the hall, and the moment they caught sight of me, cruel smirks crossed their faces. Earlier that day, in a morning class, I had been on the receiving end of their group prank, and it looked as though they were up for more humor at my expense. I quickly ducked into my room, threw my books and keys down, and turned to shut and lock the door behind me. Marco, the biggest and most muscular of the three, was standing outside my door as I pulled it shut. He shoved his foot into the door frame. The look on his face was an evil grin of contempt. I pulled harder, but my attempt was comparatively weak. The door slammed wide open with the three of them standing there.

"Having a good day?" Brian asked with a sneer. He was as broad as Marco with a beefy chest, his thick curly mullet damp with sweat at the ends.

"Look, guys, you had your fun earlier this morning, just let me study," I pleaded, hoping they would go away. I reached for the doorknob to try and shut the door again.

Marco grabbed me by the arm. "What's the matter, faggot?" he laughed.

The word was a slap in the face. I had not heard that slur since high school. Panic flooded me and I snarled, "Fuck off." I tried to yank my arm out of his grasp.

Menzo's smirk widened. He stood there shirtless, clad only in a pair of blue checked boxer shorts. At 5 foot 7 he was my height, but his strapping build and huge pecs intimidated me. In any other circumstance, Menzo's body would have been enthralling.

"Wanna play?" Menzo taunted as they walked into my room. Marco still had me by the arm and flung me so that I toppled back onto my bed.

I was begging desperately now, looking up from my bed. "What are you guys doing? Just go away, I have studying to do."

They laughed. "C'mon, Voges, you wanna have some fun, don't you?" Menzo grunted. Marco grabbed me off the bed and yanked me back up. Brian took hold of my other arm and swung it around. Within seconds he had my left arm locked behind my back. Menzo went back over to close the door to my room, which had been left ajar. The four of us were alone. Terror set in, and within a moment I found myself shoved to my knees.

"Come on, guys, please let me go, please." Menzo walked up to me, leering. The other two held me down, preventing any movement. Menzo slid his boxers down to his ankles, his semierect dick hanging within inches of my mouth. They all snickered.

"C'mon, faggot, you wanna suck on it, dontcha?" said Menzo, taunting and pushing forward. His penis slapped against my face, smacking my mouth and sliding up my cheek repeatedly as I jerked away. I inhaled to catch my breath, but the rank odor of male sweat and jockstrap was all that filled my nostrils. I reared my head back, but Brian and Marco thrust it back into the stench that was Menzo's crotch.

The thought of Menzo's dirty cock in my mouth and taking even slight pleasure in devouring his manhood was too much. The magnitude of the assault kept my arousal in check as I was being forced against my will.

Luckily, a noise in the hall distracted my captors. In a dizzying moment, I somehow slipped out of their hold and found the strength to fight my way loose. I made it to the door and exploded into the hallway, bolting down the steps for the lobby of Morlan.

The whole episode freaked me out, leaving me humiliated and victimized. The word *faggot* kept ringing in my head. I had been maligned with that slur in high school, and to hear it again made me afraid. Adding to my angst was the question, *What if I am a faggot? What if I am gay?* Instinct prevailed as I closed myself off to the idea. I resolved that I could never be gay. The torture of Menzo, Brian, and Marco stifled any attraction I had for men, which I felt would only mean more pain.

Not knowing where else to turn, I went immediately to Dan and told him what had happened. We decided that I should move into an empty dorm room in another hall to remove myself from their immediate line of fire. This thrilled my bullies to no end; they could not wait to be rid of me. The day I got the keys to my new dorm room I returned to retrieve my things only to find my clothes, my belongings, everything I owned strewn around the hallway. Never had I felt more helpless and frightened. I thought I had escaped all of this drama after graduating from high school; now my torturers were back as football players, bigger and stronger.

Later that evening Dan stopped in to see my new lodgings, partly out of duty but also out of concern. Seeing my dejection, he offered a rescue: "Come on, I want you to meet some friends of mine," he coaxed, and we headed up to the Phi Kappa Tau house. It was pleasant to be invited, and I looked forward to it, as I had not had a chance to visit since my euchre training the month before.

There I met Ted and Chris, his closest buddies and fellow sophomore brothers. Ted's dark features enhanced his mock Mafia swagger while Chris's doughy build complemented his soft demeanor. They were an odd combination of pals at first glance, but there was some kind of underlying bond that brought these men together.

All of us sat around Ted's room on the lower floor of the house, testing his new stereo speakers to '70s classic rock while we drank beer. Other brothers popped in to investigate the racket. I recognized some of them from around campus. Rob, for example, was the intense cigar-chopping card shark I had met on my first night, and we had run into each other at the radio station over the past few weeks. Div, a willowy track and field runner, sat next to me in psychology, where we were always taking turns napping while the other took notes. As we chatted about movies, music, cards, and whatnot, I realized that all the brothers were really cool, diverse guys. I had speculated that their kindness was out of pity but soon realized that they were sincere and genuine.

Over the next few weeks I got to know more of the brothers of Phi Kappa Tau. I saw so many different personalities linked together with a common bond of brotherhood. I wanted to know more: What was this brotherhood that held them together? The brotherhood was not like the cliques I had experienced in high school, or the alpha-male gangs down at Morlan Hall. I thought fraternities were supposed to be groups of drunken jocks who had keggers and played foosball. Phi Kappa Tau fraternity was not a stereotypical *Animal House* frat. You did not have to be a certain type or fit a profile to be among the brothers; it was cool to be yourself.

Phi Kappa Tau fraternity saved me from the victimization of Morlan Hall. For the first time in my freshman year I felt secure and positive about my relationships. Former hallmates like Marco, Menzo, and Brian realized that any attempt to hassle me after class on the quad would be thwarted because I was hanging out with Div or another fraternity brother.

"Let me know if they give you trouble," one of the brothers said with a wink. "You know we've got your back. Ask any of the guys."

That February I considered pledging Phi Kappa Tau and other fraternities on campus. I went to various rush parties and gave it serious consideration. The Phi Kappa Tau brothers were the main force behind my decision to pledge. On the final night of rush, when asked to submit my top three fraternity choices to pledge, I went "suicide"—I submitted a lone bid to join Phi Kappa Tau.

The following Friday was Bid Night, where you find out what fraternity chose you to become a brother. I waited anxiously to hear my name called in the crowded room full of prospective fraternity men. Halfway through the list, I heard my name: "Jonathan Vogel." In the background I heard the loud cheering of the Phi Kappa Taus. I joined 12 other freshmen that night and was finally on the official path to being a true brother.

The Phi Kappa Tau brothers took the process of introducing new members to the fraternity with distinguished regard, honor, and significance. Hazing was not tolerated like at some fraternities; all our activities centered on bonding and understanding the meaning of brotherhood. The next six weeks were full of welcome surprises and meaningful experiences. For example, the Monday following Bid Night we had our first group exercise. We were summoned to the fraternity house at 7 A.M., sleepy-eyed and prepared for God knows what, and then—surprise—the brothers took us to breakfast. We were then paired off with various brothers for study hours. The effort was not only to further our education but also to get to know one another. A less academically worthy example was when our class kidnapped one of the older brothers for fun. The kidnap was thwarted when I was taken hostage and held for ransom by the brotherhood.

During the six weeks every activity came with the same lesson: "Always trust your brothers, watch over each other, and be there for one another." Such a fundamental message is what bonded us together. We studied our chapter's history: Founded in 1910, Phi Kappa Tau began as the Rechabite Club, an independent men's social group on Bethany's campus. Those founding men were looking for fellowship and character. We were a continuation of that acceptance and fraternal love. My respect for the brotherhood only grew stronger along with my devotion toward Phi Kappa Tau fraternity. The words of the fraternity song, which we sang at the end of every weekly meeting, embodied not only my growing love of Phi Kappa Tau but also the core of our brotherhood. We would gather, our arms intertwined, circling the room, and sing slowly:

WE ARE BROTHERS NOW AND EVER
UNTIL THE DAY WE DIE
AND WHEN THAT TIME COMES ROLLING ROUND
AND WE BID OUR LAST GOODBYE
THERE IS ONE THING SURE AND CERTAIN
LET US BOW OUR HEADS IN AWE
WE'LL MEET AGAIN IN HEAVEN SOON
IN THE NAME OF…PHI…KAPPA…TAU

That May I joined the ranks of Phi Kappa Tau fraternity. I was even recognized by the brotherhood as New Member of the Year. As I left campus at the end of my freshman year, I was part of a brotherhood of men who could not be more different from one another, and I was accepted. A lot had changed since the sexual assault by the football players in Morlan Hall, but I still found myself with a sense of unsteadiness. I had successfully blocked out many questions about my sexuality, but over and over I was unable to answer the question *Who am I?* Instead I continued to ignore the persistent, nagging feeling, pushing it deeper, only to have the question surface again and again. Phi Kappa Tau fraternity was the only answer I could find.

The summer gave me time to reflect on who I was. Up until the point I met the brothers of Phi Kappa Tau, I had not been able to feel comfortable and proud being me. Physically I had dropped 40 pounds, cut my hair short, and felt good about the way I looked. I had become more social, more outgoing, and more driven. Phi Kappa Tau had been the catalyst for my newfound pride, which allowed me to begin to explore the question *Who am I?* The same strength also made me fearful: *What if I am gay?* I asked myself. *What would people think? Oh, my God, and the brothers?* That summer I wanted to rip my hair out dealing with all these questions and the ultimate answer, *Yes, I'm gay.* But I was not ready to tell anyone.

During my sophomore year in Phi Kappa Tau I felt a close kinship with one of the brothers in particular. Micah had been a new member with me. He had an olive complexion and dark hair; he was short but sturdy and had a vicious, intellectual wit. We gravitated toward each other and found a lot of comfort in each other's company. Often we consoled each other and vented our frustrations about classes and life in general. Micah would pull out his bottle of Jack Daniel's, pour us a strong Jack and Coke, light some candles, and we would talk. Billy Joel's "Captain Jack" was always on hand: "Captain Jack will get you high tonight / And take you to that special island." Whether it was the way he would grab my hand when telling a story or when he would wrap his arm around my shoulder, I sensed an attraction between us. I could not tell if the attraction was just a strong bond of friendship or if it was something else. Either way, the closeness was not something I shared with any of the other fraternity brothers.

Things came to a boiling point for my sexuality the weekend before Thanksgiving break that year. Micah visited my room at the fraternity house, visibly upset. His twin brother was suffering from some medical problems, and Micah had been particularly rude to him on the phone. He was just being his usual flippant self and realized only after hanging up how ignorant his comments had been. Micah stood at my door, the Jack Daniel's bottle in hand, and sang aloud, "Captain Jack will get us high tonight." Almost everyone was already gone for the Thanksgiving holiday or had gone out for the evening. As was our ritual, I invited him in, we lit some candles, put on Billy Joel, and I let him unload. We had left my door ajar for a while as we talked. Some of the remaining brothers stopped by as they went out for the evening, and after they had left Micah closed my door and turned down the lights.

"I really don't need them to hear this," he shrugged, and returned to the edge of my bed, now sitting next to me. We continued drinking and chatting, emotions welling up, and for comfort we embraced each other. My heart leapt with each hug, the next lasting longer than the one before.

At one point we found our arms around one another again; we were hugging and crying. His hand was gently stroking my back, thoughtfully at first, and then, so subtly, the nuance changed. Each stroke grazed my back sensually, and I instantly became giddy and nervous. *It's just the liquor,* I told myself, then corrected, *No, you ass, it's something else.* I was being aroused by a man. The answer was simple: *I'm gay.* Those words made me feel tense. Micah sensed my hesitation immediately, pulled back, and looked cautiously into my eyes.

"Are you okay?" he said.

"Yeah, just a bit buzzed," I replied, trying to shake my fear. This was not Menzo forcing me to suck his penis back in Morlan Hall. *It's okay, he's a brother, and he's safe,* I kept telling myself.

There was silence as we gazed at one another in the candlelight. His hand gently caressed my back, even more tenderly now, his dark eyes scanning my face.

"Is that okay, or do you want me to stop?" he asked me quietly.

My heart pounded against my rib cage, ready to explode from my chest. "No, you're fine," I said, finally able to reply as I slowly dared to graze his thick brown hair with my hand.

He leaned in and kissed me gently on the mouth. The Jack on his breath was almost sweet, and I found my tongue slipping inside his mouth as if to get a better taste. Suddenly I felt no fear, and within a moment we were undressing one another, slowly, tenderly. Finding ourselves naked, we explored each other's body for the first time. Our kisses were ravenous and sensual.

This is so right, so natural, I heard my mind whisper soothingly. *You want this. There's nothing wrong with what you're doing. Relax and let the moment take you.* We took pleasure in one another with no shame, filling the void that had been there for so long. That night I lost my virginity to a man, and more important, to one of my brothers. I had no regrets. Finally, after all of the hiding, the questions, the uncertainty—everything made sense.

Micah and I spent the night in each other's arms. In the morning as we dressed, I felt the alarming sense of certainty that I was gay. Both of us also understood the reality of the situation, that some things needed to stay secret. It was best this way; we were in a fraternity—what would the guys think? These were our friends, our brothers. How would they look at us if we admitted to liking men "that way"? My sexual awakening presented a new uncertainty. What had been a night of unbridled joy became intensely stressful and disorienting. I did not know what to do next.

Micah's self-preservation kicked into overdrive. After that night he would do anything to avoid interacting with me. The two friends, the two brothers who had been each other's support system, were now isolated from one another. Any meeting we had, no matter how social, was dangerous in Micah's mind. One drunken evening in late December he pushed me away abruptly as I moved to give him a hug.

"What are you doing?" he exclaimed in disgust and alarm.

I drew back, stunned. I fumbled drunkenly, "Micah, what about our night? What about us?"

He grabbed my shirtsleeve and yanked me to the side. He glanced around furtively and hissed, "Whatever you thought happened—it didn't."

His words stung. I reeled back, he left, and I ran to my room, collapsing in tears. I never felt so lost as over those next few months. Micah and I were both dealing with our sexuality, and neither of us seemed comfortable being gay. We were afraid and confused. Perhaps my sudden lack of discretion had scared him away. Now that I had had a taste, I hungered for him—not just for the physical sex but also for the support of being with someone like me. His rejection was a blow to everything I had come to expect from the brotherhood. I thought we were supposed to trust, support, and watch over each other.

Finally, after months of holding each other at arms' length, we came to a compromise. We knew that in order to survive the fraternity, we would need to be discreet, to trust one another, and support each other as allies. We would live the lyrics of our fraternity song, "Brothers now and ever." Eventually we found our way back to secretly exploring our sexuality. Our time together was our moment of safety, a shared special bond.

By the fall of 1994 my secret was coming out on campus. That semester I had chosen Harvey Fierstein's gay-themed play *On Tidy Endings* for my senior theater directing project, and I knew that I was most definitely gay. I still was quite closeted and actually dating a woman. My guilt about hiding my true self and my lack of attraction for women led to us break up. My girlfriend's friend whom I had cast in *On Tidy Endings*, had suspicions about my sexual tendencies, and rumors started. My theater confidants had come to know about my sexuality over the years, but the fraternity didn't. I was deeply fearful of rejection. I was not sure if the brothers would look at me as a liar or a pervert if they knew the truth. Then there was the fear of the entire campus finding out. The pressure was incredible. I needed to tell the truth once and for all. I could no longer live quietly—too much had changed inside.

Coming out on a brother-by-brother basis was the game plan. My roommate, Tom, was among the first brothers I chose to tell. Lanky with shaggy strawberry hair, he was a junior and a true smartass. We had become close over the past three years, sharing times at the radio station and in the student paper's darkroom. When things became difficult for us in our lives, we would often vent and kick the other back to reality.

Late one October night, I chose to out myself to him over an evening of intoxication at Bubba's Bison Inn, Bethany's local drinking establishment. "I've got to tell you a secret about me, and you can't freak out," I slurred drunkenly.

He blinked, caught off guard. His eyes narrowed. "Are you going to tell me you're gay or something?"

My mouth hung slack at his candor. I felt completely terrified. *Is it that obvious?* I wondered. I quickly attempted to regain my composure and drew a deep breath. It was now or never.

"Yeah, I am. I'm gay." I exhaled hard and felt relief wash over me. I had finally said the words to one of my brothers.

Tom paused in thought, and with a huge grin said, "Hey, it's you. You're cool. I support you." Then, in true Tom fashion, he cracked, "Just don't be checking me out in my underwear." We shared a laugh and celebrated my outing with a shot of tequila.

I was bolstered by Tom's response. My next move was to tell the seniors who had joined the fraternity at the same time as me. Again the tension was unnerving. But I figured that these brothers had known me for nearly four years—surely they would see me as the same Phi Kappa Tau brother. Any worries I had were in vain. Each brother shared an unquestioning loyalty to me whether I was gay or not.

I was on a roll. The easiest brothers to tell were the underclassmen, usually after we had all had plenty of beer. "Hey, man, you're my brother," one guy exclaimed drunkenly with a bear hug of affirmation. Others gave similar affirmations and words of support. A few of the brothers even thought that having a gay brother was an honor, a value to the fraternity brotherhood.

Not everyone took the news well in my fraternity, however. One of the juniors I told looked stricken, backed away, and mumbled, "Hey, well, whatever, just as long as you don't hit on me." Another seemed to accept the news well but was caught later making inappropriate comments to some of the other brothers. The hardest to come out to were Pete and Ed, neither of whom took the news well. Both of them were my "littles," meaning that I had been their brotherhood mentor when they were new to the fraternity. Pete was stunned, and while he immediately pledged his support to me as my little, he was visibly ill at ease for some time. Ed, on the other hand, was infuriated that he was not the first to know, and he felt betrayed. He eventually came around to understand how difficult a choice it was for me to come out to the fraternity.

Bethany is a small campus. The gossip ran rampant, and pretty soon my coming-out was top-of-the-tabloid news. My brothers never strayed far from my side, and they still had my back. Coming out did not gain me any special privileges. At first I may have been treated slightly differently, but the final outcome was what I had hoped for: acceptance and the realization that being gay was one aspect of me. As my brother Tom so eloquently said, "You're still Jon, right? You're not going to dress in pink and dance naked across the lawn?" Then his mischievous grin would appear and he added, "At least not sober."

The year after I left Bethany College, the campus landscape continued to change for the better. A few other brave souls came out that next year, and there was even a gay and lesbian student alliance formed on campus. Social acceptance and tolerance were blooming on the small campus in conservative West Virginia. I like to believe that my fraternity, Phi Kappa Tau, and I contributed in part to the progress.

Phi Kappa Tau enabled me to begin slowly coming out to my family. The brothers, like my family, never stopped loving me. Micah, however, chose to remain in the closet until after we had both graduated. I understood and respected his choice. Our sexual relationship continued well beyond our senior year. It was comforting that I had a sexual partner who was also a fraternity brother. Micah and another one of our brothers, a sophomore named Frank, became involved during our senior year, and we all moved to Chicago after graduation.

Life and its many surprises have pulled Micah and me in different directions. We still keep in touch, however, and look fondly on the time we shared as brothers and lovers. I am eternally grateful to have had the love of Micah at such a crucial time in my life.

Today, my gay Chicago friends are sometimes surprised by my affiliation with a fraternity, particularly when they notice the tattoo on my leg with the Phi Kappa Tau letters and fraternity shield. When they hear me talk about my college fraternity experience, they can see that the brotherhood helped me grow into the man I am today. I am forever honored that I am a member of Phi Kappa Tau. As our fraternal song goes, "Brothers now and ever / Until the day we die."

Leaving the Door Open

by Raymond A. Lutzky, Rensselaer Polytechnic Institute, Troy, N.Y.

In Mr. Urban's fifth grade class at Siwanoy Elementary School, I was a stylish young pupil wearing a white sports jacket with padded shoulders. Some would figure this was a little dressy for a 10-year-old, since most of my peers wore T-shirts and jeans. I thought the jacket made a nice statement—the perfect fashion accessory. I wish someone had told me I was gay back then. I needed Harvey Fierstein to tap my white padded shoulder and say in his darling gravelly voice, "Excuse me, honey, but I need to tell you that whether you know it or not now, you're a raging queen." Sadly, Harvey and I never met in fifth grade, and I thought I was "just sensitive," not gay. I cried when I realized in sixth grade that the jacket did not fit anymore.

The summer between my junior and senior year in high school, I had my awakening with a kiss. His lips touching mine for the first time changed my world. The kiss kindled a fire in me that I would not be able to put out. We never kissed again, and he denied that he was gay. I kept my emotions bottled up through my senior year in high school, but not a day went by that I didn't remember that first kiss or what it meant to me.

I arrived at Rensselaer Polytechnic Institute in August 1998 from my hometown in the suburbs of New York City. Online in a chat room I had met a few other gay RPI students, several of whom had already told me how closeted the campus was despite being 70% male. I found it easier to find gay students at RPI on the Internet than on campus.

One of the guys I often chatted with was named Chris. He was a junior and captain of the RPI ambulance team. I was still nervous about meeting gay people in real life, and chatting with him online about being gay was a huge relief. One day after chatting online for a while, Chris said that he was in a fraternity. A third of all men at RPI joined fraternities. I could not possibly imagine myself in a fraternity. With a background in theater, I was not really the fraternity type. I confided in Chris that I felt alone on campus with my only social outlet being the computer.

His next message read, "Come up to my fraternity; we're having a rush event." I had never been to a fraternity house and was excited by the invitation. Still, I worried that meeting him would not be the right thing to do, especially at his fraternity.

"Are you sure that's okay?" I replied. He had also mentioned that he was not out to his fraternity brothers.

"Yeah, it'll be fine," he typed. "Just please don't say anything." He continued, "We're having Tiki Night. There's a barbecue and volleyball. It'll be fun. Come over."

That afternoon, I walked over to the house of Lambda Chi Alpha fraternity, often known for short as Lambda Chi. The whole event was rather nerve-racking. Finally, Chris and I met among the crowd for a brief moment. Sadly, the rest of the time we avoided each other with only a glance now and then. It was too weird meeting him from the online world in the real world. I was glad, though, that I had ventured beyond my computer. I soon got sucked into the fraternity recruitment machine. The brothers of Lambda Chi Alpha were truly amazing guys, and I really enjoyed hanging out with them. My name became part of their rush database, and I was invited to many other events that week. Without realizing it I had been hooked into Greek life.

Lambda Chi Alpha gave me a bid, asking me to join the brotherhood. The gay issue had never come up, and I was not going to bring it up. I trusted the brothers and had the feeling that the fraternity was full of reasonable men who might be accepting somewhere down the road. It was a risk I was willing to take—the fraternity allowed me to be part of something greater than myself. I was so proud to be called a brother of Lambda Chi Alpha.

One evening word came that the new initiates were to meet in the fraternity library. We were told it was an important announcement that needed to be shared openly. We sat around the large oval conference table.

"There's something we need to talk about, just so that it's clear and you guys understand," began Jim, a sophomore with a lot of respect among the brothers. He was flanked by two of the other chapter officers. I could sense his frustration. Out of nowhere he said, "There are no gays in this fraternity. We've had some in the past, but they have graduated and left." I sat there totally perplexed. A few of my fellow new brothers seemed to understand, and they gave each other meaningful looks. I wondered what had sparked the need to have a meeting to say this.

I turned and asked John, another freshman, "Where did this come from? Did something happen?" John told me that during rush a lot of the other fraternities would refer to Lambda Chi as "Rammed a Guy." Rumors had been circulating among the new brothers, and I had not really been aware of it. Fraternities would often do name-calling and spread rumors to persuade students not to join rival fraternities.

Shocked by the whole ordeal, I don't remember much of the conversation that evening. Lambda Chi Alpha's "gay reputation" on campus was a mystery to me. I had no idea that there had been other gay brothers in the fraternity, although I knew of at least one brother who was gay and closeted, Chris. Two brothers, if I included myself. *What would happen if these brothers knew that they were wrong, that there actually were gays in Lambda Chi?* I wondered.

It didn't take long to find out. The week of my fraternity initiation, Chris finally decided to come out to the brothers. He chose to tell the fraternity during a private ceremony called a "candle pass," where brothers sit in a circle, pass a candle around, and one by one share their innermost thoughts about the fraternity. Brothers would bond by opening up and would often express closely held sentiments about one another. It happened rather quickly. Chris was handed the candle, and he candidly told all the brothers that he was gay. He said he wanted to be honest and help the fraternity understand he was still a good brother. Most people did not really get the point. In fact, right before Chris was handed the candle, a brother near me muttered under his breath, "Don't say you're gay." The brothers already knew that Chris coming out would reinforce a reality that they dreaded.

Despite being an excellent brother by fraternity standards and values, Chris became alienated from the fraternity after coming out. His experience made me seriously consider my own coming-out. I was ambitious to be a leader in the fraternity. I had already been elected secretary and desperately had my eye on the presidency. The fraternity was a way to prove myself. Coming out would not be a bonus.

"Hi, I'm Frank," said the 25-year-old fraternity alum sitting among the brothers. Some time had passed since initiation, and I had never met an alumnus. But here was a handsome, masculine blue-eyed alum with his hand outstretched to me. I shook his hand, and the moment was electric. I was unable to get any coherent words out of my mouth. He had come early to visit prior to the fraternity's Founders Day Formal, an annual dinner followed by a dance to commemorate the occasion. I got strangely quiet and felt paralyzed. The connection was exhilarating and reminiscent of my first kiss in high school.

"Oh, yeah, he's gay," one brother told another after Frank had left the house that evening. Bells went off in my head. Nobody had said that while he was there. He must have been one of the ominous "gay alums." I desperately wanted to see Frank again but had no clue where to find him. My face must have said it all.

"What's wrong, Ray?" asked Mike, my big brother, noticing my forlorn look.

"Nothing, really…the night's just not going how I wanted it to," I said vaguely. Mike replied with a smile and slapped my back.

"Let's go downtown," he suggested, leading me out the door of the fraternity house. We went to one of the local bars where a fellow Lambda Chi brother was tending bar. As a 19-year-old with a low tolerance for alcohol, I was way too drunk somewhere around my second or third "house of pain" cocktail.

Upon returning to the fraternity house that night, I slithered across the floor on my back, shouting, "I'm a snake! I'm a snake!" Mike simply lumbered over to a chair and dropped down. I pulled myself off the floor and onto a nearby couch. We sat in the empty room and stared at some infomercial on the television.

"Hey, Mike," I said, whipping my head towards my brother.

"I'm gay," I blurted out. "Wow, I really threw you for a loop there, didn't I?" I said, laughing, and staggered to my feet.

Mike sat there stunned and quiet. Then with another laugh and a broad smile on my face, I passed out.

The next day I didn't actually remember my revelation to Mike. The whole evening was an intoxicated blur from the moment I had met Frank to my night out with Mike. My stomach felt awful, though, and I wasn't for sure if it was just the alcohol or the growing pain of staying closeted. Mike decided to keep the entire matter between us and chalked it up to one to many "house of pain" drinks.

Founders Day Formal was the next evening. I knew that Frank would be in attendance along with many other alums coming back to campus. Just for Frank, I paid supreme attention to my tie, hair, and suit jacket, even though I was going alone. My hope was that I would catch Frank's attention. The vibe I received when we first met was definitely one of curiosity and flirtation. He was probably trying to figure out if I was gay.

I arrived at the banquet hall and took my place at a table of younger brothers. Anxiously, I looked around the room, waiting for Frank to arrive. Dressed in a pristine Navy uniform complete with white gloves, Frank came through the doors. *Wow, what an entrance,* I thought. His broad shoulders were complimented by the tassels and his blond hair gleamed in the light. Several alumni who I would later learn were also gay accompanied him. The fellow alums hurried him to a distant table before I could intercept him. I sat through the dinner dejected.

"Hey," a deep voice said to me from behind my chair. "What's up?"

I turned from my chair to see Frank standing there smiling at me. I immediately stood up and gazed directly into his eyes. "Nothing much…nice uniform," I said coyly.

"Thanks. Would you like to dance?" Frank replied with a mischievous grin.

Out of the corner of my eye I could see the fellow alumni members of Frank's entourage aghast at what was happening. I was swooning.

"Uh…yes," I uttered barely audibly. I nudged myself forward.

Together we walked out onto the dance floor toward the DJ booth and the masses of people dancing. Being asked to dance by a man in uniform and a fraternity brother, I was on cloud nine. There would be no denying that I was gay now.

Frank and I blended in rather well, dancing for a long while, until the

DJ played the obligatory slow song. I did not have time to choose whether I should sit down. Without missing a beat, Frank reached for my hand and led the way. He placed his other hand firmly on my waist.

As we swayed on the dance floor, now joined by only two or three other couples, the full reality of what was happening sunk in. All eyes were on us, and for the first time in my fraternal life I was afraid of my brothers.

"Am I making you uncomfortable?" Frank asked, bringing me back to reality. I managed a weak "uh-huh" and a nod, looking painfully in his eyes. Frank understood, and we left the dance floor.

He mentioned that a number of the alumni were planning on going to a local gay bar after the formal, and he wanted to know if I wanted to join them. Going to a gay club that night with Frank was far more important than the consequences of my actions in the fraternity. I leapt at the opportunity, surprising him with my openness to the idea. Frank had me from the first handshake to the tassels on his Navy uniform—I had a bad case of puppy love.

We went out with a large group of fellow Lambda Chi alumni, all of whom were gay. Many had graduated in the last five years and were amazing, brilliant people who were very accepting of a new 19-year-old addition to Lambda Chi Alpha.

I remember kissing Frank at the side of the dance floor, passionate and longing for more. I became lost in his embrace, and all my fears about being gay vanished. Frank was sensual and strong, and he fulfilled every one of my boyhood fantasies.

The fellow alumni were there not only to enjoy themselves but also to act as chaperones. Although Frank and I had a great time kissing, drinking, and dancing, they made sure we both went home alone.

The next day Frank and the other alums left. My obsession with Frank waned as soon as I realized I was alone. The full reality of what I had done hit me like a ton of bricks. I was gay, and now my fraternity knew.

Luckily, Chris was around to explain the legacy of the Lambda Chi Alpha gay brothers. Basically, my chapter had seen a host of strongly involved, motivated, and absolutely wonderful gay members who were mostly open about their sexuality. However, by the time I had arrived at RPI, the tide had shifted and the acceptance had regressed into homophobia. I was glad to have Chris there to support me. He understood what it was like to come out in the fraternity.

Chris and I immediately went from distant brothers to good friends. The fallout reaction to my coming-out was a mix of emotions. A few of the brothers were supportive. When I made a formal announcement a few months later, many of the brothers showed respect by shaking my hand, and some followed with a hug. Other brothers were not the least bit pleased. The brothers considered my coming-out a threat to the image of the fraternity and their ability to recruit, to compete athletically, and to get a date on Saturday night. It was not a comfortable place, with many of these brothers choosing not to speak to me. At times I felt like my brothers had left me in the darkness without a candle.

Inspiration comes from the strangest places. What got me through all this was the National Conference of Lambda Chi Alpha International Fraternity. The national conference allowed undergraduate members to come together from all across the United States and Canada. I had always dreamed of being the chapter president of the fraternity, and this was an excellent conference to learn the ropes. What really put a gleam in my eye was the keynote address of the awards banquet that year by the recipient of the Cyril F. "Duke" Flad Award. It was basically Lambda Chi's Man of the Year, and this year the winner was an aspiring heart surgeon. He received a standing ovation, a plaque, and $5,000 in fellowship money. But more than the money, the winner got the microphone for as long as he wanted, and subsequently, the ear of over 500 attendees.

I decided then that I could win the Duke Flad Award in 2002. Then I would be crowned champion of the fraternity, and all my brothers would need to accept me. Winning the coveted award would prove that I was a good brother, a quality Lambda Chi Alpha man. Making myself invincible was the best way to deal with the brotherhood's doubts and my internal pain of not knowing if it was okay to be gay. I wanted to prove myself.

Walking out of the awards banquet I thought through a winning battle plan for the Flad Award over the next three years. My plan was clear: I would become chapter president. I would become friends with the new university president at RPI and generally create a shining image for our fraternity. I would achieve the prestige of being honored as Rensselaer's Greek Man of the Year and president of the Order of Omega. Quite simply, I would be Master of the Universe, the best brother ever, anywhere, period.

No longer did I have time to be gay. I had more important fraternity-type things to do. I focused on the blank lines on the Flad nomination.

Each line needed to be completely filled with awards, involvements, and accomplishments to prove that even a gay brother could be the best brother of Lambda Chi Alpha. I needed a host of awards, scholarships, citations, and honors. I rehearsed my acceptance speech in the shower a hundred times. In each speech I would share undisputable proof that even though I was gay, I could still be a good brother, the best brother in the fraternity.

By my junior year I was officially considered "connected" on campus by my fraternity. I was heavily involved in many campus activities and well known to the campus community as a Lambda Chi. Chris had graduated the previous year, and I was now the lone gay brother. With all my campus leadership experience, I was determined to run for fraternity chapter president. I saw this as a golden opportunity to finally realize my dream.

Divided down the middle, the fraternity questioned having an openly gay president. The conflict reached a fever pitch by the time of the election, and it was obvious that lines had been drawn. I lost the election.

Disappointed that I had failed, I slowly realized that the fraternity would need time to accept an openly gay brother as fraternity president. There were some serious discussions questioning why it was such a bad thing to have a gay brother, and the fraternity was slowly waking up. Most brothers realized that I was the most active Lambda Chi brother on campus and was largely responsible for increasing recruitment numbers through my student orientation involvement. More and more, brothers were coming to the conclusion that being gay ultimately did not matter. Brothers began to reach out to me again.

Everything really began to change for the better when I met Joey. He was one of the guys I had gone after during rush and convinced that Lambda Chi Alpha was a great place to be. With curly blond hair, bright blue eyes, and a ton of ambition, Joey was absolutely beautiful, and he was only 17 when he entered Rensselaer as a freshman. He visited the fraternity more and more during rush, and he was a shoo-in to get a bid.

There was a party the night after all the new members, including Joey, had gone through their fraternity induction ceremony. The entire night I noticed Joey following me around the fraternity house as I continued to get more and more drunk. I watched him out of the corner of my eye and got a devilish idea.

"Hey…man, I'm wasted," I informed Joey, who nodded and giggled in his own drunkenness.

"Listen…I'm going to need to leave my car here and walk home…but *you're* coming with me," I told him in a commanding, older brother tone.

"Okay, sure!" he replied cheerily.

Oh, boy, I thought. *I would never have done this if I wasn't drunk.*

Joey and I left the fraternity house about half an hour later and stumbled back to my on-campus single apartment. We fell back on the couch together and watched something mindless on TV. While we sat there, I edged my hand onto his leg, where I gently rubbed my fingers over the denim of his jeans.

Before I knew what was happening, Joey and I were facing each other on the couch, our lips locked together. I could feel the longing, the passion coming from Joey and found it incredibly erotic. It was all I could do to keep from tearing his clothes off that night.

"Have you ever done this before?" I asked while kissing the side of his delicate neck.

"No. Please don't tell anyone," he said, enjoying every moment of every kiss. We drifted further into the sexual intensity of exploring each other the entire night.

When we awoke the next morning, I felt very guilty. I had taken advantage of a 17-year-old brother from my fraternity. I could not get over my shame. In my moment of guilt, I made a critical error.

"We shouldn't do this again," I said, coldly.

"Why?" asked Joey, who looked more heartbroken than I realized at the time.

"Well…you see, it's not really a good idea for two brothers to get involved with each other," I offered. Joey looked despondent.

"Oh, um…okay. I guess you're right," he said in a levelheaded way.

Joey did not speak to me for six weeks. It was dreadful. I could not believe what I had done to my new brother Joey. I had truly hurt him. He avoided me at fraternity functions and ignored my instant messages online. Eventually I pleaded with him, apologizing profusely for how I had hurt him. I begged that we at least speak again.

The thought of Joey being gay made me feel less alone. He gave me an outlet to understand myself. I was lucky that we were able to work through it together and keep our brotherhood intact. Joey still was not out to the fraternity, but we were there for each other.

After the Joey incident, I forced myself to concentrate on how I could make a positive impact on campus to help others who might be gay. My influence on campus was useless unless I could create greater awareness for students like Joey. I knew what it was like, and I did not want others to feel alone.

The opportunity was magical: The perfect educational program combined being gay with being in a fraternity. That semester I organized various campus organizations to join together to sponsor a lecture titled "Out and Greek: Being Gay, Lesbian, Bisexual in a College Fraternity." The program featured national activist, author, and educator Shane Windmeyer, who specializes in sexual orientation issues within Greek life and who founded the Lambda 10 Project for Gay Greeks. I sat proudly as Shane delivered a poignant speech full of humor, understanding, and passion for being gay in fraternities and sororities. During the program, Shane also brought volunteers onstage to find out their GPA or "gay point average." Joey turned out to be one of the volunteers, and it made me grin inside. My hope that evening was that if only one student got Shane's message that "It's okay to be gay and Greek," then I would have made a difference.

The "Out and Greek" lecture was a huge achievement for RPI. The campus buzzed for weeks. I felt inspired by the momentum and more than anything wanted to make my own speech to a crowd of 500 Lambda Chi Alpha fraternity brothers at the national conference. I was on my mission and wanted everyone to know that you can be gay and be a good fraternity brother. It was Duke Flad or bust.

The clock was ticking. I called in all my favors to complete the references and recommendations for the Duke Flad Award. Some of these contacts I had spent years developing on campus, including the president, alumni, deans, student leaders, and other staff. My application was complete. I put every ounce of my determination into ensuring that my qualifications could not be overlooked. I offered my absolute best for consideration and hoped it was good enough.

The answer to my Duke Flad application came at an odd time—I had graduated from Rensselaer and I was interning at a session of the Undergraduate Interfraternity Institute at Rutgers University. The five-day leadership school is a high-quality dynamic experience that shares the values of Greek life. As an intern I was helping the facilitators and students with logistics. On the final night of UIFI, I received a call from Joey.

I remember standing in the parking lot of the Rutgers's Zeta Tau Alpha sorority house while Joey told me some of the best news I had ever heard.

"Hey, Ray!" Joey shouted. "I wanted to tell you that I told some brothers that I'm bi," he said proudly.

"Wow, Joey! I'm so proud of you, that's amazing." I was thoroughly overjoyed realizing the courage it takes to come out. "Congratulations!"

"Yeah, well, I thought it was time, and I'm more comfortable now than I was…well…a year ago," he said with a laugh. I laughed too.

Later that night I drove back home for the summer from UIFI. I broke down and cried, feeling drained, exhausted, and elated with the news from Joey. When I finally arrived, I staggered into my house and then to my room. A small red light on my answering machine was flashing and immediately caught my attention. I drifted across the room to check my messages.

"Ray," the message began, "this is Father George Dirgahli, otherwise known as 'Doc' in the Lambda Chi Alpha world. I've been trying to reach you to tell you that you've won a graduate fellowship for 2,500 bucks, and I understand you're coming to Syracuse University for that…"

He continued but all I heard was between the lines, what he did not say: I had won a fellowship but I had lost the Duke Flad award.

I called Doc back and thanked him for the message. I told him I was looking forward to meeting him at Syracuse for my graduate fellowship. Inside I was devastated that I had lost the Flad award. I had failed. I would never be able to make that speech at the national conference to Lambda Chi Alpha International. Those 500 men would not hear that it is okay to be gay, and I could not prove that you can be gay and still be a good brother. I had lost my opportunity to make a real difference, to reach even one person. This horrible news completely overshadowed the news of Joey coming out.

But then it hit me—one person. Suddenly I realized the achievement, my success: Joey. He was finally able to come out. My goal to help one person come to terms with being gay had become a reality. The revelation gave me a sense of pride. I had passed along the brotherhood values that Chris had displayed in coming out years earlier. He ultimately challenged the brothers and opened the door to truth and brotherhood. Now I had graduated and Joey remained with the door open, as an openly bisexual brother. Through my leadership and being an example for my brothers, I was able to show Joey that it was okay to be gay and show the other brothers that you can be gay and a good brother. I did not need to win the Flad Award or any awards or titles to change people's beliefs and perceptions. Simply being who I am and living my life openly and honestly was enough.

Bonded

by Michael A. Knipp, Roanoke College, Salem, Va.

"Listen," she said as she stood on the opposite side of the freshly stripped mattress in my bedroom, surrounded by high school memorabilia and a collection of Pez dispensers. "I know that you've been pretty capable of doing things on your own for a while now, but college is going to be different. You're not going to have Mommy there to help you out."

I stopped folding my underwear. I moved toward the closet, trying not to make eye contact. I pulled out some sweaters.

"Mother," I gushed authoritatively as I put the clothing in my duffel, "I know! I'll be fine. I can cook, I clean, and I can do my own laundry. I've had plenty of practice. I'll be all right."

"I know, I know," she said, trying to reassure herself. "But you're my baby. I don't know what I'm going to do without you."

"You'll do the same things that you do when I'm here, except, well...I won't be here."

"It's just that..." she hesitated. "It's just that I've never been to college, and you're the first one in our family to ever make it that far, so I don't know what to expect. I worry about you."

"What are you worried about?" I asked.

"Well, for one, the drinking." I should have seen this coming. "I've seen those *20/20* specials with John Stossel about wild parties, binge drinking, and alcohol poisoning. And it's all because of those fraternities. Those boys have no regard for themselves or their schoolwork. They just party all day."

I tried to hide the excitement in my eyes for fear of a longer lecture.

"Mike," she said in her maternal tone, "just promise me that you won't get involved with all of that nonsense. Promise me that you won't join a fraternity."

"Um," I started. I could not lie to her face. She's my mother. I returned to the closet, buried myself face deep, and reached for more sweaters. "Okay, I'll make you a deal. I promise that I'll spend the first semester studying and doing well and—"

"But—" she interrupted.

"And," I cut her off, "when it comes time to rush I'll make sure that I do the right thing and learn all I can about the brothers, and the fraternity, and the rules, and everything else. I promise I won't do anything stupid. How 'bout that?" It was the best I could do.

"Just be safe," she responded, a little disappointed. "I don't want Barbara Walters doing a follow-up special on you."

"Deal," I said. And with that, we packed the rest of my belongings into the box and loaded up the truck. I was off to the first day of the rest of my life.

When I arrived at Roanoke College for freshman orientation, I was in awe. I had dreamed about that day my entire life, and here I was, finally living it. I could not believe my eyes. For the first time, I felt absolutely enlightened. I was about to embark on the most supreme adventure that I had ever been offered. There was not a word in my lexicon to describe my feelings.

The campus was a sprawling, neoclassical, meticulously groomed area that housed 1,700 students. The Evangelical Lutheran Church-affiliated private institution boasted a superb graduation rate, distinguished alumni, and a major namesake—all reasons that I chose Roanoke College. Around 11 that evening those standards started to fly right out my third-story window.

Mom and Dad returned to my room to say their goodbyes, Dad with a handshake and Mom with teary eyes. They headed toward the elevator door through the narrow fluorescent-lit hallway. My mom stopped, turned, and glared at me sharply.

"What are you going to do tonight?" she inquired.

"Probably just go to bed," I lied.

She turned, walked past the two remaining doors between my room and the elevator, and pivoted once more, for the last time.

"Michael," she called out desperately.

"Yeah," I said, sinking into myself.

"Be careful," she whispered defiantly. Then they both disappeared.

No rules. No parents. The party scene was about to commence.

That night I found "fiesta central"—the place to party—and off I went. It was a huge fraternity bash. I stopped and took it all in for a moment. I was about to meet real fraternity guys for the first time. I could not fuck it up. I wanted to make a good impression. No, that was wrong; I had to make a good impression.

I must have stood there for a steady minute and a half, just staring up the stairwell that led to the second-floor apartment. Suddenly, one of the guys tapped me on the shoulder from behind.

I swiveled around to meet this muscular fraternity guy with Welsh features and sparkling hazel eyes. He looked every bit the fraternity guy that I imagined: Abercrombie cargos, Wallaby shoes, a North Face windbreaker, and the quintessential ball cap emblazoned with the Greek letters KA. His dark hair was perfectly ruffled as if he were a page ripped from the *YM* magazine summer surfing pictorials. In that brief second, I doubted that I was ready for this. I looked nothing like a fraternity guy. My nearly albino Irish skin and reddish hair did not fit the image. I had just beaten puberty while he had a full 5 o'clock shadow.

"Are you just going to stand there and smack it all night, fag, or are you going to come up and party?"

"Ugh," I mumbled, startled. I was obviously embarrassed, but I attempted to recover. "Yeah, I was just waiting for my friend."

"Dude, you just got to campus," he said in his macho manner. "How many friends can you possibly have by now?"

The other guys standing around him, all fraternity guys who shared similar physical traits, laughed.

"I mean my roommate," I said.

"Well, get your ass upstairs, frosh," said another fraternity guy with blond hair and flawless features. "There's lots of poontang for you."

More haughty laughs and high fives echoed from the chorus of fraternity guys.

I followed the guys up the steps. *Poontang,* I thought. *I hope not.*

After that initial party, only a few weeks passed before I became close friends with one of the fraternity members of the Kappa Alpha Order. At first our friendship was based on social and recreational activities—like drinking and pot smoking. But it soon evolved into the beginnings of a brotherly bond.

Three months later I was given a bid to join the fraternity Kappa Alpha Order. I accepted. I was relieved to know that these guys liked me—that they wanted me to be a part of their prestigious organization. It was also liberating to know that my efforts to befriend the brothers had paid off, but not without a corollary: Thanks to the fraternity I now had a nasty drug habit, only a few months into my first college semester. I was spiraling downhill. I was becoming everything my mother had warned me against.

In the months that followed I combusted. My grades suffered and my finances were depleted while I accumulated credit card debt. Somehow through those hazy weekdays and hazier weekends, I managed to spend a thousand dollars on personal narcotics. My parents were concerned because I was distant and calling less frequently. And when I looked at my eyes in the dimly lit dorm mirror, a pale, sunken-faced zombie glowered glassily back. The constant harassment of pledging did not build my self-esteem either.

There was a reason for doing all of the drugs and drinking excessively, but it wasn't a reason I could tell anyone—my sexuality was unspoken. I felt the fact of it clawing at me and turned to alcohol and drugs as a coping mechanism. I had successfully duped the brotherhood into thinking I was a regular heterosexual while what I considered to be "unnatural" sexual thoughts ran through my brain. I figured if I continued to pop pills and snort some blow, I would not have to deal with reality and the sinister mess of my life.

After I was initiated as a member of Kappa Alpha, I took my newfound fraternity as license to do whatever I pleased. I was no longer the chapter bitch. I did not have to do what the brothers asked, recite the Greek alphabet on cue, or stand at attention in a musty basement having obscenities shouted at me. It was my time to shine.

I seemed to shine my best when I was heavily intoxicated. I yelled and screamed, laughed and cried, and started fights that someone else inevitably had to finish. All of this typically occurred in the same evening. Since I joined the fraternity, my behavior had already gotten me into trouble. The dean of the college placed me on probation for vandalism and reckless driving. My mom would not be proud of what I had become. I was out of control, and the brothers knew it. My behavior had become so unpredictably irregular that the fraternity had no other option but to consider my expulsion.

Attending a small private school has serious implications when your social life is at stake. I was aware of that when I joined Kappa Alpha. If I were thrown out of the fraternity, I would be ostracized not only by the brothers but also by most of the campus for being incompetent. The brothers decided to intervene.

"Mike," said our portly president, nicknamed "Big J," beginning his intervention speech. "We've told you time and again that you can't keep doing what you're doing and remain a vital part of Kappa Alpha Order. Your conduct is disruptive to the image we are committed to as a fraternity."

I lifted my shamed face a few times to gesture silently for mercy. Instead of pleading, I remained silent. My time to speak was over.

"You've left us no choice," Big J continued in his burly voice, "but for us to reprimand you severely for the negative image you've brought upon this brotherhood. I hate doing this. You're our brother, but I don't have any other choice. You've made your bed..." Big J was right. Now I had to lie in it.

Finally the decision was handed down. I was sentenced to weekly substance abuse meetings and anger management classes. I was placed on suspension from fraternity parties until further notice, which wound up being the rest of the semester. I reluctantly but graciously complied. My sexuality could no longer be an excuse for my rowdy, reckless behavior. I needed to confront my demons. The whole process made me feel miserable: I could not face the fact I had let down my fraternity, my family, and myself.

After Christmas break, I emerged as a reinvented individual. I returned to school with remorse for my actions and wanted to glide smoothly onto the right track. The punishment was exactly what I needed to be slapped back into my harsh reality. I did not want to end up like the 40-year-old attendees at the Narcotics Anonymous meetings. I felt

different—refreshed and alive. I had beaten the addiction and come back
to prove my worth to the fraternity. Despite this, my secret homosexuality was still locked away, and it ate away my conscience daily. No matter
how hard I tried, the demon remained alive.

A year passed, and I gradually proved to my brothers that they could
respect me. I poured every ounce of my time into the fraternity and making it a better, stronger place. As a result I was chosen the next year as one
of the top leaders of the fraternity. Their choice to select me was redemp-
tion for my past. The more I led the fraternity, the less time I would have
to deal with my sexuality. Plus, I gained support from fellow brothers and
had earned my place.

Proving myself as a leader slowly allowed me to become more comfortable with my character. Being gay became less background noise and
more part of my reality. With so much turmoil before, I worried that my
homosexuality would be used to scapegoat me for removal. Now I had
something to offer the fraternity, and the members' acceptance showed
me that I was a valued brother. Pride and courage swelled as I pondered
the idea of letting the brotherhood know about my sexuality. My own
self-esteem improved greatly and my internal fear subsided. I decided to
tread lightly and see what would happen.

That semester I started to live my life a little more loosely in regard
to being gay. With the help and support of some girlfriends I had come
out to, I began going out on some dates with guys privately. It was a
huge step. I tried my best to be honest and yet be discreet for my fraternity brothers. I would give a date my room phone number. If another brother picked up the phone when he called, I would explain the call
as a friend from home. The brothers did not have any reason to suspect otherwise. But after a few brothers overheard phone conversations, they started to wonder. Two of the brothers, L.B. and Nicky, were
the first to question the calls. L.B. was my roommate, a short, well-
built Southern Baptist guy. We shared bunk beds, L.B. on the top bunk
and me on the bottom. Most nights he could hear me talking on the
phone. Nicky, the other brother, lived directly across from us in a room
scented with beer and boxer shorts. The two of them frequently discussed what I was hiding.

"Come on, Mike," L.B. said as we were pirating songs on Napster. "I'm
your little bro. You can tell me."

"Dude, it's really nothing," I assured him, trying to avoid the conversation. I began to worry if they thought the gender of the callers was male or female.

"Nothing, my ass," he laughed. "I heard you talking last night in your bed. That didn't sound like nothing to me. Nicky, come here," he shouted across the second-floor hall. "I know Mikey is keeping something from us."

Nicky, a soccer-toned, perpetually tanned international relations major, who was perpetually doing homework, put his books down to join the ambush.

"I know he is," said Nicky. "I heard him talking the other day, and I know it wasn't his mom." They thought the caller was a woman. I was relieved, but still I tried to be honest.

"Guys, seriously, it's no one important. I'm just talking to somebody. We're not dating. It's just—"

"It's just phone sex, is what it is," joked L.B., nudging Nicky.

"Just drop it. Jeez." I tried not to get defensive, but their prying got the best of me. I went downstairs to smoke a cigarette.

A few minutes later Nicky arrived on the stoop outside. He apologized for being so pushy. We both brushed it off, but tension was building inside me and I desperately wanted to lay it all out on the table. The guilt and faulty attempt at honesty was more than I could handle. Nicky could probably handle the news, but L.B. was a different story. If I told Nicky, I feared he would accidentally let it slip. Then L.B. would freak out because his roommate was gay. A couple of days later I reached my breaking point. To hell with it, I had to come clean.

"Nicky, I have something to tell you." We were on the stoop, and he could see I was scared shitless.

"Mikey, you know I'll always be there for you," he offered. "What is it?"

I had gone over this moment a million times in my head. There was no easy way to say the words, although they were there; I had to come out with it.

"That girl that I've been talking to on the phone…" I paused. It was on the tip of my tongue. *Just say it already,* I pleaded with myself.

"It's a guy." I blurted.

"Oh," he said, visibly confused.

I haven't asked God for many things, but at that precise moment I prayed that Nicky would not turn his back on me. I needed him to accept me as gay. I wanted the same support, love, and brotherhood as before. I needed him to be my brother.

"Mikey," he said after the longest 30 seconds of my life, "Dude, that's okay. You're my big bro. You'll always be my big bro. There's nothing that you could do that would make me think differently of you." I felt a huge pressure lift. A few moments passed. "Even if you are a homo," he added humorously. We laughed, and then he jabbed me in the torso. It was a jab of approval, and it was comforting to say the least.

Once I had my fraternity brother Nicky on my side, I felt for the first time that everything would be okay. Coming out to my other brothers was different, however. We were sleeping in the same rooms, showering in the same stalls, and changing our clothes together. Unlike with the girlfriends I had told, I feared the fraternity brothers might feel threatened by a gay brother. Still, I hoped my brothers would be able to accept me as an equal and not fear my sexuality. I certainly didn't want to be viewed only by my sexuality. While some of my brothers were attractive, I would certainly never jeopardize brotherhood for fulfilling a desire—brotherhood was a matter of trust, commitment and responsibility.

In February 2002, the end of my junior year, my fraternity chapter hosted our statewide Province Council meeting. Every Kappa Alpha Order fraternity chapter in Virginia gathered at Roanoke College. The meeting was an opportunity to discuss and reacquaint members with the laws and values of the order. Such was the daytime agenda, at least; by evening, with over 200 fraternity men, disorderliness inevitably ensued. The weekend was a blast and a thrilling celebration. We each felt like true bonded brothers brought together by the fraternity family.

That weekend I met a fellow Kappa Alpha brother whose bond would extend further than our fraternity might expect. My relationship with Mitch actually began online. We knew about each other from chatting online in an M4M chat room on America Online. We had never had the chance to meet even though he attended Virginia Tech, which was only 45 minutes away. I had no clue that Mitch was a brother of Kappa Alpha. When I saw him at the impromptu party at our fraternity house, I immediately recognized him from his online profile. Our eyes connected for a moment, then in unison we shifted our heads away out of concern for being spotted. We didn't speak at all.

The night quickly became confused, and I lost track of Mitch as lots of guys came in and out of the fraternity house. I went to another off-campus party, and there he was with his soft blond curls and permanently blushing cheeks. Most of the guys were drunk and playing a beer pong game called "Beirut." Mitch was standing on the other side of the room watching the game. This was my chance. I pushed through the droves of sloppily intoxicated freshman and upperclassmen to Mitch's position behind a potbellied beer pong player.

"Hey," I said, for lack of better words.

"Hey," he replied, equally at a loss.

The conversation was awkward, but how else do you begin dialogue between two closeted fraternity brothers? We were both aware that we had met online and we were still processing the idea that we were, surprisingly, fraternity brothers. The fact that we shared that bond and that I was not the only gay KA gave us reason enough for us to talk. In addition, I was attracted to Mitch and knew he felt the same.

"Did you have fun today?" I asked.

"Yeah, it was okay. Kind of long, but I'm having fun now," he said.

"Really? I'm not. This place is too smoky," I said. He chuckled, knowing what was happening. I had known it before I trudged through the spilled beer to get to him.

"Too smoky, huh?" He played along. "Well, this looks it for the night. Unless you have a better idea."

A better idea, I thought. *Come on, frat boy, don't be coy.*

"Well, there's no one in my room right now," I offered. "And it's definitely not smoky."

"Sounds good," he agreed. He was horny too.

Brad, another brother at the party, was leaving at the same time. He drove Mitch and me to the fraternity house. He was unaware of what was happening and followed us upstairs to my room, making himself at home. Brad, who was always friendly, chatted idly for over 20 minutes. Mitch and I added minimally to his banter to encourage him not to stay longer. Brad finally left after a few awkward moments in conversation when Mitch and I did not respond. When he left he looked at me oddly, like a mother who knew her kid was lying about something. Brad knew something was up, but he couldn't put his finger on it. Afterward, I figured, I would be forced to debrief him about my sexuality.

No sooner had the door clicked shut than Mitch and I went at each other. We had to hurry because the place was teeming with fraternity brothers who might barge in through the shared bathroom. There was a lock on the bathroom door, but it was old and could be forced open with the slightest tug. To add to the danger, L.B. was MIA. He had a key to our room and could interrupt without notice. Mitch and I swiftly took off the necessary clothes, keeping most of them on just in case we had to reorganize ourselves rapidly. Mitch's bare thighs, so soft and pink, were enough. We kissed and gave each other head. He nearly gagged when I finished. I tried to defuse our embarrassment.

"You're a good kisser," I complimented.

"I try," he boasted. I rolled my eyes. He was cocky. Not what I expected, but hey, I just got laid, so I didn't complain.

After this first sexual encounter, Mitch and I wanted to see each other more. I had hoped that we might begin dating, but he was content having sex and returning home to high-five his buddies for the "girl" he just bagged. He was still afraid of his brothers discovering his affinity for men. After a few months of sporadic visits, school ended and Mitch graduated, moving home to Richmond. I brushed Mitch off as a fling to be forgotten.

Just when I had my priorities back in order and put Mitch in the past, my secret came out in the fraternity. I was outed in early May at my big brother Jan's graduation party. I was drunk and stupid, accidentally flirting with the male cousin of a friend. Subconsciously I probably hoped that someone would tell the world for me. That drunken flirtation was my release from bearing the burden.

To my surprise, the news was welcomed by most of the fraternity. My brothers already seemed to be unofficially aware. The culmination of my coming-out was entirely anticlimactic. The simple truth is, I had been afraid for no reason. My brothers had always stood by my side, but I automatically assumed the worst when it came to my sexuality. No matter what the issue was, my brothers supported me. I could not have asked for a better response.

Then came the real climax. In mid July, as I was settling into my summer job on campus, Mitch called. He said that he had accepted a job in Roanoke and would be relocating to my area in a few weeks. Although I was dating other guys at the time, I was overjoyed at the prospect of possibly dating him and making a commitment to one another. After all, we were fraternity brothers, and that seemed like a verifiable cornerstone for a solid foundation in any relationship. Mitch was emotionally distant before, but I kept telling myself that there were reasons, including the distance between us at the time. After he moved to Roanoke that would all change.

That summer Mitch and I simply got to know each other, the way we should have started when we first crossed paths. At the onset of autumn I began my senior year. I had entirely too many commitments on my plate. Mitch and I were spending many days a week together. He did everything with me: fraternity events, parties, and meeting more of my brothers and friends. But Mitch was still apprehensive about people finding out he was gay. I knew it would take time and tried my best to understand his feelings. I allowed him space to be comfortable with our relationship. Increasingly, though, I started to feel like I was an embarrassment to him. He had met all of my brothers and friends, but I had never met any of his. I invited Mitch everywhere with me, but when he had to be someplace, I was left uninvited. His lack of interest in our relationship and my feelings ultimately turned me off. We were at different points in coming out, and I did not want be with someone who would not call me his boyfriend.

Of course, between arguments and making up, Mitch and I would have sex. We were on and off again frequently that year. Since I was always busy with campus activities and classes, our time was limited. We would go to dinner, maybe, but it usually ended with the same sex—sweaty and physically satisfying. Still, I wanted more. I needed to be told that he loved me more than anything. Often Mitch said those words, but I would have to ask first.

Spring arrived, and I was preparing to graduate from Roanoke College with a degree in English and a minor in Spanish. Mitch and I had discussed our future. I wanted to move to New York and write for a magazine. He was undecided about his plans. Either way, we had both concluded that whatever our future was, it probably did not include each other. Our career goals were different, and our contempt for each other had grown. We hung on to our relationship and brotherhood connection to combat loneliness, but the time had come to say goodbye.

"I guess this is it," Mitch said as we walked to the back door, carrying four years' worth of accumulated junk up the steps.

"Yeah, I guess so," I said. Really I wanted to scream. Almost a year together, and all he had to say was, "I guess this is it"?

"Look, Mikey," he tried to comfort me, "you've got your things, and I've got mine. It's probably best this way."

"Best?" I repeated. "Best for who? I don't have anything left. School is over, and I don't have a job. God knows what'll happen."

"You'll be okay," he said. "I promise."

Yeah, I've heard that before, I thought in disdain. Without many more words, we kissed goodbye.

Ironically, that day when Mitch dropped me off I knew without a doubt that I was in love forever. I had loved him when we were together, but I was not completely certain until the moment he left me that day. I saw the same apprehension in his eyes when he pulled out of the driveway. We had had our share of hard times, but our bond was stronger than ever. I cried secretly for days. I would call Mitch at night, longing to be in his bed, our warm bodies entangled, his hot breath on my neck. From our phone calls I realized that Mitch loved me too. I could hear the sincerity in his voice—this separation was hard for him as well.

It always dumbfounds me how I managed to stay alive at college. Then I think back to the fraternity brothers, who propped me up when I was falling. I remember the brothers who listened and said I was okay when an outsider called me "fag." I recall the men of Kappa Alpha Order who swore to stand by me through it all. I will forever be a KA. Brotherhood is the greatest feeling in the world.

Fairy-tale endings do happen, despite angst and trouble along the way. Mitch and I have made our relationship work and have since returned to being together. We share a connection, a bond that has forced us together. We understand each other. No matter how hard we try, we can never distance ourselves. That's a beautiful thing.

What makes my experience even more worthwhile is that every morning I get to wake up next to my favorite Kappa Alpha man. His hair is ruffled, his breath is less than sweet, but he is all mine. Often he will roll over and whisper into my ear, hot breath on my neck, and ask, "Do you love me?"

My chest fills with anxiety. My heart skips two beats. I cock my head back and look into those bright blue eyes over his scruffy mug. Without hesitation, I give him the answer he is fishing for.

"I try," I say smiling. And then he kisses me, every time like the first.

Bonds of Acceptance

Next on NBC Nightly News

by Gabriel Grice, University of Colorado, Boulder

I grew up in a home where a meal was placed in front of me at the family dinner table six nights a week precisely at 6 o'clock. My mother and father, who have been married for 27 years, both grew up in the South in extremely devout Catholic and Baptist families. My brother, two years my senior, was a slacker, a juvenile delinquent, and a troublemaker. On the other hand I was a straight-A student, a National Honor Society chapter president, and a responsible individual who always tried to please his parents. We lived in Telluride, a quaint ski resort town in southwestern Colorado. Our home was warm and inviting, especially on winter nights.

Our family tradition was to eat together every evening. Dinner was commonly the time when the family would discuss the day's events and worldly proceedings that extended beyond our own lives. Tom Brokaw and his *NBC Nightly News*, delivering consistent discussion topics, seemed more like a distant family member than someone on TV.

From time to time the topic of homosexuality would come up. One cold winter evening I vividly remember hearing a heartwarming story about a lesbian couple who decided to adopt two boys. Tom attempted to make the story neutral, but there was a slant: These children had somehow been given a new life that was less than desirable. My dad's face turned redder until he stood up and shouted, "Turn off that despicable perverted television story!" No one said another word about homosexuality for the remainder of the meal. I wanted to run away.

At that point in my life I knew I was gay. I was 14 and scared by my attraction to men. I didn't have the same sexual attraction to women. My hormones were raging and I had nowhere to turn. Trying to discover oneself in turbulent times is always difficult. My father's comments only made it worse. If my sexuality were ever discovered, I feared I would lose my family.

Late in the spring of 2002, I was only one month away from graduating from high school. Growing up in rural Colorado, I had never had much exposure to any aspect of gay life. I had never told anyone about my sexual feelings. The only people who had suspicions were my closest high school friends, Tamera and Amy. On the last day of high school they cornered me in the hallway. "Gabe, how come you've never really dated girls in high school?" asked Tamera. Shocked, I did not know what to say. Without waiting for the moment to get awkward, Amy hugged me and in a gentle encouraging voice whispered, "Gabe, we just want you to be happy, whatever that means to you. Get out of here, and for God's sake, don't look back."

For the first time in my life, I felt my sexuality was not as despicable as I had imagined. In that moment I had a small breakthrough: It was time to make a choice. The power to control the path of my life would soon be mine. I knew things would be different in college.

I had decided to attend the University of Colorado at Boulder. My family wanted me to remain as close to home as possible, but I wanted to get as far away as I could. "You can be a car ride away, but I won't pay for you to go to school a plane ride away," my dad always said. As a compromise we agreed that Boulder would be an ideal place to attend school.

Colorado, as a whole, is very conservative; Boulder, on the other hand, is not. "The People's Republic of Boulder," as the city is affectionately referred to by the locals, is an accepting and tolerant place for a young gay man to be.

The summer before college, my parents encouraged me strongly to consider joining a fraternity. Both my parents were Greeks, my dad a Pi Kappa Alpha and my mother a Kappa Delta. I remember meeting my dad's fraternity brothers when I was a kid. I recall the conversations vividly: "Hey, Richard, do you remember when…" or "Yeah, I'll never forget what happened to so-and-so's girlfriend…" I enjoyed hearing the stories, but I feared that if I joined a fraternity, I would never be able to be openly gay. Fraternities are for straight, butch guys, right? It was time for *me* to start deciding exactly who I was, not a fraternity or anyone else.

The class work in college was challenging, and in my personal life I had new obstacles to maneuver. I was new to the game of dating men, so I was very cautious. Gradually I became more comfortable. The whole process took much more energy and time than I had imagined. Before I knew what had happened, I met my first love, Brian. We found each other online and seemed to hit it off well. On a crisp and cold November morning I ducked past all my friends at the dorm, put my down jacket on, and walked to Starbucks to meet him. I was in love from the moment I saw him. He was exceptionally cute, with curly hair, a square jaw, and dark blue eyes. We were sitting together having coffee, and under his breath he said, "God, you're beautiful." Our relationship instilled confidence in me for being gay, and I wanted others to know.

That fall semester I had decided not to rush any fraternity despite my parents still insisting that I give it a try. Becoming more comfortable with my sexuality was my first priority. The semester was winding down by that point and I was beginning to realize that my progress was limited. Of course, I had my relationship with Brian, but it was often turbulent, and I had not met many friends. I was hoping for more out of college.

Early in December some guys who were starting a Delta Chi colony on campus approached me. I decided to see what it would be like to hang around fraternity guys. I started attending colony meetings and information sessions about what the fraternity would be like. I felt like I was starting to connect with them—until the very last meeting of the semester. I was walking back to the dorms with three of the other colony brothers after the meeting. We walked past a guy who was dressed in tight jeans and a white see-through linen shirt. He was talking on a cell phone and using flamboyant hand gestures. I would not have noticed him, but it was December in Colorado and freezing outside. The other brothers took keen interest in his mannerisms. After he was out of earshot, one of them said, "Dude, who the fuck does that guy think he is?" and another replied, "Yeah, I don't know what that shit's about." The final edict was, "Fucking queer!"

I clammed up, horrified. *If they say that kind of stuff behind someone's back,* I thought, *What are they going to say about me when they find out I'm gay?* I wished them good night, turning down another path to walk home, knowing full well that I would never speak to any of them again. Fraternities were just as I had expected.

Coming back after winter break I was refreshed. Everyone on campus was going to the campuswide Spring Marathon party. It was still January and spring was months away, but the celebration was an opportunity to drink.

Out of nowhere I heard, "Oh, my God! I *love* those Diesel shoes you're wearing!" That's how I met Kevin. He was a half-Japanese and half-Argentinean fashion major, and an openly gay Sigma Pi brother. Whoa! I was shocked at the revelation he was out in a fraternity.

Some people would call Kevin a flamer. Considering how he introduced himself, I suppose I could understand why. He was exceedingly colorful—after all, he was a fashion major. To this day I do not know any male fashion majors who are straight.

Over the next few weeks Kevin and I spent a lot of time together. He was hilarious to be around. One afternoon I met him after class and we walked to his fraternity house, where his fraternity brothers greeted us.

"Hey, fa-a-ag!" one of the brothers said as we walked onto the lawn.

Kevin replied, "Shut it, breeder. Shouldn't you have a sorority girl hanging around your neck?"

Frat boys hanging out joking about Kevin and his openly gay lifestyle was surprising to say the least. The Sigma Pi brothers obviously had a routine of needling each other back and forth. Kevin's sexuality was something ordinary to them, and the jokes were never at Kevin's expense. I thought, *If Kevin can do this, then why can't I?*

The week after I had met Kevin's fraternity brothers, rush began. I knew I was ready for the next step, to rush. I settled on two fraternities: Pi Kappa Alpha and Sigma Pi.

Pi Kappa Alpha was my dad's fraternity. I owed it to him to check it out. I quickly learned about the frat's standards from the president himself during a rush event. The president sat in front of the rushees with a bottle of Coke and a bottle of Jack Daniel's and said, "Pike is about balance. Watch and learn, gentlemen!" Then he opened his mouth as wide as possible, held both bottles over his mouth, and started guzzling.

"Go-go-go-go-go," erupted the brothers. "Wahoo!" I laughed to myself at the lame attempt to display masculinity. After hanging out some more I left Pike late that January evening with two distinct impressions. First, gay guys were not wanted in the fraternity. Second, alcohol was more important than brotherhood. Pike was a miserable disappointment.

Now more than ever I was determined to join Sigma Pi. But even with Kevin being openly gay, I was not ready to come out to the fraternity brothers. Sigma Pi offered me a bid shortly thereafter, and I accepted without hesitation.

The following week at the bid day party, Kevin pulled me aside.

"Gabe, I have something to tell you. Please, please don't be afraid, because you have no reason to be," he said.

Obviously concerned, I asked, "What's up, dude?"

He replied, "They know."

How could they know? I wondered. As it sank into my head, I turned pale. I found out later it was not too hard for the brothers to do simple "gay arithmetic": They had put two and two together when they saw me hanging around Kevin and his gay friends.

A torrent of thoughts rushed through my mind. *Should I admit it? No, I'm not ready! Maybe I should deny it? Then I'd be living the same lie and hiding from the same fears my whole life!*

"Why are you so afraid for them to know?" Kevin asked.

"To tell you the truth, I don't know. I've lived my life going out of my way to make sure people didn't know. I'm just not used to it," I replied.

Kevin smiled and said, "You really shouldn't be so worried about it. They've known since you started to rush the house. If they had a problem with it, you wouldn't have been given a bid. Take a minute, and then come back inside."

I had never had so many people know that I was gay before. I felt like I had lost control of it, but I also realized that there was nothing I could do about it. Instead I would wait. The brothers could come to me if they had any questions or issues with my being gay.

The strategy seemed to work well. I knew someone would confront me eventually, but I had no idea when. My pledge brothers and I were becoming very close. I knew everything there was to know about each one, including information on his family and girlfriends. None of the pledge brothers had ever asked me about my sexuality.

A month later we all went to a party in an old house that should have been condemned 15 years earlier. I was standing around the keg watching the cheap, foamy beer pouring into our cups when Court, one of my pledge brothers, finally broke the ice.

"So do you have a boyfriend, Gabe?" His question was unexpected but sincere. Whew! I had assumed the first question would be, "Gabe, are you gay?"

In my heart I felt I could trust Court and the other pledge brothers. In this instant, I found the courage and the opportunity to come out. I responded without fear, "Yeah, I do."

"That's cool. How long have you guys been dating?" Just like I had done with their families and girlfriends, my pledge brothers wanted to know more about my life. The brotherhood made it easy for the first time in my life to talk about my sexuality.

One of the pledge brothers joked, "Well, we all need a token gay guy." He put his arm around my shoulder in fraternity style.

Another pledge brother quickly pushed him off of me and said, "Fuck you, dude, he's no token. To me, he's just one of the guys, nothing more, nothing less." With his hands on my shoulders and a broad smile, he gave me a hug and said, "I couldn't care less. You're my brother, man."

The entire experience was a huge relief. My fellow pledge brothers were playfully arguing over who accepted me more and for what reasons. I couldn't have asked for a better response.

At the weekly chapter meeting the next night I told all of Sigma Pi fraternity. During open business, someone typically shares something good that happened that week. With all eyes on me, I nervously walked to the front of the room and said, "This week has changed my life. It's not easy being openly gay for anyone. But it's because of the support I get from this house that I feel comfortable telling you. I know you all know already, and that's fine. But I want all of you to be comfortable with me too. I thank you for what you do and for being my brothers. It's because of this fraternity that I have the power to live my life the way I want. It makes me proud to be a Sigma Pi." My eyes became teary and I smiled. All the brothers began clapping slowly, followed by cheers that turned into whooping and hollering—the typical frat-boy expression of approval.

As my pledge semester progressed, however, I realized there were still men in the fraternity who were not as comfortable with my sexuality as

I thought they would be. These brothers would have one final vote before I would become a brother in the fraternity. Still, I felt a duty to try and win over the brothers who were hesitant and uncomfortable. My challenge was to learn more about these brothers and be more than "a gay" in their eyes.

Kyle, a tall, heavyset brother from Washington, came from a deeply devout Mormon family. Homosexuality is condemned and even persecuted among Mormons. Even though he wasn't a practicing Mormon, he still held many of the Mormon beliefs. Since I had come out he had been very standoffish with me. My big brother, Nate, called me one night and said, "Gabe, I don't want to scare you, but there's something you should know. I've been talking to Kyle, and he said that he was going to vote no on you during the pledge vote because you're gay." I was angry. Nate continued, "But don't worry—if he does, I'll personally kick his ass."

"Just because I'm gay?" I asked. I tried to think of something else I might have done to upset Kyle.

"Yeah, that's pretty much it," he replied. "I would recommend spending time with him and making him understand that your sexuality is only a small part of who you are. Being gay doesn't define you. You need to show him a different side of you, the side he hasn't seen."

Over the next few weeks I made a point of spending time with Kyle, almost to an obnoxious degree. The sophomore spring formal proved to be a cornerstone in the brotherhood between him and me. He invited me out on the deck for a cigarette that evening. Smoking was not my thing, but I knew it was a good opportunity to get some time alone with him. He opened up and told me about his steadfast convictions about befriending a homosexual.

"Gabe, I've never met a gay guy before. I've always been told that homosexuals are disgusting and an insult to all that is beautiful and right." He paused, looking puzzled by his own words. "But I think you're a great guy and someone I consider worthwhile in my life as a friend and a brother." I patted him on the shoulder. His words came from a place of conflict and meant more than I could have imagined. I respected him for sharing his feelings and for recognizing that I had something to offer him and the fraternity.

"Thanks for your honesty, Kyle. It means a lot to me, and I'm glad that you're a brother and also a friend," I said. Joking, I told him that I thought we had the beginnings of an MTV *Real World* television series. Kyle laughed and responded, "Gabe, you're gay. There's neither pride nor shame in that. To me, you're a man and a brother."

Finally, with Kyle on my side, I had the acceptance I wanted in the fraternity. Many more discussions with other brothers ended with similar honesty and understanding. There was only one more obstacle preventing me from being completely open about my sexuality: I had to come out to my family, my parents.

Clearing that hurdle would be a huge undertaking, and I was not sure I was ready. But Sigma Pi was in my corner, and the brothers would give me the necessary support. The friendship was stronger than anything in my entire life. If my family kicked me out and never wanted to see me again, the fraternity would be my family. I decided to write my parents a coming-out letter. I cried a lot rereading and rewriting the letter before sending it. Part of it read:

MY LIFE HAS BEEN A LIE. I'VE IGNORED A FUNDAMENTAL PART OF WHO I AM BECAUSE I FEARED ITS REPERCUSSIONS. IN AN EFFORT TO DEFUSE THE LIES AND LIVE A BETTER LIFE I NEED TO TELL YOU—I'M GAY. EVERY TIME I SAY THAT WORD, OR WRITE IT DOWN, A FEARFUL THOUGHT RUNS THROUGH MY MIND—THE THOUGHT THAT THOSE WHO HAVE LOVED ME ALL MY LIFE MAY LOVE ME LESS BECAUSE OF SOMETHING THAT MAKES ME WHO I AM, AND THAT I ULTIMATELY CANNOT CHANGE. THIS IS, YOU COULD SAY, MY DEEPEST, DARKEST, AND AT TIMES MY MOST LAMENTED SECRET. THE WORST PART WAS THAT I WAS ALONE AND HAD TO FACE IT ALL BY MYSELF. I'M TIRED OF BEING TWO-FACED, TIRED OF LIVING TWO LIVES, TIRED OF LYING. WORDS CANNOT ADEQUATELY DESCRIBE HOW SCARED I AM AT THIS VERY MOMENT.... I NEED YOU GUYS IN MY LIFE NOW MORE THAN EVER.

Five days after I had sent the three-page letter, my parents had not called or e-mailed me. I expected the worst. I picked up the phone and called home to have my mother answer in tears.

"Gabe, we're so disappointed," she said. That was the only thing she could manage before she had to put the phone down.

My father picked up the phone and said, "Gabe, I don't believe you. I'm disappointed in you, but we'll get through this; you'll get over this. We'll get you the best therapy. I've been in contact with a group of people in Boulder who are ex-gays and they want to meet with you. No matter what happens, though, I do love you. You have to pray. It's not too late. God will forgive you."

My family's intention to send me through intensive antigay therapy, counseling, and even an "ex-gay" camp sent me into panic. After hanging up the phone, I broke down, lying on my dorm room floor, crying and shaking. I had to talk to someone. Fortunately, Court lived on the other side of the dorm.

Grabbing a baseball cap, I positioned the brim low across my face to hide my tears and dragged myself to his room. He knew immediately what to do and say.

"Dude, it's all right. They'll come around," he said after I had told him the details of the phone call. Tears streamed down my cheeks. He consoled me with a hug, and I'll never forget what Court said next.

"When people find out something like this, they may not be able to accept it. You need to work with them to tolerate it. You can help them when they need it, but you can't force them to accept anything. Until then, live your life as you see fit," he said. This compassionate response changed my life.

My parents' reaction to my coming-out shook my life to its foundations. I was unstable and started to drink heavily. My brothers were the only source of support. I needed to rely on those I could trust, the fraternity. I realized that alcohol was not the solution, brotherhood was.

Considering my family's staunch religious convictions, I doubted that my sexuality would ever be completely acceptable. I first needed their tolerance and to pace my expectations. Court had been right, and the fraternity stood by me in this awful time with my family. Through extensive counseling my family has learned that they cannot change who I am. Slowly they have moved to a level of tolerance.

In fall 2003 my parents came to Boulder and met my fraternity brothers. All of them were very pleasant, and my parents were well received. Driving them back to their hotel room, my father asked guardedly, "How come your brothers didn't blackball you?"

"Why would they?" I asked.

"Because you're gay," he replied.

It was an opportunity to push the envelope gently.

"Well, because they know that it is only a small part of who I am. They love me and accept me for what I stand for and what I believe in. We share the same set of values. They support me and believe in me. They can look past something that other people can't. In your eyes it's a glaring flaw, but to them, it's a characteristic that distinguishes me and contributes to the brotherhood's diversity."

Stunned, he had no idea how to reply. Sometimes agreeing to disagree is the best way to move forward. I knew that my words would keep them up all night thinking.

When it comes to my family, I know my parents will never be comfortable or openly accepting of my life. As their son I have to respect their understanding and learn to cope. We continually challenge one another, and just as with my fraternity brother Kyle, I try to make my family see me for more than my "gay self."

Without Sigma Pi, I never would have been able to come out to my family or develop more fully as a gay man. Over a hundred men support and love me as their own regardless of my sexual orientation. Even during my horrible breakup with my first love, Brian, the brotherhood was there to hold me up. Who would have thought that a fraternity would give a gay man the self-confidence, self-esteem, and power to be openly gay?

To Live a Lie

by Joseph Zagame, Penn State, State College, Pa.

"Joe, tell me what your favorite part of the female anatomy is," asked Tom, my fraternity brother.

My mouth dropped open. The question was totally unexpected. Tom had an overwhelming sense of masculinity, humor, and compassion; he was an inspiration for me. I did not want to disappoint him with my answer. My discomfort probably showed; I was a tiny, sexually ambiguous kid from Long Island. My heart sank. What would I say? "I like the breast," I said finally. The brothers cheered and roared. I had successfully fooled them. Any more hesitation would have drawn suspicions about my sexuality, so I said what they wanted to hear.

Pledging a college fraternity gave me little time to deal with my sexuality. I knew the answer to the collegiate "Who am I?" question, but I maintained my veneer of heterosexuality. I used the fraternity to avoid coming to terms with my sexuality.

Kappa Alpha Order inducted me into the fraternity at the end of my first semester in fall 2002. Consumed by fraternity life, I was now a part of Penn State's massive, all-encompassing Greek system. I needed to somehow maintain the false image of heterosexuality, so I began dating a sorority girl, Melissa. She had busty looks and a sexpot image, and she had shown interest in me. No one would ever suspect I was gay with Melissa at my side.

Walking into the fraternity house one afternoon, I heard Tom yell, "Hey, Joe! Your girlfriend is banging." He had a way with words that challenged me to think of a way to top him with my response.

After laughing and giving him a "yeah, I know" I said, "Yeah, she is definitely a good piece of ass."

Presto! The plan worked. Never once did anyone doubt my heterosexuality. The horrible side effect of this process, however, was the development of an intense case of internalized homophobia. I would do anything to insult others perceived to be gay. I would put down people with antigay jokes and blatantly homophobic harassment, a reflection of my growing self-hatred.

The following year, one of my brothers asked a common question during one of our meetings: "Does anyone here have any objection to this rushee becoming a pledge in our chapter?"

I responded, "He talks kind of gay. We definitely don't want any fags in our fraternity."

In reality, the only gay person I did not like was me: Joseph Zagame, a dishonest, closeted homo. My gay feelings continued to surface, and I would trick myself into believing that I was heterosexual by drinking. But my feelings and my internal struggle would still be there the next day. I was setting myself up for a train wreck.

The last fraternity party of the semester was when I saw Eddie. He had been involved in the same leadership organizations on campus as me, and although he was a member of another fraternity, we seldom spoke. I was drawn to his handsome looks, extraordinary smile, light brown eyes, and gym-built body. Eddie approached me first with casual conversation at the party, and for some reason I felt he was flirting. I flirted back, or maybe the alcohol did it for me. The more interested I got, the more I had to drink, and I drank a lot.

"Do you want to walk back to the dorms together?" Eddie asked right before the party ended. He was drunk, I was drunk, and deep down I think both of us were looking for the same thing.

"Sure, let me go get my coat."

Eddie and I took the scenic route back to his dorms, making idle, drunken chatter along the way. Eddie insisted I come in: "My roommate went home for the weekend. You're more than welcome to stay over."

Without any doubt, I knew what Eddie was offering me. It was what I had been hoping for all night by flirting with him. Now, as I leaned against his door, my heart beat faster, and I took a step inside.

Not too much later we were lying on his bed naked, his tender lips pressed against mine. His steaming breath gave me new life. His body felt beautiful against mine. I will never forget that moment. I felt alive for the first time in my life.

Once I sobered up, I felt embarrassed and vulnerable. What had I done? What if my fraternity brothers ever found out? Sneaking out of the room while Eddie was asleep, I went back to my dorm room. I ended up in the shower, trying desperately to scrub the gay off me. I did not want to be homosexual. Falling on my knees in the shower, I began to cry. I thought, *You'd be better off dead than gay.*

Luckily, I didn't act on any of my suicidal thoughts. My Catholic upbringing condemned suicide but encouraged the power of confession. I couldn't start by telling my fraternity brothers, especially being the one who chastised "fags." I came out to a good friend of mine who was not associated with the fraternity, and I felt safe. The spring semester came to a close, and that summer I came out to many close friends back home and to my family. The 180-degree shift was a thrill, but still I feared telling my fraternity.

I returned to campus that fall for my sophomore year. I decided that coming out to the fraternity was not an option. Back in Long Island I would live the gay scene; on campus I would remain closeted. Living in the fraternity house that semester, I felt immense pressure to maintain the straight frat-guy persona. I ended up avoiding the brothers entirely, coming to the fraternity house late at night only to sleep. I was completely paranoid: I thought that if I made one false step, my secret would be revealed. Fraternity brothers started calling me "Shady Joe" because I never associated with them anymore. During that time I started dating a guy named Brad. He hated the fact that I was in a fraternity. He figured that fraternities by nature were antigay institutions.

Eventually rumors started to get around the fraternity house, and the word *gay* was linked to my name. One evening I walked into the dining hall and heard my name being called aloud. Three of my fraternity brothers were gesturing me to come over to their table. I walked over to say hello.

"Joe, we have a question for you. We heard this rumor about you, and we were wondering if it was true. Someone said that you were gay," my fraternity brother Steve asked with a disgusted look.

My heart jumped in my chest. I went on the defensive. "Definitely not. Why the hell would you even believe such a thing?" I demanded angrily.

Without waiting for a response I turned and stomped away. I hoped my rage was visible to all who dared to question. Outside the dining hall, alone, tears started to trickle down my cheek.

Things started to get really bad as more rumors spread. I decided that my time at Penn State was coming to an end. I needed to get out, and so I applied to other schools, including some universities in New York. I assumed it would be easier if I were closer to my friends and family in my home state. The only thing left would be to rough out the remainder of the semester and await my transfer.

"Faggot!" my brother Steve yelled at me, much like I had used the word during my freshman year. He was 6 foot 4, and his imposing gaze down at me made it all the more degrading. Every single day, whenever I saw him—in a bathroom, in the hallway, even on the street—he would say that word. My anger grew, and eventually I could not take it anymore.

I came home late one night from a party. Like an annoying parrot Steve once again said, "Faggot." Unable to restrain myself, I walked over and punched him in the face. The brothers stopped me from getting in another blow, and held Steve back from escalating the fight.

"Why did you do that?" Tom asked.

"You wouldn't understand," I said, aloof and confused. That punch was the final straw. I realized that I could no longer live the lie. It was time to finally come out to my brothers.

The following day was our fraternity chapter meeting, and charges would probably be brought against me for hitting a fellow brother. Everyone needed to know I was gay—not the next day or the day after, but at the meeting. Standing up in front of the brothers, I read from a piece of paper to all of the fraternity. My nerves were shaky and I could barely speak clearly. My eyes became moist.

"Brothers, there is something I want and need to tell you all, something I believe you all deserve to know about me." I paused to catch my breath. Rubbing my eyes, I proceeded, "I am gay. I hope you can all respect me and know that I am still the same person." I sat down quietly. Nobody said anything. The room was silent for what seemed like a lifetime.

The president stood up and said, "Would anyone like to add anything?" No one said anything, and so the president said, "Chapter is adjourned."

Chapter ended without any charges being pressed, and immediately afterward I went to my room, avoiding the brothers. Honestly, I thought that would be the last time I showed my face in the fraternity house—I was prepared to leave.

My fraternity brother Tom was the first one to come to my door. Asking to come inside, he expressed his strong support for me and recognized the pain of the struggle I was clearly going through. His acceptance meant something special to me. From the first day of my fraternity life, I worked hard not to disappoint Tom and often looked up to him. His love granted me strength and courage in my despair. Then, shockingly, brother after brother came knocking on my door. Each told me in his own way that he was okay with my being gay. The love of the brotherhood I experienced then was the strongest feeling ever. Each brother lent me a greater sense of pride in being gay and a Kappa Alpha.

So much had changed so quickly. Questions naturally came up about my sexuality from each of my brothers. I was never bothered by the questions and saw them as an opportunity for us to get to know each other all over again. I tried to answer from my heart and with humor. There were stupid questions, like "Are all left-handed people gay?" But there were also good ones, like "When did you first realize you were gay?" Educating my brothers about being gay allowed them to know me more fully and for us to become true allies.

Much of the homophobic banter in the house ceased, and I felt included in the fraternity once more. I went to parties, socials, and other fraternity activities, and for the first time I was myself. I didn't understand the full impact of my coming-out and how accepting the brothers were until the fraternity spring formal.

"Hey, Joey, are you bringing your boyfriend?" asked Tom. I had told him about my relationship with Brad shortly after I had come out.

"Of course not. The brothers definitely would have a problem with that," I said, not even thinking twice.

"Well, I spoke with most of the brothers, and they just assumed you would bring him. It seemed like they'd be okay with that," he said. Again,

I was blown away by the response of my brothers. I never would have thought they would be comfortable with me bringing my boyfriend to the fraternity formal.

As Tom suggested, I brought Brad to the formal. He was reluctant, of course, based on his extreme dislike of fraternities. Personally, I thought that some of my brothers would react negatively, but I was wrong. The fraternity truly surprised me. Every one of my brothers introduced himself and his date to my boyfriend and me. Brad's perspective on fraternities totally changed that night. Likewise for me, it was a pivotal moment to understand the positive influence that I had on the fraternity and that the brothers had on my life.

Their acceptance turned my life around. I had found an inner peace and never contemplated suicide again. One of the brothers pointed that out to me this past year. "You aren't the same person you were last year. You seem different—not because you're gay, but because you're happier," he said.

Approaching my junior year at Penn State, I am indeed happier. I am no longer living a lie. I learned that brotherhood is brotherhood. It is about accepting your brothers in spite of their differences. And that once you respect yourself, others will respect you too. My fraternity's acceptance has changed me as a person. I'm happy to be who I am and happy to be part of the Kappa Alpha Order.

Two Opposite Tales

by Jack Trump, Indiana State University, Terre Haute

"Sean, what's up? What's the matter?" I asked.

"I need to talk to you. Can I come over?" Sean asked between sobs.

"Just tell me what's wrong," I replied, clutching the phone closer to my ear.

"Jack, I can't talk about it now. Can I just come over?" he implored.

"Yeah, sure, where are you?" Sean had never acted like this before. Was he hurt? I had grown especially close to Sean over the previous semester when he rushed the fraternity. The tone of his call was disturbing.

"I'm in the car. I'll be there in a few minutes," he said, and hung up.

I thought about the relationship that I had developed with my fraternity brothers. I had just moved back to campus after winter break, and I was excited to be back for resident assistant training. I had missed my friends and my fraternity.

Prior to my college years, the only impression I had of fraternities was that they were a breeding ground for alcoholism and immorality. That changed after I met Sandro, my Brazilian roommate, my first week on campus. Sandro was a pledge of Phi Kappa Tau. He was a nice guy, but I was not exactly thrilled to be rooming with someone who was in a fraternity. Sandro's friends were colony members trying to bring a chapter of the national fraternity to campus. I was a little reluctant to hang out with them at first, but after getting to know Sandro and hanging out with his fraternity, I started to inquire about fraternal life. I liked what the fraternity stood for and hoped that the concept of brotherhood was not just a ploy. Besides, I had always wanted a real brother, and this was an opportunity to have a fraternity of brotherhood—for life. The friendships that I developed with these guys grew stronger as the semester progressed. The value of brotherhood was evident not only in their words but also in their actions. To my surprise, I received a bid to join the fraternity, and I was also voted president of my incoming pledge class. Later I learned that I was the "rush crush"—the new member most sought after by the fraternity.

The facade that I created regarding my sexuality was impenetrable. Although I dated girls here and there, I never sought anything intimately or sexually serious from them. I often characterized myself as a chameleon, able to change with whatever was expected of me. In high school I was forced to acknowledge that I was attracted to other boys after developing a major attraction toward my best friend, Ryan. I could never bring myself to say anything or act on those feelings. My heterosexual facade was always in place, and I became skilled at selectively editing my life to show only certain aspects that I knew others would most readily accept. Some call it manipulation; for me, it was necessary for survival.

The phone rang again. It was Sean.

"Jack, I'm here," he said.

"Okay, I'll be down in just a few minutes," I answered.

When I went to let him into the residence hall, I was confronted with a different person. No longer was Sean the strong and confident brother I had come to know. He appeared defensive and withdrawn. He looked as though he had just run a marathon, his face haggard and tearstained. He fell onto my bed and we just sat there for a while in silence. I wanted to do something, to give him a hug, to fix whatever was wrong, but I forced myself to wait patiently as he struggled for words through his tears.

"Take your time, Sean," I said. "I'm not going anywhere." I sat on the bed next to him.

"There's something I want to tell you," he said. He struggled to collect himself.

"I don't know how to say this, so I'm just going to say it." He took a breath. "I'm gay." The words hit me like a slap. In that moment, I wanted to pretend that it hadn't happened and to have him leave. I was worried that my facade would collapse and that I would be forced to deal with my own sexuality. I didn't know what to do or say.

"I'm really sorry, Jack," he said, as if he had let me down.

I loved Sean like family, and I did the only thing I could: I reached over, hugged him, and said, "Sean, trust me. It doesn't matter." We both cried, and the response to my acceptance was heartfelt for both of us. Before I had a chance to contemplate my inhibition, my own emotions took over, and I continued: "It doesn't matter to me because I'm gay too."

I said it, I actually said it, I thought again and again in my head. Sean was the first person in my fraternity to know; he was only the fourth person I had told in my whole life. Then it hit me: My facade had fallen apart on campus. I was panicking on the inside, but for Sean I struggled to maintain what little composure I had left. I had given up control and revealed all of me. While I knew I wanted to be there for my brother, I felt exposed, like in one of those dreams where you go to class naked.

"Jack, they know." Sean broke away from the embrace, his face grave and his lip curling as if to cry again.

"What do you mean, 'they know'? Who are they?" I replied. He began to sob. "Sean, what's going on? Who are they?" I demanded. "Your parents? Who?" But I knew the answer before he responded. I could see my own fear reflected in his eyes. Sean was afraid of the reaction and rejection by our fraternity brothers.

Although Indiana State was not an overtly homophobic campus, this was pre-*Will & Grace*. There were certain unspoken rules to be followed, especially in the context of a fraternity, and this would surely break several of the masculine heterosexual norms.

"The fraternity knows." He sighed, stifled a sob, and went on, "I was using Jim's computer. It was no big deal. Everyone uses it. Someone must have been looking at gay porn on Jim's computer, but it wasn't me, I swear!" He gestured wildly. "They started doing this witch hunt in the house to figure out who it was. Of the six of us staying in the fraternity house over break, I was the one who got blamed." I believed him.

He told the whole story of how he had been accused and had locked himself in his fraternity room. He did not leave except to eat, shower, or use the restroom. He knew that I would be back from break early for RA training and that I could help him find a safe place to stay. Sean had figured I would protect him. His brothers, our brothers, had reacted poorly to their "discovery." A few guys had thrown garbage on Sean while he tried to get to his car, defamatory comments were left on the whiteboard on his door, and other brothers had stopped speaking to him.

"Jack, I know what I have to do. I'm going to come out Sunday night at the fraternity meeting before the rest of them find out." Sean was desperately trying to maintain control and keep what dignity he had left after the ordeal.

"Sean, are you sure this is something you really want to do? Are you ready for this?" I asked out of concern for me as well. I knew the inevitable was beginning to unfold, and I could not stop it. Sean had had no say in the way he was outed, but I would not allow the same to happen to me.

"Jack, what am I supposed to do? I'm worried about what's going to happen when everyone else gets back. The handful of people that were at the fraternity house over the break will surely spread rumors if I don't do it first." He sighed. "I was honest about being gay when they asked, and I'm probably going to get booted out for it." He was still shaking, but his eyes began to harden. He had made up his mind, and the decision had been made for me too.

"You're right," I said. "There's not much of a choice. Sean, I need you to know that no matter what happens, you're still my brother." I would not let him face our brothers alone.

I spent the next few days in a haze of doubt. I spent most of my free time with Sean to support him as best as I could. Sunday night and our first fraternity chapter meeting of the semester came too quickly. I knew what I had to do, but would I have the courage to stand by my convictions, or would fear paralyze me?

My fraternity house was a truly historic, well-kept building representing traditional Greek life. One of my favorite places was the fraternity chapter meeting room. It was a beautiful, expansive room with a vaulted art deco ceiling. All the fraternity activities centered on this area—it was the heart of the house. Despite the overwhelming size of the room, there was always a sense of closeness when I entered it in the presence of all the brothers. Tonight, of all nights, I still felt the rush of excitement walking in. I had not seen many of the brothers since the fall semester, and I had missed the camaraderie.

The meeting progressed normally with chatter about the winter break and events for the upcoming semester. I had good memories of the fraternity over the past three years. There was Super Bowl Sunday my freshman year when we had rented a location at the student union to watch the game, rooting for Green Bay. It was the first time I truly felt happy and a part of the lives of my brothers. There were brotherhood weekends, where we focused on connecting with each other and bonding by sharing our feelings. I also cherished watching a brother fall in love and then consoling him after he got dumped.

The time for the gavel to pass had come. Each brother would hold the gavel and he could speak his mind without being interrupted. Sean had made prior arrangements with our president to speak first. I wanted to be happy for Sean, proud of what he was about to do, but I could not get beyond my fear. I desperately hoped that his coming-out would be well received and that I would be proud of my fraternity.

My mind was tuned in for three words—"I am gay"—but beyond that I wasn't tuned in to what Sean was saying. I could tell from his body language that he was terribly nervous. I picked up pieces of his speech here and there, including a reference to another gay brother in the fraternity. Finally he said, "Now you know," and with his head down he handed the gavel to the next brother and left the house. A few minutes of silence fell over the room, broken by our president explaining that we would discuss what Sean had just said. I asked that I be allowed to speak first.

I talked about my frustration and disappointment with the fraternity. I tried to reconcile the good memories I had of the fraternity brothers with the violent character of the people who had harassed Sean over winter break. It was confounding to think that a fellow Phi Tau would do those things to him and still consider himself a brother. It was frightening that others could witness such incidents and do nothing to stop them. I told the brothers that I was disgusted with the current state of our brotherhood. "When we were just a colony and there were only a handful of us, we actually cared for one another. We talked so much about not being 'that typical fraternity.' We weren't just okay with difference; we were all about it. Come on, people!" I said, troubled by their despondent faces. "Before we had our charter, we knew what brotherhood meant. Even if we didn't agree with somebody, it didn't change the fact that he was a brother. We've finally gained the fraternity charter that we worked so hard for, but somehow that must have meant forfeiting our brotherhood along the way—because this is not the fraternity I remember joining." My point was becoming clear. "Sean's given so much to this fraternity, for God's sake. He won Outstanding Associate of the Year at the Omega Awards. He busted his ass for you, the fraternity, and he didn't have to come out to you. He shared this part of his life with you, and you decide to treat him like this?"

I handed the gavel to the brother on my left for his response. The gavel moved its way around our circle and the words expressed varied among support, frustration, indifference, and hate. No one held back his true feelings. While it was difficult for me to hear many of their words, I gained respect for the brothers who were unashamed to say what they thought.

After more than three hours of discussion, the gavel found its way back to my hands once again. Almost every person in the room looked mentally drained, and there was an unspoken consensus to move on with the discussion and reach some sort of resolution.

I stood up and said I had one last thing to say. "It's important that I say this," I told them. All eyes were on me, and I felt my hand pull back into a fist around the gavel. I would now deliver the death blow to my once-perfect facade. Just as I was finding my words, someone stood up and said, "Jack, sit down! Let's get on with the damn vote."

I looked at him and said, "No, you sit down. I have something important to say. Sean said that there is someone else in this fraternity who is gay, but he didn't say who." I paused to catch my breath. "Take a look at the person sitting next to you. What if he were gay? We all call ourselves brothers, but what does that mean? How strong is this so-called brotherhood if we're so quick to turn our backs on one another? Sean didn't murder or rape anyone; he simply told us something about himself that we didn't know. He is still the same brother as before. I would even argue that his bond of brotherhood is stronger now because he took the risk of sharing something very personal. So what now? Do we turn our backs on him? Most brothers have said they want to see him booted out because you think he lied to us or because your so damn worried about what will become of our fraternity reputation if we have a gay brother. He said there is someone else in our circle who is gay. Who is it? Put yourself in that person's shoes. Do you honestly think he would come out now, knowing how you would treat him? Let's be honest." There was some awkward movement. It was obvious the brothers were considering that someone else might be gay. "What if it was me? What if I was the other gay brother? I'm an RA, I'm part of this fraternity, I'm a leader in several student organizations, and my hometown is only half an hour from here. If it were me, would you understand? It isn't that Sean was lying to us, it's that he just wasn't ready to come out. Instead he was outed." Barely pausing, I went on. "I'm going to make this really easy for you so you don't have to go on another witch hunt. I am the one Sean was talking about. Yes, I'm gay. So go ahead, take your stupid fucking vote, because I really don't care anymore. If you really don't want us here after tonight, then I will gladly leave." I was on a roll and there was no turning back. "But I'll tell you something: There's going to be a time when you don't have that choice to avoid someone simply because he or she is gay. Then what? Will you quit your job because your supervisor is gay? Will you move because your next-door neighbors are gay? Think about it. Oh, and also, there are more than just two gay brothers in this fraternity, but because of your homophobia you'll never know how many."

I set down the gavel firmly and left, not even looking at another brother on my way out the door. I was not going to wait for the fraternity to kick me out. The magnitude of my actions hit me when I stepped into the cold. *I can't believe that I actually told the brotherhood. Before tonight, I was still in control. Now that's gone.* As I walked away from the fraternity house, I heard a group of brothers coming out the door yelling for me to wait up. I yelled back, "What are you doing? You need to go back inside and be part of the vote. You're still part of the fraternity."

"Jack, we don't care about that vote," one brother called back. "It's cold as hell out here, and you're not walking back to campus in this." I was in disbelief. They told me to hop into one brother's tiny red pickup truck. The four of us crowded into the cab as we headed back to campus. Being together in the confined space spoke volumes about their comfort with me after my revelation. One brother looked over at me and said, "Nothing to worry about, buddy; there wasn't a vote taken."

The night that Sean and I came out was one of the last times we ever spoke. In time the brothers came around, but Sean felt that the scars from the earlier homophobic rejection were too much to overcome. He felt the fraternity had not done enough to heal those wounds. I have tried to understand why my friendship with Sean ended so suddenly. I can only suppose that he saw me as one of them because I stayed in the group that had hurt him so severely. Perhaps the fraternity did not make reparations when he needed to feel support from the brotherhood. To this day the question still lingers.

Either way, I owe my brotherhood to Sean. I would never have come out had it not been for him, and perhaps I would have remained skeptical of that central tenet of fraternity life—lifelong brotherhood. He brought about my coming-out, and he sparked conversations about being gay that I would never have imagined in the fraternity. His brave act allowed me to be myself and to be openly gay.

After that night the fraternity brothers gradually learned an important lesson about diversity, and they opened their minds to accept my being gay and a good brother. Nevertheless, when Sean and I tell our stories about that night, I'm sure we tell two opposite tales. One of my professors always said, "We are the rooms in which we live." Put more simply, "We are our life's experiences." Sean's experiences were different than mine because of the homophobic behavior he witnessed firsthand. I cannot begin to understand what he went through and the pain he felt at being outed. Sean had his reasons for leaving, just as I had my reasons for staying.

Standing Tall and Proud

by Richard P. Peralta, DePaul University, Chicago

Fresh out of the closet in high school, I often felt like an after-school special. Everyone seemed to know about my being gay. I was out and proud, almost six feet tall, well built, with spiky frosted black hair. My favorite attire was a navy muscle shirt with the slogan MAKE HIM BEG emblazoned across my pecs. Fluorescent blue and pink buttons on my backpack read, I'M NOT GAY BUT MY BOYFRIEND IS and CAUTION: FAG ON A RAG! My high school locker was defaced with the word FAG scrawled on it. Reactions were mixed, but I never wanted to be known only as gay. Being the token gay guy from my high school class of 2001 was not my goal. I figured college would be different.

The fall of my freshman year at DePaul University, I became a founding father of a colony of Sigma Phi Epsilon national fraternity, often called Sig Ep. DePaul is the largest Catholic university in the nation and the largest private institution in the Chicago area. Most men joined the new Sig Ep colony because the fraternity gave them a sense of purpose. My reason, on the other hand, was the fact that during rush Sig Ep did not judge me for being gay. They did not place me in a box along the spectrum of the Kinsey sexuality scale, wondering if I fit any gay stereotypes. They merely got to know me as "Dickey," my affectionate nickname. I never came out to the brothers as a whole. I let them figure it out on their own through conversation when I felt it was appropriate. There were two other queer brothers already in the fraternity. If I didn't make a big deal about being gay, I knew the chapter would not care either. I left behind my blatant high school T-shirt slogans and buttons, and my physical traits made me the all-American fraternity man. Sig Ep brought out the best in me.

Shortly after the acceptance of my bid to join Sig Ep, the brothers and I were eating at the student union, referred to on campus as the Max. We were gorging ourselves on food like most college men do when my brother Mark casually asked, "So how was your date last night?"

Mark was a calming individual who studied bio. He was relatively short in stature and often amusing on account of his klutzy habits. Mark was the average type of guy anyone would feel comfortable befriending on account of his big heart.

"So?" he asked again.

I panicked for a second and then responded nonchalantly, "It went well, actually." I didn't know for sure if he knew I was gay or how he knew I had gone on a date the night before. As he was heterosexual, I assumed that he would move the conversation on to other topics.

"So where did you go?" he said, kicking my leg under the table and smiling. Mark did know I was gay. *What was he up to?* I wondered.

I answered his question honestly, aware that the brothers in earshot were listening as they devoured their dinners. I talked about the film, where we had dinner, and the lack of chemistry, making sure that the pronouns were ambiguous. I had learned my lesson being the token gay in high school and figured that I wanted the brothers to know me first as Dickey, not for the gay label.

"What was his name again?" Mark asked comfortably and loudly over all the noise, emphasizing the gender pronoun.

The sounds of chomping halted as Mark and I continued eating. When I said his name, three spoons dropped simultaneously as the rest of the table looked at me. One brother at the end of the table apparently had not heard the conversation and continued contently chomping along. The other brothers' faces looked shocked.

Finally the brother at the end stopped eating for a moment, and with his mouth full he said, "Big deal, he's gay. Are you going to finish your fries, dude?"

I passed my fries down the line as I saw everyone look around, share shrugs, and return their focus to eating and their previous conversations. I smiled at Mark and he returned a goofy chuckle. For some brothers, tolerance was the first lesson. For others, acceptance came as easily as asking for more fries.

By and large, the Sig Ep brothers made me feel shockingly normal about my sexuality. I even took another guy as my date to the fraternity semiformal that year. Still, the brothers had some concerns, a few avoided me, and there were always many questions.

One time a brother was passing me in the halls, his arms loaded with books. He made eye contact over the tall stack and asked, "Hey, I'm on my way to bio, but I was wondering how old you were when you knew you were, y'know?" I would always answer the questions openly and honestly. Another time on the way home from intramural football practice, as we were walking and throwing football passes, a brother asked, "So, wait, I heard you had a girlfriend on and off for three years in high school. Is that true? How did all that work? Did she turn you gay, man?"

The questions never bothered me. I was glad the brothers appeared to be genuinely interested in my life. The brotherhood was stronger due to the fact we could bond over our lives truthfully. Homophobia was not able to destroy our fraternal love, close friendship, and loyalty to one another. Most of the fraternity brothers did not fear my sexuality—rather, they found it reassuring to know someone gay.

The closeness was mutual, and the questions revealed a comfort with our masculinity beyond words. I even had a fraternity brother who eagerly offered, "Hey, Dickey! Want me to set you up with my girlfriend's brother's best friend's second cousin who's gay too?" And my favorite question, which usually came late at night after drinking with an intoxicated brother's arm around my shoulder, "So, dude, do you, like—" he would burp and continue, "Do you, like, have a boyfriend that you, like, do stuff with, man?"

The brotherhood of Sig Ep transcended the stereotypical boundaries of Greek life. It made me feel safe and that I was part of the family. Unfortunately, a few of my brothers had issues with the gay thing now and then, but the defining rule was one of respect. Some gay men who were non-Greek would give me the cold shoulder for my fraternity involvement, assuming the homophobic stereotypes were true of every Greek. My lesbian non-Greek friends were more supportive than the gay men. These women actually empowered me to challenge the notion. I did not have to be a stereotype of a gay man or a fraternity man. The brothers inspired me to simply be myself and bring both worlds together. By junior year I found myself more accomplished than I ever dreamed.

Active in Greek life, I had met a number of fellow Greek leaders through conferences, parties, visiting other universities, friends, or chatting on Greek networks online. I made a large number of Greek friends online who would instant-message or touch base through blogging. That is how I met Rolin, chatting online about our fraternity chapters and comparing the two experiences. Rolin was in another social fraternity and was closeted. Unlike Sig Ep, which has a nondiscrimination statement inclusive of sexual orientation in the national fraternity bylaws, Rolin's national fraternity does not have such a policy. He would often ask about my brotherhood and the positive experiences of being out in the fraternity. He also shared his fears about coming out, especially on his campus in the South. He hid his sexuality by acting as heterosexual as possible. He even told me that he had purchased every *Girls Gone Wild* video. We both appreciated the companionship and found support in one another. Plus we were both leaders on campus and in the fraternity. Rolin served as interfraternity council president on campus and vice president of his fraternity, and I also held leadership positions in the fraternity and on campus. Even as an out gay man and a closeted gay man, both of us had been recognized by our fraternities' national headquarters for our leadership. The fraternity devotion we shared was our common bond that brought us together, and the love grew from that point on.

Although Rolin and I were years apart in our coming-out processes, our personalities blended so well that he soon became more than a friend. He was handsome, of average build, and about 5 foot 5, with hazel eyes and tiny freckles that only added to his good looks and charming smile. We quickly developed a long-distance relationship via the Internet and telephone.

"Can you call me before you go to bed tonight?" he said one night over the phone.

"Of course I will," I whispered back.

"Good, because I want to hear my boyfriend's voice before dreaming of him all night."

I blushed. "Oh, so I'm your boyfriend now, huh?" I chuckled.

"Only if you call me yours," he replied.

"Are you sure you want to do this, tiger? I've been burned my share of times," I said cautiously.

"Don't worry, babe, I'm not going anywhere for a long time. People like you and me are few and far between. Nothing would make me leave you," he said, and reiterated how much he loved me. We had a connection that simply cannot be put into words.

Distance was a challenge to our relationship, along with the fact that Rolin was closeted. It was never easy, and the closet would naturally limit our relationship. We would spend hours on the phone, lying in bed, my limbs wrapped around my pillow.

"We need to take it day by day, baby," he assured me on many calls. "Someday we'll get to where we want to be, but for now we have to do what we can, travel when possible, and finish school." He was content with the relationship and was not ready to come out in his life.

My fraternity brothers, on the other hand, were mixed about my relationship with Rolin. Dennis, one of my brothers in the fraternity, was always watching out for me and my shifting love life. He was Filipino too, slightly shorter than me, but was always the brother I looked to for advice.

One night as I sat there upset about Rolin, Dennis patted my back and asked, "Are you sure you want to be doing this? I mean, with Matt and all. You finally got through that mess."

He had to bring up Matt, my ex-boyfriend. That relationship ended because Matt felt his coming-out process was progressing faster than he could handle, and leaving me would slow things down. Before Matt was Peter from Massachusetts, who came out only after the push from our relationship. And before Peter was Greg of Wisconsin, also closeted and who ended up down the road at Northwestern University as a brother in Phi Kappa Psi. My history of closeted suitors worried my fraternity brothers. Dennis had made his point clearly. Still, Dennis and the other brothers supported me and threatened to kick anyone's ass if they hurt me.

Then came the recurring conversation that ended my relationship with Rolin. The brothers had warned me, but I had hoped Rolin was ready to be what I wanted in a boyfriend. "Why can't you come to formal?" I said over the phone as I bit my lip.

"Because, Richard, I'm not ready. Don't you understand? You've been there before. I'm not ready for that kind of environment, with everyone knowing I'm gay."

"But you'll be safe," I shot back, "and the guys have been wanting to meet you."

"I can't, baby. Not just yet," he said firmly. "I know I'm not going to be ready to come out anytime soon as an undergrad in my fraternity. I may never be ready."

While our connection remained whole, having our lives apart with him deep in the closet took a toll. We ended our relationship and instead played the on-and-off game and "I love you, but I hate you" for the next year. We called each other only when intoxicated—after enough booze we would profess our love, inflicting further pain the next day. During our split my use of alcohol and nicotine increased while my motivation in class waned. My performance suffered everywhere, and my fraternity brothers were concerned. Efforts to date other men were hopeless.

My love for Rolin was real. The pain I felt was over the turmoil he grappled with regarding his sexuality. Why couldn't his fraternity brothers support him? Brotherhood should be there in times of need. He had unselfishly given so much to the fraternity. It was not fair.

None of my brothers understood what I was going through. No matter what, they only wanted me to be happy. Each time Rolin had turned me down to be my date to the fraternity formal, the brothers wanted to kick his ass. They loved me that much. They could not understand why Rolin would not feel safe.

Finally the brothers convinced me that I had to make a choice. Besides hating the world, society, closed-minded bigots, Texan presidents, the church, and everything else that oppresses the queer community, I had to choose to be strong. That's when I decided to take a stand on behalf of Rolin. His fraternity had to hear about the pain of the closet and know that there are many men like him out there. I decided that I would make a positive difference by contacting Rolin's national grand fraternity president. The e-mail read:

THE FUTURE OF GREEK LIFE CAN ONLY SURVIVE IF THE GREEK SYSTEM RECOGNIZES THE DIVERSITY OF OUR COLLEGE CAMPUSES. I'M PROUDLY A MEMBER OF A FRATERNITY THAT DOES *NOT* DISCRIMINATE BASED ON SEX- UAL ORIENTATION AND I FEEL THAT YOUR FRATERNITY'S WAYS ARE COUN-

TERPRODUCTIVE TO THE FUTURE OF COLLEGE GREEK LIFE TODAY AND ITS
LEADERS OF TOMORROW.

I explained in the e-mail that the fraternity had a strong leader in one
of his chapters who struggles daily with being gay in fear of what may
happen if he came out to his brothers. I reiterated that this leader had
been nationally recognized and had accomplished a great deal for his fraternity. If he was given the necessary support from his local and national fraternity, he could have an even stronger and more positive impact on
the undergrads and alumni of the fraternity. I copied the e-mail to the
rest of the national headquarters staff. I had no clue if I would be successful or even receive a response. At least I tried to change the status quo.
Believe it or not, the first response I received was from the national fraternity president himself. His e-mail read:

I DON'T BELIEVE IN SUGGESTING THAT SOMEONE THAT IS HOMOSEXUAL
DO ANYTHING OTHER THAN WHAT EVERY OTHER MEMBER DOES, AND
THAT IS, KEEP THEIR SEXUALITY TO THEMSELVES. I PERSONALLY BELIEVE
THAT SEXUAL PREFERENCE IS SOMETHING THAT ANY INDIVIDUAL SHOULD
KEEP TO THEMSELVES AND SHARE ONLY WITH A MATE SELECTED FOR LIV-
ING TOGETHER. I KNOW OF NO REASON WHY SOMEONE SHOULD NEED TO
"COME OUT OF THE CLOSET" CONCERNING EITHER THEIR HETEROSEXUAL
ORIENTATION OR HOMOSEXUAL ORIENTATION. FOR EXAMPLE, THIS LAST
TUESDAY I HAD DINNER WITH FIVE STUDENTS, ONE WAS CHINESE, ONE
WAS JEWISH, ONE WAS BLACK FROM THE CARIBBEAN, ONE WAS WHITE,
AND ONE WAS PUERTO RICAN. WHATEVER THEIR SEXUAL ORIENTATION, I
HAVE NO IDEA AND COULD CARE LESS BECAUSE THAT IS NOT MY BUSINESS,
NOR DO I CARE.

Then other national fraternity staff members responded, desperately
wanting to know who had "the audacity to write such filth." I was disgusted. No wonder Rolin felt like he could not come out. I would never
have guessed a national fraternity would be so homophobic.

This week I begin my senior year, and who knows what the future
holds for Rolin and me? Everyone has a time and place to come out. I
cannot control that for anyone but me. Some of us are visible pioneers
while others, like Rolin, are struggling for any acceptance. There are
many men in the same quandary. It is not at all easy being gay and
Greek today.

Some fraternities will have to lead the way to educate on issues of sexual orientation and the acceptance of gay brothers. Sig Ep and other inclusive fraternities should stand tall together for the promise of brotherhood. Gay or straight, we should be equally proud to be Greek.

Finding Courage

by Adrian V. Herrera, California Polytechnic State University, San Luis Obispo

I don't act like that, so am I gay? I would often ask myself when I was growing up. Somehow I always knew I was gay, but I convinced myself I never fit the gay mold. I came from a traditional Filipino family and have two older brothers. My father is a U.S. Navy veteran. Six feet tall and 165 lean athletic pounds, I participated in lacrosse, rugby, and wrestling in my high school just outside Baltimore, managing to suppress any overt signs that I might be gay.

Whenever I would see a gay person in high school, I would look at myself and think, *I don't have a lisp. I don't have any effeminate features. I can't be gay.* I was clearly in denial and certainly not ready to come out.

Eventually college brought me to California and got me out of the closet. I began my freshman year in 2003 at California Polytechnic State University in San Luis Obispo, or as most people call it, Cal Poly. The location was perfect—rolling hills and the Pacific Ocean—and I was finally able to come out slowly on campus without any worries about my family.

The second week of school I was eating lunch with my roommate as part of our daily routine. My roommate was a Mexican-American from Northern California who loved the Oakland Raiders. I would always poke fun when the Baltimore Ravens won or the Raiders lost. The cafeteria was packed that day, but we managed to find us an empty table, where a group of three guys soon joined us for lack of finding another place. We all introduced ourselves and made small talk. One of the guys responded immediately when I mentioned where I was from.

"Maryland? What made you come all the way out here to California?" he asked.

"Because the engineering program out here is pretty damn good…and it's California, bro!" I answered.

All of us got along instantly as we ate and talked about sports and the campus. They mentioned that they were in a fraternity called Tau Kappa Epsilon, also known as the Tekes.

"We have a barbecue for rush week with our fraternity later if you want to swing on by," one of them said. "You should come—it's free food!"

My roommate and I decided to check out the fraternity—mainly for the free food. These three guys seemed pretty cool, and they were a diverse group. One was Mexican-American and went to my roommate's rival high school. All were transfer students from different parts of California, and one was originally from Wyoming. My only knowledge of fraternities was based on MTV's *Fraternity Life:* drunken guys trying to hook up with girls and occasionally getting into fights. I had never heard of gay men in fraternities and did not know how that would go over. I decided I would not lie about being gay if I was asked.

When we arrived at the University Union that afternoon, the rush week barbecue was bustling with students. More than 20 booths crowded the union, and guys were everywhere trying to drag men to their fraternity. The smell of barbecue filled the air as we walked down the rows. It was exactly how I pictured college to be: young people hanging out and having a good time. Eventually we walked by the TKE booth. Many of the fraternity brothers introduced themselves, and somehow one brother and I got stuck on the topic of college football.

"I'm from Maryland, so of course I love the Terrapins. I almost went to University of Maryland," I explained.

"You came all the way from Maryland?" he said in shock. He then proceeded to tell me, "Maryland will lose to Florida State this year.

Florida has the offense and the defense this year to match, buddy."

We had a 10-minute debate about college football. The brother was Indian-American and from the Bay Area. After learning that I was an engineering major, he introduced me to another fraternity brother. This guy was a general engineering student from Washington State. He gave me a heads-up on the rigorous engineering program and Cal Poly. All the other fraternity booths were trying to get guys to join without even learning about them. None of these guys were even trying to get me to join their fraternity. They just wanted to hang out with me. They were not pushy or superficial. Their approach is what made me come back and finally decide to rush TKE.

After I had gone to all of the TKE rush week events, I was invited to a formal interview. I could not believe I had made it that far. It was the last step in the process before you receive a formal pledge bid to join the fraternity. One of the brothers told me to dress professionally so that I would make a better impression than everyone else. I wore a blue dress shirt and khakis. I forgot to wear a tie, but I figured I would still be one step above the other guys.

I arrived for the interview and waited on the back patio with a few other students. Many of them seemed nervous, but I really wasn't. I thought, *What is there to be nervous about?* Then I remembered that nobody had ever asked if I was gay. It had never come up. I had never lied about it, but I lacked the courage to tell the truth. I became nervous too. The dress shirt was creeping up my neck, and I was getting hot.

Five minutes later I was sent inside to the main room. One seat in the middle of the room was left open for me. Five brothers were on the other side of the room sitting on a couch. I sat down and thought, *Man, they are going to interrogate me!*

The questions were pretty traditional, and I am a natural talker. I talked about high school and my family. Then I hesitated—what about my sexuality? In the end I thought, *What the hell have I got to lose?* I mustered all my courage. When the president asked if there was anything else I wanted to say, I thought this was the only opportunity. So I said to the brothers, "I'm not sure how your fraternity feels about homosexuality, and I'm not sure if you want me in your fraternity, because I'm gay."

I felt a tremendous sense of pride. I never dreamed I would have said "I'm gay" to a bunch of fraternity men. I felt like I had made myself vulnerable, but I was not about to go back into the closet. Honesty was the best policy.

One of the fraternity brothers told me later about the meeting where they discussed all the formal interviews. There was a rumor that a gay guy was trying to get into the fraternity. Nobody knew who it was, so I guess it was true that I did not really fit the gay mold—most people cannot tell that I am gay. The president calmed everyone down and began discussing the interviews. Each rushee has his photo placed on a large board so the members would remember the person from rush week. When he came to my picture, blue dress shirt and khakis, no tie, the president said, "This kid is in a unique situation. He is one of the coolest guys we have, but he has some reservations about all of this because he is gay. He doesn't want you guys to judge him, and he doesn't know how you guys feel about homosexuality."

The discussion grew heated. Some were blatantly against the idea of pledging someone gay: "What would the other fraternities think? We'd be the gay fraternity," said one opponent. Other brothers did not care about the image and saw a gay pledge as another aspect of diversity. "We always claim to be such a diverse house. We always pride ourselves on our diversity," said one brother. "This is a test of that. We have an opportunity where we can really become a diverse house, and look at you guys."

One of the brothers I had first met in the cafeteria that day asked, "If you guys didn't know he was gay and just knew his character and his credentials as a person, you would let him in, right?"

Some brothers didn't really care. Their main concern was more about my well-being. "Would he be comfortable in this house as a gay guy?" one asked. Another said, "Would he get offended at comments about homosexuality?" "Will he be treated differently during pledging because he's gay? " asked another.

I did not know all this at the time, but I guess the brothers talked long into the night about me and about homosexuality. The fact the conversation took so long shows their genuine brotherhood and their strong fraternal values.

A few days after the interview, I received a call from the president asking to meet personally. "Hello, Adrian? I just need to talk to you real quick—are you in your dorm? Can I come over for a minute?" I told him it was cool and hung up.

Man, was I nervous. *Why does he want to meet with me?* I thought.

Why doesn't he want to meet with my roommate? Are they going to beat me up for trying to join their fraternity? What have I got myself into? Finally he arrived, his face expressionless. "The reason I wanted to meet with you was because I wanted to talk to you." He looked concerned. "You act more mature than most of the guys in the fraternity. And to think you're only 17." I remained silent and nodded. He went on to say that the brothers discussed my sexuality at the meeting. He took a deep breath and said, "The brothers don't care if you are gay or not. You're a cool person. That's what we liked. Being gay is only one part of you. You don't flaunt it like most of them would." He paused and smiled. "You and your roommate are both receiving a bid. Please don't tell him, because campus policy states that you guys can't know until bid night."

Wow, I did it, I thought. They had accepted me for me. But there was more.

The president continued, "It's your decision, though. It's going to be really hard in the Greek system because it's heterosexually oriented. Other brothers may make gay jokes and comments, but know that each one of them wants you as a brother. We are going to back you up no matter what."

I thanked him for his consideration, and he left me to think about my decision. Honesty had paid off, and I wanted to see this as an opportunity rather than an obstacle. *Should I do it?* I wondered, and then the question began changing: *Why shouldn't I?* My decision came quickly. TKE fraternity accepted me unconditionally and had moved a step forward to embrace diversity. I was honored to accept the bid.

Now I'm in a fraternity. My reasons for joining are clear: the brotherhood, the challenge, and, of course, the good times. Many of the brothers who did not support my bid earlier have changed their minds, once they got to know me as more than the gay guy.

Joining TKE is one of the best decisions I have ever made. I know that my fraternity brothers are always there for me. I have formed a bond that I will treasure for as long as I live. And it never would have happened if I had not found the courage to be honest and open.

Odd Man In

by Mark Bigelow, Northwest Missouri State University, Maryville

Growing up in rural Missouri, I was the tall lanky kid who always stuck out. With a crooked smile and shy at times, I preferred to be low-key. I was happy with what I had, but always knew there was more out there. That is why I went as far away as possible in Missouri for college.

I entered Northwest Missouri State University in the fall of 1995. Like most freshmen I lived on campus. Northwest was a smaller school, with an enrollment of 6,000, tucked in the far northwest corner of the state. As a university Northwest was constantly walking a tightrope between traditional Christian values and modern progressive thinking, usually favoring the former.

I remember in our first floor meeting. As softly as I could, I said, "I am Mark Bigelow. I'm from Laddonia, Mo." As I said my name, that one guy—the one who can walk into a room and own everything, the one with the perfect eyes, hair, teeth, muscles, and bone structure—leaned in to the group around him and whispered, loud enough for me to hear, "He's got to be a fag." I was not surprised. I had dealt with that sort of thinking all my life. I just rolled my eyes and went on.

My first exposure to fraternities was a bit overwhelming and definitely not a welcome experience. During the first few days of my freshman year at college, It was impossible to avoid anything Greek. There were the Delta Chis, "the pretty rich boys"; the Phi Sigs, "the jocks"; and the Kappa Sigs, "the smart guys." I could not pass through a crowd without getting information about everything you ever wanted to know about Greek life. The whole experience reinforced many of the stereotypes I had of fraternities. I felt like these Abercrombie-wannabe frat boys were car salesmen, each equipped with high-pressure sales tactics, offering to be your best friend because their fraternity had what you needed.

First a pretty preppy fraternity boy with an incredible smile approached me and said, "You want all the hot girls you can get?" I thought to myself slyly, *Yeah, if you're going to be there.*

Second was the "defying mainstream America" fraternity guy—the one who has no labels on his clothing, uses no products, and tries so hard not to fit in that he actually does. He asked, "You want to meet some really down-to-earth guys?" I thought, *Yeah, more posers like you, sure.*

Then came the "deer in the headlights" fraternity guy, spreading unyielding enthusiasm my way. Rather dorky and chubby, he was having his first time being in charge of anything. To impress his brothers and desperate to get any interest, he rushed up and said loudly, "You want free pizza?" I thought he would need a Valium later just to calm down.

Finally was the fraternity guy who was so good-looking, cultured, and well-liked that you were almost jealous of him. He was exactly all you ever wanted to be and had the charisma and charm to make it all seem real. As sincerely as possible, he offered, "Do you want what you've never had?" He was dead-on with what he had to offer: What I had never had was a sense of belonging. I had never felt like one of the guys. The fraternity could offer me the one thing I always longed for—brotherhood, camaraderie, and acceptance among men.

It was a definite temptation. In the end, the only question unanswered remained, *Could I be openly gay in a fraternity?* Still, I was not buying into fraternity life, not even from him.

My world was different in 1995. I had never seen a positive gay role model on campus or in my life. I presumed being openly gay would mean discrimination, if not a death sentence. That perception made it more difficult to admit my sexuality to myself or to others. I had not told anyone, but I knew I would in time. I also assumed that a fraternity would definitely not be a welcoming place.

My first three years of college were spent entirely focused on residential life activities on campus. I quickly found acceptance there and the openness to be myself. I became involved in my residence hall, and the next year I got a job as a resident assistant. My responsibility was to establish a community conducive to a variety of lifestyles and interests for a floor of 50 men. My job was perfect and allowed me ample opportunities to meet new people and grow as an individual. I always looked for other ways to get involved on campus too, such as designing advertisements for the school newspaper and serving on various campus committees. I was content with my contribution to the university. I was also becoming more comfortable in my own skin with my sexuality: I was able to integrate all aspects of who I am, including being gay.

In the summer of 1998, I decided to live in a house off-campus with my best friend, Karen. She belonged to a sorority and was a short firecracker of a woman. She could get anything she wanted by flashing her baby blue eyes. She was strong in her convictions and never one to mince words; I loved that she was never afraid to tell you exactly what she thought. She talked constantly about the positive influences of the Greek system, and she had many friends who were in sororities and fraternities. Due to my insecurities, I had never explored Greek life outside the barrage of encounters during rush week as a freshman.

Thanks to Karen, I had the opportunity that year to meet a few of the men of Tau Kappa Epsilon. She had an impeccable talent for being one of the guys: One night I was cooking dinner at our house for her and me, and her guest list kept expanding. First the list included Karen's blond-haired, blue-eyed sorority sisters. Then it grew to include all the fraternity guys who would follow her sisters around hoping for a date. I ended up cooking for about 20 people. The first TKE I met that night was Grant. He was always ready to lend a hand. He was not the most attractive guy in the crowd, with crooked teeth, a little acne, and a bit of a gut. But he never tried to be anything else; he capitalized on his imperfections, integrating them into his personality.

After dinner he helped me collect the dishes and asked, "Hey, Mark, why aren't you in a fraternity?"

I looked up. "I don't know, just never felt like it would be a good fit for me."

He moved closer and rather offhandedly said, "Well, you would be a good fit for us."

Puzzled, I stopped what I was doing and asked, "How do you figure?"

He grabbed a cloth to help me dry the dishes and explained, "Teke is an accepting organization. Tonight, without thinking about what you could get out of it, you welcomed us into your house. That's what we're all about."

Cautiously, I kept Grant talking about his fraternity. I was excited about the prospect of joining, but I knew Grant probably had not figured out that I was gay. I agreed that I would think about TKE some more. The ultimate question was how the fraternity brothers would react to finding out I was gay. I had become comfortable with being gay, but it wasn't the first thing I told people about myself. Karen knew, and so did other people on campus. I told people when I felt comfortable with them, and I usually got the classic response: "Well, I assumed you were."

I still had a week to make a decision about joining TKE. The more I thought about rushing, the more excited I became about the idea of brotherhood. I started attending rush functions, even though at first I had to force myself to leave the house. Soon the camaraderie I felt among the brothers assuaged my fear about being accepted.

TKE did not have a fraternity house on campus due to a horrible fire two years earlier. Faced with adversity, the brothers did not give up but rather banded together. The brotherhood was not defined by a physical house like most fraternities. Instead, the individual men defined TKE and who they were as a fraternity. After several TKE rush events, a brother named Ken, a wild skater boy, came up to me, "Hey, man, it's about time you decided to join."

"Yes, it is a long time coming," I said. "I don't know what I was so afraid of."

He leaned in and said, "I know what you were afraid of, and it's okay. You have a lot of supporters, including me. Don't worry."

Much like when I was growing up in rural Missouri, I stuck out like a sore thumb, trying hard to fit in but always failing. I wanted to believe Ken and did not pursue the topic further. I feared that hiding "my little secret" was hopeless.

I was out one night later that week and ran into Derek, a friend who had graduated two years earlier. I had forgotten that he was also a TKE alum. He had been my resident assistant when I was a freshman. I knew he was always willing to stick up for what was right, accepting people for who they are. When I had come out years earlier, Derek was one of the first people I had told, and he was completely supportive. I pulled him aside during our game of pool and asked, "So have you heard?"

"I've decided to join TKE," I said enthusiastically.

He hugged me excitedly. "It's about time!"

"Well, don't get too excited. I think there might be some people that will try to block my membership. I'm sure guys either know or assume that I'm gay. They might not want to be known as the gay fraternity," I said.

Derek looked me square in the eye and replied, "I know how you feel, but take a chance and trust that you'll get in." It was a simple concept: I had to trust that Grant, Ken, and Derek—three brothers from different walks of life—along with the other brothers of TKE would look beyond my sexuality and make the appropriate decision. They were right: A few days later I enthusiastically signed my bid to join TKE.

The first night as a pledge, I remember pure terror. The brothers greeted me warmly, but I imagined whispered remarks: "Oh, I think he might be gay," or "Something's different about him." I did not want to hide my sexuality from the brothers, but I also wanted to succeed so much that I didn't want to admit it either. I did my best to play the part of a good brother and fraternity man. There was a group of brothers I never quite meshed with. They were the übermasculine, beer-guzzling, weight-lifting guys whose sole purpose in college was to have a good time. We would mostly fake getting along. I would laugh at gay jokes, bring girls to our parties, and not question traditional gender roles. Such a facade made me feel as though I would never belong.

As homecoming approached in mid October, I was spending more time with my fraternity pledge brothers. I really enjoyed the relationships and felt close to most of them. Nevertheless, one brother, Brandon, made my skin crawl. Rather average and physically dumpy, he had a shaved head, intense dark brown eyes, and no respect for anything or anyone around him. He enjoyed taunting me. The worst was when all the pledges were working on our homecoming float at an agricultural supply store on the edge of town. We were all making small talk, asking about our classes and the previous weekend. Brandon was being obnoxious and said he had a great joke to tell us. I don't remember the gist of it except for the punch line: He loudly said, "faggot," and the joke ended.

None of us were quite sure if he had actually told a joke or just put some words together and called it a joke. I looked at him, smirking in disgust. It was not one of my better moments.

Brandon was disappointed with our response and looking directly at me, saying, "What, you don't find that funny, Mark?"

I said sarcastically, "Um, yeah, I get it. Ha ha ha!"

I turned to walk away and overheard him mutter, "Why do they let fags in here?"

Brandon continued telling the joke all day. Some guys in the fraternity laughed while others did not. I tried to not let it bother me—that was exactly what he wanted. At the end of the day, Tommy, our pledge class leader, approached me and asked, "Is everything all right?"

I looked at him and said, "As far as I know. Why?

"Well, some concerns have been raised today," he replied. "I think we all need to sit down and have a discussion tonight." My stomach started to knot. I knew this could not be good.

The dreaded meeting took place in a Conoco parking lot. I was to be the topic of conversation, and I was the last to arrive. Walking up, I felt like a "dead man walking." I could not help but remember the recent news that had hit the front page of all the papers: the hate-crime murder of a young gay University of Wyoming student named Matthew Shepard. I imagined the absolute worst and lost all trust I had in the brothers. I was shaking and sweating as I waited for the meeting to start.

Tommy, always very direct, said, "So, Brandon, I hear you're spreading around that Mark is gay."

Immediately all eyes were on my sweaty face. I was scared to death. Brandon snapped arrogantly, "I have a right to speak my mind and say what I know to be true. Earlier today he didn't laugh at my gay joke. He has that prissy walk and talk. I know he's gay."

At this point I realized that somehow I had entered the center of the circle. The laughter, yelling, and footsteps all around me oddly became intensified. I felt trapped, and my first thought was to look for an opening in the circle to escape. Scanning the circle, car headlights occasionally illuminating the scene, I saw looks of surprise and disappointment on my pledge brothers' faces. I found my opening, right where I had been standing. The missing link in the circle was poignant: As pledge brothers, the goal was to unite—no beginning, no end, like a circle. The truth had now broken the circle. Brandon went on, "We got a faggot in this group, and you all better be on guard."

I stood motionless, keeping my dignity. I was not going to let him tear me down. Then the question I feared rang loudly. Brandon, asked, "So, Mark, are you gay?"

I held my stance as time stood still. I knew what I needed to say, but I felt all alone among my brothers. I closed my eyes, fully intending to say defiantly, "Yes, I am!" Instead, I insisted, "No, I am not gay." In the same moment Tommy said loudly, "Who cares anyway if you are or not. We love you."

I was stunned to hear the words, "We love you." Brandon was no longer a threat. He was powerless. The brothers immediately gathered around in a show of support. I was wrong to let my fear destroy my trust in my brothers. The fraternity had kept me in the circle of brotherhood. I was amazed at the outpouring of acceptance, but inside I truly hated myself. My cowardice ruled out the option of telling the brothers the truth. I felt ashamed thinking I had had to lie to survive.

I went home physically, mentally, and emotionally exhausted. Throughout the evening my pledge brothers came by to offer support and check in on me. I assured them I was unscathed and wanted to forget the whole situation. My sexuality was never questioned again.

A few weeks later I was initiated into TKE. That last semester I was able to participate as a full-fledged member. I would attend fraternity meetings, serve on committees, and help promote a positive image of TKE. I felt accomplished and proud to be a brother even though my lie remained.

The end of my senior year arrived. I could not believe my time in the fraternity was over. We had a senior send-off party, and one of the older brothers, James, a very plain and whiter-than-white conservative dualistic thinker, found me and pulled me aside. We had never really been close as brothers, and his tone was uncharacteristically somber.

"Mark, I just want to apologize. I was one of the people that didn't want you to join TKE. I assumed things about you and worried that it would hurt the fraternity," he said. "Whoever and whatever you are, you're my brother. That is what brotherhood is all about. You are a stand-up guy, and I see that now."

We had a few laughs, and for the first time I really felt as though I was not the odd man in the fraternity. It showed me that I did fit into TKE, and I was one of the individuals who contributed to the identity of the fraternity. The only regret I had as I left was that I did not trust in the brotherhood enough to tell them that I was indeed gay. I simply was not ready.

One year later at homecoming, on a visit back to campus as an alumnus, I finally came clean and told the brothers that I was gay. I had needed time to live openly and honestly with who I am before I could tell my fraternity. As I should have known, the brothers did not really care. Most of them responded, "It's about time" or "I am glad you finally felt comfortable enough to share that." They understood how difficult a process it had been for me to come out. None of them faulted me for lying.

TKE fraternity offered me the one thing I always longed for—brotherhood, camaraderie, and acceptance among men. They loved me unconditionally. This support led me to want to give something back to TKE as an alumnus, and as a graduate student at Oklahoma State University I found the perfect opportunity. Through an advertisement for people interested in forming a chapter of TKE at OSU, I contacted Tom, who had transferred from another university where he was a TKE. Since OSU did not have a chapter, he volunteered to form one. He was excited that I had called and said, "A representative from nationals will be here next week. You should come over and we can all talk."

When I got to his house I was greeted very warmly by Tom. Jeff, the representative from TKE national fraternity, had just arrived too. The three of us sat down to contemplate a strategy. Jeff, a tall, well-built man, was a dominant figure in the way he spoke and the way he carried himself. Not letting Tom get a word in, the conversation was mostly between Jeff and me. At one point Jeff asked, "So, Mark, do you have a girlfriend?"

I was a bit taken aback but replied, "No, I'm gay. But I am not dating anyone."

I'm not sure I would call it an awkward silence that followed, but I could tell something was not right. He carried on and said, "Well, that's good. I'm glad you feel comfortable being yourself."

When we parted ways for the evening we exchanged numbers and Jeff said, "I will be in touch in a week or two."

After not hearing from Jeff for a week, I called him. "Hey, I was just wondering where we were and if everything is okay," I said.

Apologetically he said, "Sorry, I have gotten really busy. I'll give you a call soon." After two more weeks of waiting I called back. Jeff said very matter-of-factly, "Thanks anyway, but I don't think I'll need your help, and I think you know why."

Jeff's response on behalf of the TKE national fraternity didn't mirror the acceptance in my own TKE fraternity chapter. My attempt to give something back to TKE was a disappointment.

I almost hadn't joined TKE because I assumed that being gay outweighed my value as a contributing brother. I was wrong many times in this regard, and I learned the valuable lesson of trusting oneself and trusting others. I would never be the odd man out because I finally found acceptance, a sense of belonging, and brotherhood.

The Row

by John Skandros, University of Southern California, Los Angeles

Dear Johnny,

You are 22 years old now and approaching the end of your college career. I remember the past and I think of you, so lost, so unhappy. Tears run down my cheeks as I reminisce of your sadness. The immutable longing for self-identity will soon cease. You will attend a wonderful university where you will be accepted into the School of Cinema-Television. You will meet life-changing professors and colleagues who will guide you, challenge you, and identify with you. You will join a fraternity where you will forbid yourself from adopting an assimilationist strategy to please others, with intentions of helping destroy negative perceptions of homosexuality around you. You will develop your creativity to fuel your desire to study and create progressive media for future generations...

I wrote this to myself as an assignment for the first gay and lesbian class ever offered at the University of Southern California School of

Cinema-Television. What shocked the students in the class the most when I read it aloud was that I was in a fraternity, a brother of Delta Chi national fraternity, to be precise. Many of the students believed the prevailing stereotypes that the Greek system on campus was merely a homophobic heterosexual haven. Nobody thought a fraternity would allow for someone who was gay to be open and accepted as part of the brotherhood. Such is the perception on most college campuses.

My fraternity had a unique bond. My being gay presented opportunities for us to better understand one another. Many times the brothers would poke fun at me for being gay; I would simply return the favor: "So, are you hetero-flexible?" I asked. Usually I would get blank stares, smiles, and odd looks, like "What are you talking about?" I never imagined a brotherhood so strong that we could use humor and understanding to support one another. Responses to that question often led to more laughter, a sense of comfort, opportunities to build bridges, and ultimately acceptance of being gay.

I came to USC in the spring of 2001. Raised in the suburbs of Las Vegas, I did not know a single soul in Los Angeles or on campus. During my freshman year I was housed in the Radisson Hotel, right across from the campus, due to a shortage of residence hall facilities. My family was raised on an elementary school teacher's salary, so I did not come from wealth like many of my fellow students. The thought of the luxurious accommodations on the seventh floor of the Radisson had me anxious with excitement for my first year at the university.

Together on the seventh floor there was an eclectic mix of students from diverse backgrounds and ethnicities. I even spotted another gay guy living on the floor. I had been out since the age of 16 but decided that I needed to "cover up" any seemingly gay characteristics. Being labeled first as homosexual on campus was not what I wanted. Instead, I hoped people would get to know me for more than the gay label.

During the first residence floor meeting, a delightful Asian girl from our seventh-floor community came up to me and said, "You're gay, right?" My new leopard bedspread must have given me away, and I knew that my plan to cover up my more effeminate characteristics would not fly in California, especially around women, whose fine tuned gaydar seemed very advanced. So I responded proudly, " Yes, I am gay." I could not deny who I was.

The next question from the floor meeting that evening was, "Are you going to 'the row'?" The row was where all the fraternity houses were, 28th Street, lined with stately old mansions one after another with racks full of Cali Cruiser bicycles. I had contemplated venturing to the row because of a fraternity guy named Chad, a closeted gay fraternity brother of Delta Chi. We had met online prior to my coming to campus. He had told me about Bryce, who was openly gay in the fraternity. An openly gay guy in a fraternity defied many of the stereotypes I had—most important, that frats were adamantly homophobic. Plus, I was not attracted to booze and hooking up with girls on a regular basis. I figured the row did not serve any useful purpose for me. Still, I figured I would challenge my preconceived notions, trust Chad, and spend the evening on the row with my new seventh-floor friends.

The row was a different world. Going up and down glamorous 28th Street was amazing—rush week was well under way, with the glitz of fraternity insignias all over. The doors to the houses were wide open, and loud music blared. There was endless entertainment and the obligatory heterosexual key to any successful fraternity party: sorority women. Each house spent thousands of dollars, and one fraternity in particular was rumored to have a $22,000 rush budget. They rented out nightclubs and sushi restaurants, and they even hired bands to play at their exclusive rush parties. Sigma Nu hired Vanilla Ice to perform at its party. I felt as if I had never left the Las Vegas strip, with all the women, excitement, and entertainment.

My friends and I scurried around to each fraternity house, meeting fraternity guy after fraternity guy. Never in my entire life had I seen so many gorgeous guys. The men were physically built as solidly as the fraternity mansions they lived in, each guy with perfect California sunbleached hair, a glowing golden tan, and sculpted muscular body. To top it off, they greeted me with open arms. I never felt so welcome in my entire life.

Going through rush was an easy decision after my first night on the row. There were 12 fraternities on campus, and I rushed half of them. My sexuality was not remotely an issue—at many of the parties and events I would find delightful females at my side, enticing me to become part of the row subculture. I would back away to let other men gladly take my place among the breasts. Delta Chi men were different, however. The brothers spent most of their energy trying to get to know me. Their purpose was not to entice me with scantily clad women or spend $500 for me to have a private hour-long lap dance at a local strip joint. They were interested in getting to know who I was. I admired that quality as well as the fact that they were more diverse. There were several Hispanic men, Asian men, and even the token openly gay guy, Bryce. With no hesitation I chose Delta Chi, and they chose me on bid night a week later. Overwhelming and thrilling, my college life had begun, and to my shock I was going to be a fraternity man.

Now came the big question. Being gay had not come up during rush, and I managed not to lie to anyone. Still, I knew I should probably tell the brothers. I knew that the fraternity was cool with Bryce's being gay, but I wanted to be known first as myself. I asked myself, *Do I tell them? When? How?*

Once again, I decided to try to cover up my sexuality. I was not ashamed or embarrassed, but I was concerned that I might be rejected by the brotherhood. During the first semester I made a constant effort to avoid any discussion of sexuality with the brothers. I placed an old high school dance picture with my female date prominently on my dresser. I claimed that I had a girlfriend back home. The assimilation strategy didn't fool everyone. Just like the Asian girl on the seventh floor, my pledge brother Stephen had astounding gaydar and pegged me as gay from day one. I didn't know why, but he had shown a keen interest in me. He was also closeted, and he saw through me. He had skin like porcelain, short glossy brown hair, and a healthy build with a stoic posture.

One night Stephen offered to pick me up from my room for an outing in Los Angeles. He drove up in his Saturn that he had affectionately named "Sammy." We drove around L.A. and he pointed out the details of the city. His major was urban planning, so his knowledge gave me a greater appreciation of my new home. I loved looking at the skyscrapers downtown. Compared to the artificial landscape of Las Vegas, the magnitude of the L.A. skyline amazed me. The entire time Stephen projected a playful "you're not fooling anyone" attitude, and we enjoyed each other's company.

Before the evening ended, we stopped at a desolate park to feed on some Chex Mix. Stephen turned toward me with a smile. "Johnny, I know your secret," he said.

I looked at him, not surprised, and said, "Oh, Stephen, I know your secret too." He flashed a smile, and we chuckled like two schoolgirls getting ready for prom. That night was the beginning of a lifelong friendship.

We found strength in our friendship to come out to the fraternity. I took that semester to become more relaxed with all 80 of the brothers. It was difficult to get to know all of them well, but I tried my best. My plan was to come out to the fraternity after pledge semester.

Hanging out in Stephen's room one day at the fraternity house, we ran into Matt, his roommate. He was in our pledge class, but I never had the opportunity to get to know him. Stephen told me that he had recently come out to Matt and that he had been wonderfully supportive.

Matt was comfortable with his own sexuality and openly considered himself to be metrosexual. Everything in his room was tidy and organized, from the pencils on his desk to his pajamas folded neatly under his pillow every evening. The picture frames were perfectly aligned on his walls. He fit the model of metrosexual with his impeccable styling, long shiny brown hair, and muscular body. His wardrobe was like walking into an Abercrombie & Fitch clothing store. I had had him pegged as gay due to his ability to accessorize and look so damn good. Unfortunately, I was wrong; my gaydar was off from feeding on too many stereotypes.

Still, I thought that Matt would be an easy one for me to come out to, and I was determined to tell someone. Stephen had left the room, and Matt and I were sitting there alone.

"So, Matt, I want you to know that I'm gay," I said, boldly shooting him a glance.

"I know," he said without a pause. He smiled, showing his bright white teeth, and shook his head. I was a little shocked as I hadn't expected that reaction.

"Johnny, I knew you were gay the first day you rushed," he said, putting his arm out to me. "Duh. You were wearing capri pants." We both started laughing. Matt went on telling me how much he values all brothers, gay or straight. He had a lot of respect for those brothers who came out in a fraternity. He could tell Stephen and I were much happier being who we really were. Matt was not only a straight metrosexual, he was also an ally.

Of course, when you tell one fraternity brother, news spreads like wildfire. All the other brothers seemed to know within a day. I did not experience any homophobia from any of the brothers. Several approached me to ask a variety of questions. Some of these candid inquiries frankly blew me away: "Johnny, you're gay, and that's cool. So can you help me get girls now?" Another brother asked, "So, Johnny, what's it like to be gay? Do you check out guys the way we check out girls on the row?" The most frequent question was, "Hey, Johnny, I'm going on a date with this hot girl, and I need your advice on what to do on the date."

The brothers were extremely inquisitive and interested in the whole gay thing. On top of that, they trusted my opinion when it came to getting girls. Because gay men traditionally have stellar relationships with women, the brothers assumed that I knew some ancient gay secret for attracting women. There was much humor and learning through the process. All the brothers spent time getting to know me as Johnny, not as "the gay one" or "the gay pledge." Nothing had changed in their perception of my ability to be a good brother.

After I came out, the reaction was like a domino effect. Chad, who had first introduced me to Delta Chi, had had much more difficulty finding self-acceptance and support. For six months I had counseled him about being gay, telling him that he was completely normal and okay. Finally he came out to the fraternity.

I also wanted to leave my fraternity mark in other ways, so I took on the leadership role of rush chair. It made perfect sense. Being in charge of recruitment required me to do what any gay man would enjoy: meet other men. Gay guys are sensitive, smart, and analytical when it comes to meeting new men. Being a fraternity leader made me feel important and gave me the chance to earn respect among the brothers. I must have been doing something right because after three semesters of being in charge of rush, I received the Best Chair of the Year Award. The honor made me feel accepted and proved that I could be an excellent brother who happened to be gay. I decided to write a letter to the university about my experience at Delta Chi. I explained in the letter that I was gay and proud to be in a fraternity. Part of the letter read:

My experience as a brother of Delta Chi is the primary reason that I am advocating for the fraternity to be considered for the highest honor, the President's Award. Since I joined the fraternity, there was never an issue concerning my sexuality. Moreover, I have never experienced any bigotry, hatred, or discrimination because of my sexuality. Since fraternities are stereotyped as predominantly heterosexually scripted and homophobic, I feel that Delta Chi fraternity has functioned in erasing these stereotypes, accepting people for their merits and hard work, without race or sexuality as a factor.

THIS SEMESTER WE HAD A RUSHEE WHO SAID THAT HE WAS GAY WHILE RUSHING. THE MEMBERS OF DELTA CHI DID NOT CARE ABOUT THAT WHEN DECIDING WHETHER OR NOT TO GIVE HIM A BID FOR THE FRATERNITY; AS I EXPECTED, DELTA CHI OFFERED HIM A BID, WHICH HE ACCEPTED.

That year, our fraternity was awarded the highest honor of the year, the President's Award, to recognize outstanding contributions to the campus community. We were also given the coveted Diversity Award and the New Membership Recruitment Award. My hard work had paid off. I was more than a token gay brother; I was a respected leader in the fraternity.

Stephen suspected that one of the brothers, Billy, who was among the roommates living with him, was gay. His acute gaydar was right, of course. Billy came out to both of us one evening. Hearing Billy say "I'm gay" reminded me of my first time and the relief I felt being open and honest with those around me. Six months later he came out to the entire fraternity house. The news was not a big deal. Coming out had become a common thing in the fraternity and in the entire Greek system. There were many other men who were openly gay in several fraternities on campus. Of course, there were always some fraternities where it would not be safe for a brother to come out. But the Delta Chi brothers did not care. The idea of a gay brother was not a big deal anymore.

Change happens slowly. Casual, careless comments were often thrown around the house, like "That's gay" or "What a homo." It didn't bother me, as it was just part of unconscious speech patterns. Sometimes I would confront them with a sarcastic, witty comment to challenge them. In any case, such comments were not threats but were reminders of work remaining.

One night at a local gay bar called Tiger Heat I met a closeted Greek from another fraternity. We began talking about fraternity life, and he was in total disbelief about how comfortable my fraternity was having many gay brothers. He went on to share how he was always on guard with his sexuality and clammed up around his brothers. He hunched his shoulders together for emphasis, looking miserable. More concerned about their image on campus, his brothers would often steer clear of any possibly effeminate men, worrying that they might be gay. He determined that he could never come out and be accepted by his brothers for such reasons. I felt even more fortunate that Delta Chi understood the meaning of brotherhood and that the definition extended beyond a brother's sexuality.

Fraternities can be wonderful opportunities to show that gay men and straight men can be not only friends but also brothers. I believe that the percentage of gay and bisexual men in fraternities is much higher than the Kinsey 10% theory. Homosexuality in the fraternity setting can be readily hidden, ignored, and suppressed by using heterosexist behavior as a mask. From my experience, these are closeted men who are masculine jock types who lack role models. I met many of these men hiding in the gay bars of Los Angeles.

Every semester I watched as new pledges would learn that I was gay. Many would be concerned about how they should act and what it meant to the fraternity. The strength of the brotherhood would overcome any homophobia. These same brothers would later run up to me between classes and give me a hug and treat me with utmost respect and acceptance. Delta Chi fraternity had become a family, a true brotherhood. That is the power of brotherhood and the power of living your life openly and honestly on the row.

Conclusion:

A Challenge to Fraternities to Fulfill Their Mission
by Douglas N. Case

BROTHERHOOD IS, SIMPLY STATED, A COMBINATION OF REAL FRIENDSHIP AND LOYALTY HAVING A SOLID FOUNDATION. IT IS NURTURED BY COOPERATION AND UNDERSTANDING.

Three decades ago when I was a Kappa Sigma pledge at San Jose State University in California, I memorized the above definition from the glossary of my pledge manual. Although most of the other passages I was expected to recite on command have long since faded from my memory, the definition of brotherhood remains. For me, the definition explains what a fraternity is—or should be—all about. It is because of my belief and commitment to that ideal that I have devoted my entire professional career to the enhancement of fraternities and sororities.

I had the privilege of writing the introduction to *Out on Fraternity Row*, and I am honored to provide the conclusion to *Brotherhood*. "Conclusion" connotes an ending, but I hope readers will view this chapter instead as a call to action as there is much work still to be done. As I read the stories submitted for this anthology, I found myself wiping away tears several times. Some of the tears were shed because the stories were heartwarming, but others because of the pain a student endured. I was constantly reminded that although progress has been made toward a more inclusive fraternity environment, there is still quite a distance to go before the institution known as "fraternity" fulfills its true promise of brotherhood. For many gay and bisexual students and alumni, that promise remains elusive.

One of the signs of slow progress arrived in my office mailbox almost a year ago. As the coordinator of fraternity and sorority life at San Diego State University, I receive copies of the national periodicals of several fraternities and sororities. Many of the magazines contain little that would be of interest to nonmembers, but some have informative feature articles on contemporary issues related to fraternity and sorority life. The winter 2003-2004 issue of *The Magazine of Sigma Chi* was truly groundbreaking. It was touted as "The Diversity Issue" and contained a variety of articles exploring different facets of diversity within the fraternity. For example, there was a fascinating account of the internal struggle in the 1960s to eliminate the "white clause" from the fraternity's constitution. Sigma Chi did not initiate its first black member until 1970. There was also an article from a Jewish member telling why he wears a ring with the fraternity's symbol, a white cross, and a story featuring the fraternity's culturally diverse chapter at the University of California, San Diego.

The bold words COMING OUT on the cover, however, are what truly grabbed my attention. Inside the issue were two full-page essays by two now-openly gay fraternity members. What made this remarkable was that, to my knowledge, no other national fraternity or sorority magazine had ever mentioned sexual orientation issues in such a prominent way. In fact, a few years ago, the magazine editor of another national fraternity wrote an article on gay men and fraternities that received a literary award from the National Interfraternity Foundation, but the fraternity declined to publish the article in its own magazine.

As I read the essays in the Sigma Chi magazine, I recall thinking how reassuring the article must have been to both out and closeted Sigma Chi members of all ages—and how I wished that such stories would have appeared in my own fraternity's magazine back when I was a deeply closeted undergraduate. In those days it would have been considered heresy for any fraternity to publish such an article in its magazine. As I read the magazine I thought, *Wow, we've come a long way.*

Then I received the spring 2004 issue of *The Magazine of Sigma Chi,* and it proved to be a reality check. The fraternity received an unprecedented number of letters to the editor regarding the diversity edition. Many, including some of my fellow campus fraternity and sorority advisors, wrote to applaud the fraternity. On the other hand, several were quite disturbing. One writer threatened to withhold future financial support, one requested that his magazine subscription be canceled, and another indicated that he was surrendering his membership. A fraternity alumni chapter president in Texas reported that undergraduates were burning the magazine. I quickly realized that although we may have come far, there is still a long way to go.

Cultural change within fraternities and sororities tends to lag behind the rest of society. For example, it was not until fall 2003 that the first black student pledged a traditional sorority at the University of Alabama, an institution that has been racially integrated since 1963. Fraternities and sororities are becoming more culturally diverse, but the organizations typically do not reflect the demographics of their host institutions. Given this inherent resistance to change, it is not surprising that the acceptance of openly gay men in fraternities is progressing at a much slower pace than what we would ideally hope. Nonetheless, progress is being made, and gay and bisexual fraternity men from my generation and before marvel at how things have changed. I attribute the progress that has been made to the recent visibility of sexual orientation issues as they pertain to social fraternities and sororities and to societal changes in the past decade that have resulted in greater acceptance and understanding of gay, lesbian, bisexual, and transgender people.

I take a pride in contributing to the visibility of GLBT issues within the fraternity and sorority system. In 1990, as president-elect of the Association of Fraternity Advisors, a national professional association for campus officials who work with fraternities and sororities, I shepherded a resolution through the annual business meeting that called on AFA members "to implement sexual orientation awareness, education, and sensitivity programs for the Greek community." The resolution was somewhat controversial and created a stir, but it got little attention when it was reaffirmed at the business meeting in 1999 because by then association members took for granted that GLBT issues needed to be addressed.

My informal research of gay, lesbian, and bisexual members of fraternities and sororities, summarized in an article titled "A Glimpse of the Invisible Membership" that appeared in the April-May 1996 issue of *AFA Perspectives,* also helped to enlighten the fraternity and sorority world. A far greater audience was reached by the publication in 1998 of *Out on Fraternity Row,* which was displayed prominently in bookstores nationwide, with thousands of copies sold. The book educated thousands and inspired countless men to realize that it is indeed possible to be an openly gay or bisexual fraternity member.

In addition, the Lambda 10 Project, established in 1995, has been at the forefront of promoting a greater understanding of GLBT issues within the fraternity and sorority community. Under the leadership of Shane Windmeyer, the Lambda 10 Project maintains a comprehensive Web site with valuable resources (including an impressive "Who's Out" list of fraternity and sorority members), publishes training manuals and other materials, conducts training sessions for professionals who work with fraternities and sororities, presents innovative educational programs for campuses and fraternal organizations, and moderates an e-mail discussion list.

These initiatives have sparked newspaper and magazine articles that have highlighted the experiences of openly gay, lesbian, or bisexual fraternity and sorority members. Feature articles have appeared in *The New York Times, Rolling Stone, The Advocate, Out,* and numerous college and university student newspapers and local GLBT publications.

Equally significant are the changes that are occurring in general society. The climate for GLBT students is changing on college and university campuses because students are entering our institutions with a greater awareness and acceptance of homosexuality.

Students are coming out at much earlier ages. When I was in high school there were no openly gay students. It was simply unthinkable for young people of that era to reveal their homosexual inclinations to their peers. Many, perhaps most, gay high school students in my generation attempted to deny their sexual identity, even to themselves. Most young gay men in today's world begin the coming-out process before they graduate from high school,[1] and most high school students know at least one gay or lesbian classmate.[2] There are thousands of gay-straight alliance student organizations on high school campuses throughout the nation, and the number is growing rapidly.[3] Consequently students enter college today with much greater awareness regarding sexual orientation issues. Many gay students are already "out" when they arrive on campus, and most nongay students know someone who is gay.

Societal attitudes on homosexuality are changing, especially among young people. One example is the opinion regarding the issue of gays and lesbians serving in the military. A December 2003 Gallup Poll found that 90% of voters between the ages 18 and 29 supported allowing gays and lesbians to serve openly in the military (an institution similar in many ways to fraternities).[4] Even more revealing is a 2004 survey that found that almost half of junior enlisted service members believed that gays and lesbians should be able to serve openly in the military. Similar studies taken back in 1992 when President Clinton first proposed the idea found that less than one in six male enlisted soldiers supported that position.[5]

Another strong indication of generational differences with regard to GLBT issues is the support among young people for the most controversial gay issue today—same-sex marriage. A recent national poll found that almost half of Americans between the ages 18 and 29 supported same-sex marriage, compared to less than 20% of those older than 65.[6] The youth of today believe that gays and lesbians should be afforded the same opportunities as everyone else.

In addition to the increased visibility of GLBT issues on high school campuses, there is a much greater GLBT presence in the media, including openly gay cast members in popular television shows such as *The Real World*. It is not surprising that gay freshmen are coming to campus more out than ever and that more fraternity men are more open to the possibility of having a gay brother.

Despite the greater awareness, however, homophobia is still significantly more prevalent among college men than college women.[7] It is therefore not surprising that resistance to having gay fraternity brothers remains a powerful obstacle.[8]

The stories in this anthology reflect these trends. Although a more accepting environment for gay and bisexual fraternity members exists today, things are far from ideal. The stories with the happier conclusions tend to involve students who have realistic expectations, are willing to take some risks, and are willing to educate others.

I was particularly impressed by the stories of Travis Shumake and Chris Ho, both of whom were finally admitted to fraternities on their third attempts to join.

Travis was denied a bid from Sigma Chi, where he was a legacy, for being gay and was blackballed from Phi Delta Theta because his presence as an openly gay pledge was "breaking down the brotherhood," but he chose to persevere despite "deep battle wounds." He developed friendships with younger Sigma Chi members, who asked him to join, and he eventually became an executive officer. Several of his fraternity brothers at Northern Arizona University willingly posed with him for a photograph that accompanied a feature article on gay fraternity men that appeared in the October 12, 2004, issue of *The Advocate*, the national gay and lesbian newsmagazine.

Chris was turned down by the two largest fraternities at the University of Nevada at Las Vegas because of his sexual orientation. Finally he was accepted as a pledge for Alpha Tau Omega and was named Outstanding New Member on his campus. "It took me three tries to finally crack the shell of the Greek system," Chris remarked. "But I did it—my determination held strong."

Then there is the story of Stefan Dinescu, an out sophomore actively recruited by Beta Theta Pi at the University of Connecticut, who was one of several who wrote about assuming the role of an educator. His straight brothers learned what it is like to be gay through both humorous and serious discussions. As Stefan wrote about his experiences being openly gay, "I found the entire party to be hysterical. If I jokingly flirted with a fraternity brother in conversation, he would flirt back for the fun of it. When I danced at the party, the guys started catcalling and complimenting me on my moves. My sexuality did not matter at all. I was sure that being myself would make them reject me. Instead, being gay was the hottest thing. They could not get enough of Stefan: my wit, my dancing, and my flamboyant personality."

It is not easy being a trailblazer, to be the only openly gay person in a heterosexist organization. It takes a lot patience, some tough skin, a sense of humor, and a willingness to give people second chances. Some people are insensitive out of ignorance. That does not mean they are mean-spirited or cannot change. In fact, sometimes those who demonstrate the most intolerant attitudes can be transformed into the strongest allies. There are some who may be unwilling to change their beliefs regarding homosexuality, but if treated with respect they will do likewise.

Not all gay students have the temperament and patience to be pioneers and educators. Some choose to remain in the closet to avoid assuming those roles, and others will drift away from the fraternity after coming out because they do not want the additional burden. Those are decisions that each gay fraternity member must make for himself.

Another lesson gleaned from reading the stories is that young gay men have been socialized to expect rejection. There are exceptions, but repeatedly the opposite occurs and brotherhood trumps prejudice. Having the courage to come out strengthens fraternal bonds in ways never imagined. Being willing to take risks—such as bringing a male date to a fraternity function—often brings unanticipated rewards.

Not all of the stories have happy conclusions. The Tau Kappa Epsilon

chapter at Texas A&M gave Clay Cunningham a pledge jersey, then literally took the shirt off his back at the bid day event when they learned that
he was involved in the campus GLBT student association. The national
Latino fraternity, where closeted "Carlos Cervantes" is affiliated, humiliated an openly gay member, causing him to leave the university. This
occurred with Carlos's cowardly acquiescence. In both cases, the fraternities' rationale for their unbrotherly behavior was a fear of gaining a
reputation as a "gay fraternity." As the rush chair told Clay, "The principle is one of sacrifice—a few, for the good of many."

The fact that a majority of the stories in this compilation have a positive outcome can be deceiving. People are more inclined to share their
triumphs than their despairs. Furthermore, most undergraduate gay fraternity men still choose to hide their sexual orientation from their brothers. We have come a long way, but in order to enhance the fraternal experience for gay men, there is much left to do.

There are several specific things that can and must be done to take us
to the next level of fulfilling the fraternal mission of brotherhood.
Initiatives need to be taken by both institutions of higher education and
national and international fraternal organizations, and there are several
areas where further research can provide guidance. I therefore propose
the following recommendations as a "gay fraternal agenda" for the next
decade.

ACTION ITEMS FOR COLLEGES AND UNIVERSITIES

**Establishment of Ally Programs for the Fraternity/Sorority
Community:** Progress in creating more inclusive fraternity/sorority
communities can be accelerated with the active and visible support of
heterosexual fraternity and sorority peers. An organization should be
created that is modeled after gay-straight alliances that have been so successful on high school campuses. Although some colleges and universities have "Straight But Not Narrow" or similar ally groups, few if any that
are aimed specifically for the fraternity/sorority community. Although
membership in an ally program should be open to all interested students
regardless of sexual orientation or Greek affiliation, such organizations
can be most successful if the membership is composed primarily of heterosexual fraternity and sorority members. It is important that the
organization not be perceived as a gay group. Although it will likely be
easier to recruit female members, it is also critical to make every effort to

have a gender-balanced group. On each campus, the group can organize educational programs for chapters and councils, distribute posters and buttons, and work collaboratively with campus GLBT organizations and programs such as Safe Zone programs. An example of a Greek Ally organization can be found on the Lambda 10 Project Web site.

Establishment of Greek Safe Zone Programs: Many colleges and universities have created GLBT Safe Zone programs. The purpose of such programs is to create a more comfortable environment for all members of the campus community regardless of sexual orientation or gender identity. Faculty, staff, and students who participate go through intensive training on sexual orientation and gender identity issues to equip them to serve as a resource for GLBT persons as well as those who are questioning their sexual orientation or gender identity. Participants are provided a Safe Zone symbol such as a button or decal to display so that they can be visibly identified. A Greek Safe Zone project can be a component of a campuswide program that targets fraternity and sorority members as participants. Information and resource materials for creating a Greek Safe Zone program can be found on the Lambda 10 Project Web site.

Establishment of Support Networks of GLBT Fraternity/Sorority Members: Although there are informal, clandestine gatherings of gay fraternity members on many campuses, there are few that have an organized support network for GLBT fraternity and sorority members, such as the "Pillar" program described by Grahaeme A. Hesp in the interventions and resources section of this volume. The primary purpose of such groups is to provide a forum for GLBT chapter members to share experiences and advice, provide moral support, and have an opportunity to socialize. Because privacy is a major concern, it is critical that the group be composed of exclusively GLBT members with a firm confidentiality policy. It is acceptable, however, to have a trusted and respected heterosexual faculty or staff member, such as someone from the counseling center, to serve as facilitator. Meetings should be held in a private location where closeted members can arrive and depart without fear of being "outed." In addition to meetings, such support networks can operate an e-mail list or online chat rooms to enhance communication.

Establishment of a "Gay-Friendly" Chapter Certification Program: A program should be established on campuses to identify chapters that are "gay-friendly." In order to qualify, a chapter might be required to adopt and enforce a sexual orientation nondiscrimination and nonharassment policy, conduct GLBT sensitivity and awareness programs for the entire membership at least annually, participate in a campus ally program, and have a written commitment of the entire membership to support a chapter climate of understanding and acceptance. Such programs could include a visible certificate (e.g., a framed certificate, with a rainbow-colored border, placed in the entryway to the chapter house that proclaims, "All are welcomed here"). A certification program would be a proactive opportunity for chapters to combat homophobia and heterosexism and let guests and prospective members know that the chapter is an inclusive and supportive organization.

Establishment of Fraternity Chapters Primarily for Gay and Bisexual Students: Many students who are members of minority populations prefer to join fraternities and sororities that enable them to enhance their cultural identity. Fraternal organizations for African-American and Jewish students have existed for decades, and in recent years there has been an emergence of Latino, Asian, Native American, and multicultural fraternities and sororities. Many gay, lesbian, or bisexual students who are uncomfortable joining predominantly heterosexual fraternities or sororities would benefit from joining a fraternal organization that meets their needs for mutual support. Delta Lambda Phi is a national social fraternity for "gay, bisexual, and progressive gentlemen," founded in 1986.[9] Interfraternity Councils should include and support such organizations.

ACTION ITEMS FOR NATIONAL/INTERNATIONAL FRATERNITIES

Adoption of Nondiscrimination and Nonharassment Clauses: Only a handful of national/international fraternities have included sexual orientation in their nondiscrimination and/or nonharassment clauses. Recently, Sigma Phi Epsilon (1999), Lambda Chi Alpha (2002), and Pi Kappa Phi (2002) have enacted such legislation at their national conventions, and several other organizations have policies or materials that indicate nondiscrimination because of sexual orientation. Most of these initiatives were student-driven, and unfortunately the strongest resistance came from alumni. It was the undergraduates who brought about change in fraternities in the 1960s with regard to racial and religious exclusion, and it will be up to the undergraduates in the current generation to take the lead in breaking down the barriers of discrimination. Adoption of such policies does not assure the elimination of prejudice. Because membership selection votes are often conducted by secret ballot and members are not required to justify their decisions, discrimination can still occur. Nonetheless, such statements are important because they spell out that discriminatory actions based on sexual orientation are not acceptable.

Increased Educational and Awareness Programs on Sexual Orientation: Activities that national/international fraternities should consider include educational sessions at leadership conferences on GLBT issues, dissemination of guidelines to assist chapters in supporting members who come out, GLBT sensitivity and awareness training for staff and alumni volunteers, and publication of articles on sexual orientation issues in fraternity magazines, newsletters, and Web sites.

Adoption of Policies Regarding Transgender Members: Although sexual orientation and gender identity are separate characteristics, they are related because they involve gender roles. Society has recognized the value of having organizations that meet the social development needs of both men and women. Accordingly, social fraternities and sororities are exempt from Title IX of the Higher Education Act, which prohibits discrimination based on sex. Few fraternities have given consideration on how to deal with pre- and post-operative transgender members. For example, if an initiated member undergoes male-to-female sexual reassignment surgery, how is the person's membership status affected? With more transgender people "coming out"—and at earlier ages than in the past—this is an issue that national/international organizations will soon be compelled to address.

AREAS FOR FURTHER RESEARCH

Research on Gay and Bisexual Fraternity Members: I conducted my informal research on gay, lesbian, and bisexual fraternity members in the early 1990s because there was a dearth of information on this topic. Unfortunately, research on this topic is still very limited. We need to have data to understand better the experiences of gay and bisexual fraternity members and to measure our progress toward creating more inclusive and accepting fraternal environments. I am pleased to announce that the Lambda 10 Project is embarking on a new research project to update and validate my informal findings.

Research on the Attitudes of Heterosexual Fraternity Members: There has been only limited research on the attitudes of heterosexual fraternity members with regard to sexual orientation issues. Most of the research has included brief mention of sexual orientation when examining attitudes of fraternity men with regard to broader issues of diversity. In order to change the fraternal environment and to measure our progress, we need a more comprehensive analysis of the attitudes of heterosexual fraternity members and how those attitudes can be transformed.

Research on Sexual Orientation Issues in Culturally Based Fraternities: Two of the stories in this book point out the complexity of sexual orientation issues within Latino and Asian fraternities. There are significant cultural and religious barriers that tend to hinder acceptance of gay fraternity brothers in culturally based fraternities. We need a better understanding of how to address attitudes within culturally based organizations before we can develop interventions.

As I was doing some research in preparation for this chapter, a member of Sigma Phi Epsilon, who was instrumental in the enactment of his fraternity's nondiscrimination legislation, shared with me some of the flurry of e-mail messages in support of and opposition to the resolution at the fraternity's 1999 national convention. Jack, a brother from a chapter in Texas, wrote, "As a pledge of Sigma Phi Epsilon, I learned the Cardinal Principles of Virtue, Diligence, and Brotherly Love, and I continue to apply these principles in my daily life." Jack went on to relate the story of a lifelong friend, Mark, who had attended another university and joined a different national fraternity. Mark's fraternity had abandoned him after he revealed that he was gay, and he transferred to another institution. Unlike Mark's fraternity brothers, Jack decided not to let sexual orientation stand in the way of friendship. His message continued with a story of recently attending a commitment ceremony for Mark and his partner. Jack wrote, "Neither of their parents attended the ceremony. As my wife and I entered the chapel, we headed for a pew in the middle of the church. One of the ushers stopped us and said. 'No, your seats are up front.' My friend wanted us seated as his family." Jack and Mark were members of different fraternities, but they were truly brothers in heart. It is these types of stories that explain what brotherhood—the mission of fraternities—is really all about.

In order to determine if fraternities are living up to their professed ideals, it is instructive to define brotherhood. *Out on Fraternity Row* includes this definition: "A family devotion to other men who share a common bond, friendship, and love for their fraternity and welfare of their brothers; a willingness to help or aid a brother in time of need; and shared common values of loyalty, honesty, understanding, and respect." With initiatives described above as a guide, can we genuinely strive to bring fraternities closer to fulfilling this definition of brotherhood? I do not think it is too far from our reach.

I cannot complete a conclusion to *Brotherhood* without reflecting on a story in *Out on Fraternity Row* that profoundly affected me. I continue to be haunted by the account of a closeted gay fraternity member identified as Sean. Sean was a chapter president, Interfraternity Council president, and "Most Outstanding Greek Man" who committed suicide after he was discovered in bed with another man in his fraternity house. As is disturbingly apparent from some of the stories in *Brotherhood*, suicide is not an uncommon option considered by fraternity men fearing rejection. If this book can help fraternity men understand that brotherhood equates to unconditional love and acceptance, and if the powerful stories contained herein motivate readers to accept the challenges outlined above, it will have served its purpose.

Douglas N. Case *currently is the coordinator of the Center for Fraternity and Sorority Life at San Diego State University where he has served in an advisory role with the campus fraternity and sorority system since 1978. He is an active member of the Association of Fraternity Advisors and served as the national president in 1991. Case is an initiate of Kappa Sigma Fraternity at San Jose State University. He is also an honorary member of Delta Lambda Phi National Social Fraternity and has advised the San Diego chapter since its inception in 1992.*

NOTES

1. Caitlin Ryan, "LGBT Youth: Health Concerns, Services and Care," *Clinical Research and Regulatory Affairs,* Vol. 20, No. 2:137-158.

Studies conducted in the 1970s and 1980s found that the average age that gay males self-identified as gay was 19 to 23 years old. Recent studies indicate that the average age of self-identification has dropped to 14 to 16 years old.

2. Riley Snorton, "New Poll Shows at Least 5% of America's High School Students Identify as Gay or Lesbian," Gay, Lesbian, and Straight Education Network press release. (New York City: October 7, 2004) Retrieved January 20, 2005, from http://www.glsen.org/cgi-bin/iowa/all/library/record/1724.html.

An online poll, "High School Attitudes on Sexual Orientation," was conducted jointly in April 2004 by Windmeyer Research and Polling and Penn, Schoen, and Berland Associates for the Gay, Lesbian, and Straight Education Network. According to the poll, approximately 5% of America's high school students identify as gay or lesbian, and nearly 75% know a gay or lesbian person (48% of students know a gay or lesbian classmate; 30% have a close gay or lesbian friend).

3. Gay, Lesbian, and Straight Education Network, 2003 GLSEN Annual Report (New York City: 2004): 4.

By the end of the 2002-2003 school year, 1,864 student clubs or gay-straight alliances has registered with GLSEN.

4. Paul Johnson, "Massive Support for Gays in Military, Poll Shows," 365Gay.com (Washington, D.C.: December 25, 2003). Retrieved January 20, 2005, from 365gay.com/newscontent/122403militaryPoll.htm.

The CNN/USA Today/Gallup poll, which was conducted December 5-7, 2003, surveyed 1,004 adults. Survey participants were asked, "Do you think people who are openly gay or homosexual should—or should not—be allowed to serve in the U.S. military?" In the 18- to 29-year-old age range, 91% said that gays should be allowed to serve openly. The percentage of positive responses from those aged 30-49, 50–64, and 65 and over was 81%, 74%, and 68% respectively.

5. Steve Ralls, "New Poll Shows Shift in Military Attitudes Towards Gays," Servicemembers Legal Defense Network press release. (Washington, D.C.: October 26, 2004). Retrieved January 20, 2005, from http://www.sldn.org/templates/press/record.html?section=2&record=1674.

6. Martha Irvine, Associated Press, "Most U.S. Youth Unfazed by Same-Sex Marriage" (Chicago: March 22, 2004). Retrieved January 20, 2005, from http://msnbc.msn.com/id/4580991.

The poll was taken in February 2004 by the National Annenberg Election Survey at the University of Pennsylvania.

7. L. J. Sax, J. A. Lindholm, A.W. Astin, W.S. Korn, V. B. Saenz, and K. M. Mahoney, *The American Freshman: National Norms for Fall 2003* (Los Angeles: Higher Education Research Institute, UCLA, 2003).

The study found that 34.6% of male American freshmen in fall 2003 agreed strongly or somewhat with the statement, "It is important to have laws prohibiting homosexual relationships." Only 19.2% of the females agreed.

8. To participate or for more information, go to the Lambda 10 Project Web site at www.lambda10.org.

9. More information on Delta Lambda Phi National Social Fraternity is available online at www.dlp.org.

Interventions and Resources

How to Use Stories
as Educational Tools

by Pamela W. Freeman

Breaking the cycle of invisibility begins by sharing the real-life accounts of what it is like to be gay or bisexual within a college fraternity. One by one, the visibility from each story sheds light on the truth and breaks down fear, prejudice, and persistent stereotypes. Not everyone will take the opportunity to learn by reading the various perspectives presented in this anthology. These stories can teach in a compelling, powerful way, moving people deeply and transforming their preconceived attitudes and opinions. The fraternity brothers who have provided their stories represent diverse backgrounds and perspectives. There are several ways to maximize the ability to use these stories as educational tools within a fraternity context or for other campuswide educational programs. Bringing the stories to life off the page can be half the battle to capture the interest and understanding of college students. Such activities are designed to engage participants in dialogue about the common themes:

1. **Ally Support:** It is important that a gay or bisexual brother hear openly supportive comments from heterosexual brothers.

2. **Fears of Rejection:** Closeted gay or bisexual brothers often agonize over the conflict between having a brotherhood based on trust and being dishonest with their brothers about their sexual orientation.

3. **Isolation:** It is not unusual for heterosexual brothers to fail to notice the extent to which a closeted gay or bisexual brother is feeling lonely, isolated, and possibly desperate.

4. **Benefit of Acceptance:** Recognizing and accepting a gay or bisexual brother can enhance the diversity in a chapter and actually strengthen the bonds of brotherhood.

5. **Promise of Fraternity for Life:** A gay or bisexual brother can in fact be out and accepted by his brothers, enjoy high self-esteem and status within the brotherhood, and derive the full benefit of brotherhood both while a student and as an alumnus.

In preparing this section, stories considered to most clearly show these themes were selected for use in three types of educational tools—case studies, read-arounds, and role plays. These ideas can be used in various teaching settings, from Greek Life presentations to student organizations, in training of student affairs staff, and to assist alumni in better understanding current issues facing the fraternity today. All of the activities described in this section can be used alone or can be augmented by personal accounts solicited from the audience. Of crucial importance is the selection of the teaching tool and a subsequent learning strategy that best matches the needs of the intended audience.

CASE STUDIES

Case studies are most useful when the group size is such that the group can be subdivided for small roundtable discussions. Any of the stories can be easily converted into a case study format. These two examples of case studies are also followed by a list of suggested discussion questions.

Case Study 1: "Leaving the Door Open" by Raymond A. Lutzky

Ray discovered that he was gay while still in high school, but he decided to remain closeted through graduation. He enrolled in a university that had an enrollment of 70% men, and he began to "meet" other gay people through online chat groups. Chris, whom Ray had met on the Internet, was another student at his university. Feeling lonely and unable to discuss his feelings with anyone, Ray asked Chris if they could meet in person, to which Chris replied with an invitation to a rush event being held by his fraternity, Lambda Chi. Ray, not considering himself to be well-suited to fraternity membership, and knowing that Chris was not out to his fraternity brothers, was surprised by the invitation. He agreed to accept the invitation but promised to keep Chris's sexual orientation a secret.

Fraternity rush was successful in changing Ray's mind about becoming a fraternity member, and he accepted a bid to pledge Lambda Chi. He was excited about living in the house with people whose company he enjoyed and whose values he shared. He hoped that over time he could become fully accepted by his fraternity as a gay man. Following the initiation ceremony for his pledge group, though, a highly respected active member told all of the new initiates that there were no longer any gays in the fraternity; any gays who had been members had already graduated. Ray then learned that Lambda Chi had developed a "gay reputation," and the brothers believed it had created difficulties for them in recruiting new members. Ray was shocked, knowing that there still were in fact at least two gay members—himself and Chris.

The week following the initiation ceremony, Chris decided to come out during a "candle pass" in which brothers passed a candle and shared meaningful thoughts with each other. Chris was already a sophomore and a member who was highly respected at the time, but the alienation he experienced after coming out made it difficult for Ray to follow his lead. Then, at a reunion of alumni, Ray met Frank, a gay alumnus. Frank was openly gay and invited Ray to dance with him at a fraternity dance. Ray danced and then spent the rest of the evening socializing with other gay alumni. He felt ecstatic, having met gay alumni from his fraternity whom he could admire and to whom he could relate.

The response by the fraternity members to Ray's being gay was mixed; some brothers were very accepting, while others feared that Ray's gayness would damage the image of the fraternity. Ray decided to prove that he was a worthy Lambda Chi by excelling in campus and fraternity activities. He focused on winning the national award for Man of the Year in his fraternity, and he became a campus leader through a job as Greek student assistant in the dean of students' office. Chris graduated, so Ray was now the only out gay man in his fraternity. By the time he became a junior, he was regarded as the most active fraternity member on campus, and his brothers began to accept him as a brother and friend.

One night, after a party at which Ray had been drinking, he asked a pledge named Joey to accompany him home. The two were physically attracted to one another, but after that first evening, Ray was filled with guilt and told Joey that their relationship could not continue. He realized later that he had hurt both Joey and himself, explaining that even though he was thrilled that another gay man had pledged Lambda Chi, for two brothers to become romantically involved was "fraternal incest."

This experience led Ray to find a way to educate students on campus about being gay and Greek. He brought Shane Windmeyer to campus to present his "Out & Greek" program, and Joey was a participant in the program. While Ray was not selected as Man of the Year, he was the recipient of a graduate fellowship to Syracuse University. Joey came out as a bisexual fraternity member, and Ray came to realize that as a role model on campus he had in fact had a positive impact on the campus culture for gay and bisexual students.

Underlying Issues and Questions for Discussion

Underlying issues in Ray Lutzky's story include whether pledges and actives should be expected to reveal their sexual orientation during the membership recruitment process, why gay members often get involved in campus activities and leadership roles, appropriate relationships among gay brothers of the same fraternity, and the issue of an organization becoming known as a "gay fraternity."

Discussion questions may include:

1. Can a fraternity member be a true brother and be closeted as a gay or bisexual man?

2. How can fraternities create a climate of acceptance that will enable gay or bisexual members to be comfortable with coming out?

3. If a fraternity becomes known as a "gay fraternity," how should the organization respond?

4. What ethical considerations should be addressed when two members of the same fraternity become romantically attracted to one another? Was Ray's behavior appropriate? Could he have handled the situation differently so that Joey would not have been hurt?

5. If Ray had not been an overachiever in terms of campus leadership, do you believe his fraternity would have accepted him? Why did Ray believe he had to overachieve to be accepted? What can a chapter do to help the nongay brothers accept gay and bisexual members as their equals?

Case Study 2: "Two Opposite Tales" by Jack Trump

Jack knew that he was gay when he entered college, but he had learned during his high school years how to conceal his sexual orientation. He enjoyed participating in sports and even dated girls on occasion in order to gain acceptance from his peers. Only a few of his closest friends outside the fraternity knew that he was gay, and he intended to maintain his secret.

Soon after Jack returned to the university after winter break, Sean, one of Jack's closest brothers from the fraternity, called him on the phone and requested urgently to see him. When he arrived at Jack's room in the residence hall where he was a resident assistant, Sean appeared distraught and was crying. Jack waited patiently until Sean was able to explain that his sexual orientation had been discovered. After he had been working on a brother's computer at the fraternity house during the break, it had been discovered that someone had been looking at male pornography on the computer. Sean denied having looked at the pornography, but he confessed that he was gay. He then had locked himself in his room, frightened and depressed about his future. When he left his room to shower or use the restroom, some of his fraternity brothers harassed him verbally and by throwing garbage on him. He turned to Jack for support after deciding that he must come out to the whole chapter on his own terms before everyone learned about him through rumors. In comforting Sean, Jack revealed that he too was gay. He immediately knew that his future in the fraternity would never be the same, but he vowed to support his brother.

At the next chapter meeting, Sean came out to his brothers, then left. The chapter president then asked everyone to discuss what they had just learned from Sean. Jack asked to speak first, chastising the members who had been responsible for harassing Sean during the break. After everyone had been given the opportunity to speak, it was clear that emotions of frustration and hatred were strong. Jack spoke once again, appealing to his brothers to think carefully about the vote they were about to take. He then came out himself as a gay man and left the meeting. A few of the brothers followed him, concerned about him walking home in the cold weather, and told him that no vote was being taken.

Over time the brothers came to understand that having gay members was acceptable, but their understanding came about too slowly for Sean to remain a member. Jack remained in the chapter, but he and Sean did not continue their friendship. Jack came to learn that, thanks to Sean, he had come out of his own closet and was a more genuine brother than before. Sean, though, was unable to fully recover from the rejection and harassment that he had received from his so-called brothers.

Underlying Issues and Questions for Discussion

Underlying issues include the importance of honesty in brotherhood, differences among gay members in how they respond to a climate in which they believe gays will not be accepted, the extent to which gay members are expected to adapt to a heterosexist environment, and the power of a single voice in helping to educate an organization.

Questions for discussion may include:

1. If a brother approached you in an emotionally distraught state, how would you respond? Do you believe that Jack's response was appropriate? If Jack had rejected Sean instead of supporting him, how might Sean's next steps might have been different?

2. If Jack had already been out in the chapter, do you believe Sean's experience would have occurred? What might have caused members to go on a "witch hunt" after seeing that someone had been looking at gay pornography on a brother's computer?

3. Do you think Sean or Jack made the best decision about staying or leaving the chapter? Why do you feel as you do?

4. What is heterosexism? How can it be addressed in fraternities?

5. If Jack had not spoken up at the chapter meeting, how might events have changed?

READ-AROUNDS

Presenters who are able to keep their audiences alert and engaged are more likely to be successful in getting their points across than those who simply talk "at" their listeners. One technique that has proven effective in keeping participants tuned in to the messages being presented is "read-arounds." This simple technique involves finding short, meaningful statements for participants to read when called upon during the presentation. The presenter can number the statements and insert them into the presentation to be read at a time when the message within the read-around will be especially relevant. As participants arrive for the presentation, they can be handed a slip of paper containing one read-around. For small groups, everyone present can be given one or more read-arounds; in larger groups, the persons with read-arounds can be spread throughout the audience. Following are read-arounds that have been preselected from a few of the stories in this book.

• Exposure is the best cure for ignorance, which I have learned from my fraternity brother, my pledge son. Every person needs to have experiences like mine, and if fraternities are a vehicle to make that possible, then every fraternity should have at least one gay brother. These people do not detract from your fraternity or the bonds of brotherhood. On the contrary, fraternal diversity can enhance brotherhood by adding a whole new dimension to lifetime friendships, to the growth of individuals, and to the fraternal values of humanity. My brother, my pledge son, taught me valuable lessons about diversity. Through his eyes I was able to see his reality, and as a result I am a better brother and a better person. (from "My Gay Pledge Son" by Benjamin M. Swartz)

• The word "faggot" was definitely thrown around a little more often than I could tolerate. I never joined in the gay bashing, but I still lacked the courage to defend myself or say anything. The experience only pushed me deeper into the closet and deeper into shame about who I was. (from "Cry Freedom" by "Eric Joseph")

• Over the next year, I said the words "I'm gay" many times to my family, friends, and fraternity brothers. Every time I came out to someone new, I felt that much stronger—I was developing a sense of freedom. My need to uphold some pseudomasculine straight image gradually disappeared, along with my depression. My fraternity brothers stood by me throughout the process. Coming out was the best thing I ever did, and the responses I received from those who loved me were more positive than I ever could have imagined. I was finally free of all the lies. I was a new person. (from "Cry Freedom" by "Eric Joseph")

• I had promised to be one of them, a brother—a promise I had already broken. Over and over again I had promised myself to lie: I lied to the brothers about who I was. I could not tell them I was gay because of my self-hatred, fear, and shame. The slightest hint of my truth might shatter the brotherhood. As each day passed my confusion and instability grew. No matter how hard I tried to deny my sexuality, the monsters in my closet did not ever let me forget. They whispered in my ear, "What's worse, the lie or the truth?" (from "Sexual Monsters" by M. Ducoing)

• My thought about the fraternity being nothing but one big booty call after another was going down the drain. These guys were about sex, yes, but not with each other. The stereotype of a gay fraternity that I had been battling in my mind was wrong. I had fallen into the trap of thinking, like the homophobes, that all gay men do when they get together is have wild sex. I was young, naive, and stupid, and I still had a lot to learn about these guys and what their fraternity was all about. (from "Lifestyles of the Gay and Fraternal" by Josh Ney)

• Fraternities can be wonderful opportunities to show that gay men and straight men can be not only friends but also brothers. I believe that the percentage of gay and bisexual men in fraternities is much higher than the Kinsey 10% theory. Homosexuality in the fraternity setting can be readily hidden, ignored, and suppressed by using hetero-sexist behavior as a mask. From my experience, these are closeted men who are masculine jock types who lack role models. I met many of these men hiding in the gay bars of Los Angeles. (from "The Row" by John Skandros)

• Several weeks later a few of the brothers were hanging out at the fraternity house when the topic of homosexuality arose. Weekly conversations on the Bible were common in the fraternity, and I assumed speculation about me had inspired the brothers to address this particular topic. The argument over what the Bible actually says was arduous and long. Many other brothers came by to join in the discussion and offer their strict, one-sided interpretation of the Bible. Out of nowhere, brother Sam— a short, scrawny guy with curly blond hair—stood up and handed a Bible to one of the brothers who had been most vocal in his opposition to homosexuality. "Find where it says God hates gay people in here," he demanded. Everyone sat there in shock. Sam was the total opposite of me. He was an officer in the Air Force, very politically active, and most definitely not gay. We were never close in the fraternity. I was confused as to why Sam was taking a stand for gays. *What did he have to gain?* I asked myself. (from "1 John 2:10" by Jonathan Scaggs)

• With all eyes on me, I nervously walked to the front of the room and said, "This week has changed my life. It's not easy being openly gay for anyone. But it's because of the support I get from this house I feel comfortable telling you. I know you all know already, and that's fine. But I want all of you to be comfortable with me too. I thank you for what you do and for being my brothers. It's because of this fraternity that I have the power to live my life the way I want. It makes me proud to be a Sigma Pi." (from "Next on NBC Nightly News" by Gabriel Grice)

• "Take a look at the person sitting next to you. What if he were gay? We all call ourselves brothers, but what does that mean? How strong is this so-called brotherhood if we're so quick to turn our back on one another? Sean didn't murder or rape someone; he simply told us something about himself that we didn't know. He is still the same brother as before. I would even argue that his bond of brotherhood is stronger now because he took that risk of sharing something very personal. So what now? Do we turn our backs on him?" (from "Two Opposite Tales" by Jack Trump)

• Without Sigma Pi, I never would have been able to come out to my family or develop more fully as a gay man. Over a hundred men support and love me as their own regardless of my sexual orientation. Even during my horrible breakup with my first love, Brian, the brotherhood was there to hold me up. Who would have thought that a fraternity would give a gay man the self-confidence, self-esteem, and power to be openly gay? (from "Next on NBC Nightly News" by Gabriel Grice)

"When people find out something like this, they may not be able to accept it. You need to work with them to tolerate it. You can help them when they need it, but you can't force them to accept anything. Until then, live your life as you see fit," he said. This compassionate response changed my life. My parents' reaction to my coming-out shook my life to its foundations. I was unstable and started to drink heavily. My brothers were the only source of support. I needed to rely on those I could trust, the fraternity. I realized that alcohol was not the solution, brotherhood was. (from "Next on NBC Nightly News" by Gabriel Grice)

• Coming out to my other brothers was different, however. We were sleeping in the same rooms, showering in the same stalls, and changing our clothes together. Unlike with the girlfriends I had told, I feared the fraternity brothers might feel threatened by a gay brother. Still, I hoped my brothers would be able to accept me as an equal and not fear my sexuality. I certainly didn't want to be viewed only by my sexuality. While some of my brothers were attractive, I would certainly never jeopardize brotherhood for fulfilling a desire—brotherhood was a matter of trust, commitment and responsibility. (from "Bonded" by Michael A. Knipp)

• To accept my bid I had to be straight. Pretending was not going to work, and if we were truly "all for one," they should be okay with me being who I am. It was not "all for the straight ones." "Lately, that just isn't me." I shook my head. "I can't try to be what I'm not, to you or the fraternity." I stood firm. "I'm still gay." (from "Smoking Guns" by "Travis Lin")

Role Playing

Another way to engage an audience is role playing. Participants can be asked to volunteer to read a brief scenario and act it out, then discussion can follow. It can be extremely effective to alter the outcomes slightly and have the role reenacted according to a different set of terms. Role playing can be used with large or small groups, provided adequate sound equipment and space are available.

The following excerpt has been written as a scenario for role playing, but this is only one example. Depending on the topic the presenter wishes to address, there are numerous examples to be found in the collection of stories found in this book. Always consider your audience and your educational outcomes when choosing the perfect story.

Role Play: Excerpt from "Odd Man In" by Mark Bigelow

Mark, a gay student who is out to a few of his friends, has recently become a fraternity pledge. It is homecoming week, and he and his pledge brothers are working together in the parking lot of a country store on their fraternity's float. One of his pledge brothers, Brandon, tells a joke that has the word "faggot" in it.

No one really understands the full context of what Brandon has just said, so they ignore him. He then says, "What, you don't find that funny?" Mark sarcastically says, "Um, yeah, I get it. Ha ha ha!" As Mark turns to walk away, Brandon mutters, "Why do they let fags in here?"

Brandon continues making snide remarks about "fags" as they continue to work on the float. Finally, Tommy, the pledge class leader, says that some things have been said that they need to discuss as a group. It is dark outside, except for the headlights of an occasional approaching car, and Mark feels frightened as he remembers the horror of Matthew Shepard's death. Tommy says to Brandon, "So, Brandon, I hear you're spreading around that Mark is gay." Brandon replies, "I have a right to speak my mind and say what I know to be true. Earlier today he didn't laugh at my gay joke. He has that prissy walk and talk. I know he's gay." Everyone then looks at Mark, and Brandon says, "So, Mark, are you gay?" Mark must decide how to answer. Feeling frightened and alone, even though he is in the midst of his pledge brothers, he answers, "No, I am not gay." Tommy then replies, "Who cares anyway if you are or are not. We love you."

Suggested Questions for Discussion:

1. How could members of the group have responded differently to Brandon when he first told the joke?

2. Would the fact that all people present were pledges have influenced how they reacted to Brandon? Would the situation have been different if actives had been present? Why or why not?

3. Was Tommy correct in bringing the issue of Mark's sexual orientation into the limelight? How might Tommy have addressed Brandon's behavior differently?

4. Why do you think Mark lied about his sexual orientation? Was this an ideal outcome? Why or why not?

Pamela W. Freeman *is associate dean of students and director of the Indiana University Office of Student Ethics and Anti-Harassment Programs, which includes the campus judicial system, three antiharassment teams, and the Gay, Lesbian, Bisexual, Transgender Student Support Services. With Shane Windmeyer, Freeman co-coordinates the Lambda 10 Project and coedited* Out on Fraternity Row: Personal Accounts of Being Gay in a College Fraternity *and* Secret Sisters: Stories of Being Lesbian and Bisexual in a College Sorority. *She also chairs the Indiana University Commission on Multicultural Understanding.*

The Relationship Between Hazing and Homophobia

by Pamela W. Freeman

A thorough library search leads to numerous publications about hazing but only occasional, brief references to hazing as related to homophobia.[1] One purpose of this essay is to begin to fill this void in the literature by providing observations about homophobia as a factor that can lead to hazing in various organizations, especially men's organizations. Another, perhaps more important, purpose is to stimulate discussion about a perceived link between homophobia and hazing, so that organizations will see the value of education about homophobia as a major deterrent to hazing.

George Weinberg, author of the book *Society and the Healthy Homosexual* (1972), is credited with first coining the term *homophobia*. Defined as "the fear and hatred of people who love and who are sexually attracted to those of the same sex,"[2] acts of prejudice and discrimination often result from this fear and hatred. Homophobic attitudes and behaviors are linked to *heterosexism*, described as the "system of oppression of persons who are lesbian, gay, or bisexual based on the assumption that heterosexuality is the only 'normal' sexual orientation and is, therefore, preferable."[3] Indeed, homophobia is systematically found throughout society when only the needs of heterosexuals are considered in the development of laws, policies, and social expectations. The connection between homophobia—and heterosexism as inherent to homophobia—and hazing in fraternities is explored in this essay.

In the most recent 20 years of my work as a university student affairs administrator, I have worked as a student advocate, a diversity educator, and a campus judicial system director. In each of these roles, I have had brought to my attention numerous examples of hazing that involved homophobic acts. The first example that I recall occurred in the late 1980s and involved a report from someone passing by a fraternity house in the middle of the afternoon just as a pledge was being made to run through a gauntlet of brothers as they screamed "fag" and "gay" at him. The observer reported the incident to the campus's antiharassment team under the protection of confidentiality. As a gay man himself, though, he felt that his safety would be jeopardized if he were to come forward with a formal report, so he requested that no action be taken.

In a more recent incident, a fraternity brother was initiated into the realm of those who had become lavaliered (i.e., when a brother commits his love to a woman by giving his lavalier to her) by having him get extremely intoxicated, having him wear only a woman's thong underwear, paddling him, and using a marker to write, among other terms, "pussy" and "gay" on his bare chest and back. Addressing the homophobic aspects of this case was made even more difficult because of the victim's sensitivity toward gay members in his chapter.

These and other incidents have led me to conclude that homophobia is a strong factor in the nature and extent of hazing that occurs, especially in men's organizations. Beliefs that follow this conclusion are as follows:

1. By diminishing the value of some individuals (e.g., homophobic individuals view anyone who is gay as inferior), homophobia enables members of an organization to dehumanize their peers through hazing.

2. Homophobic attitude and accompanying heterosexist attitudes lead fraternity brothers to view peers perceived to be gay as inferior (i.e., less masculine than "normal" men), further enabling the hazing of peers who may seem weak or less masculine than the expected norm for the organization.

3. Men who haze others using homophobic language and behaviors may have questions or concerns about their own masculinity or sexual identity, using hazing tactics as a way to oppress open expression of differences in sexual orientation.

4. When people with homophobic attitudes haze others, the behavior is more intense and hostile than when hazing is carried out in the absence of homophobia.

5. Elimination of homophobia in an organization can be a crucial step toward eliminating hazing.

6. Hazing will never be eliminated if efforts to address it are carried out in isolation from other social ills, such as homophobia and other forms of intolerance.

Hazing is all too common among fraternity men, supposedly having the purpose of testing the manhood and commitment of the brotherhood. Why should such behavior be a test of manhood and commitment? What is the connection? To further analyze these questions, it is helpful to turn to the literature.

Why Do People Haze?

Hank Nuwer, in his most recent book, *The Hazing Reader,* describes hazing as "a ritual that gives hazers a sense of power, entitlement, and occasionally sadistic pleasure."[4] Throughout history, such organizations as the military, athletic teams, and fraternities have attributed to hazing rituals such positive values as commitment, loyalty, brotherhood, and discipline. Described in negative terms, hazing has led to groupthink, blind allegiance, physical injury, and even death.

Often viewed as a rite of passage that is necessary for full acceptance into a group, hazing is believed by many persons to be an essential prerequisite for belonging. The desire to belong is so strong that individuals actually look forward to the chance to prove their worth to the organization by enduring the trials of hazing. Once they have succeeded and are fully accepted by the group, they are expected to carry on the tradition for future members. Hazing at its worst evolves into each individual, after attaining full member status, trying to think of ways to haze new initiates that will exceed in severity the hazing activities that they themselves experienced. The allure of carrying on the tradition often outweighs any inclination to end the cycle of hazing in an organization. Indeed, to break from the norm and try to change the culture of hazing requires a greater sense of awareness, self-confidence, and courage than is commonly found among young, insecure initiates.

The desire to haze, though, is derived from more than a simple wish to carry on tradition. In all-male organizations, hazing often is used to prove a member's masculinity, as shown through an ability to endure pain and demonstrate heterosexuality. Hazing activities that subject male initiates to name-calling (e.g., "faggot") and coming into close contact with the genitalia of other male initiates are designed to ridicule and cause discomfort. Based on an assumption that men who are masculine will find such behavior to be abhorrent, the initiates do not dare act as if they are comfortable with the activities, but they know they must comply with their orders or be subjected to even harsher punishment.

Why is it so important to prove masculinity when joining an all-male organization? The answer very likely can be explained by homophobia. Those members who haze others have as a goal to find the most disrespectful and demeaning activities possible, and people with homophobic attitudes believe that there is nothing more demeaning than for an initiate to be taunted as if homosexual. Such attitudes are derived from society at large, through heterosexist messages and hero worship of masculine-appearing men, combined with the erroneous assumption that anyone who is gay cannot be strong, athletic, and masculine. In this context, sexism is similar to homophobia in its role in perpetuating hazing. Hazing activities that shame or embarrass men for being effeminate (i.e., too much like women) are used to build up the masculine image of the ideal member of the organization—the image to be accepted into the membership. Men who do not demonstrate their masculinity through enduring hazing while putting down people who are female or homosexual risk never becoming a part of the group; they may never attain a sense of belonging. Further, men who are unsure about their own sexual identity believe that they can use homophobia and hazing to assert their own masculinity and heterosexual orientation.

Elizabeth Allan and Susan Iverson[5] discuss the power of cultural forces in influencing hazing. Members of a group who are viewed as heroes because of their positions, personal traits, or past feats are expected to perpetuate traditions, and new members strive to emulate these heroes. The result can be a culture of hazing that thrives from generation to generation. It becomes more difficult to change the culture than to sustain it, so people continue to haze.

Allan and Iverson apply theory on social norms as developed by Berkowitz (2003)[6] to explain why it is so difficult for individuals to break the pattern of hazing in their organizations. Berkowitz's model includes five steps for changing cultural norms associated with health and social justice:

1. People first must notice the event;
2. The event must be viewed as problematic;
3. People must see that they have both responsibility and capacity for changing the problem;

4. People must possess the skills for changing the problem; and

5. People must actually take action to change the problem.

Until members and initiates can take all five steps, hazing is likely to continue. There must be an incentive for an individual to take these steps, and this is where universities can focus their efforts.

How Can Universities Provide an Incentive to Change the Culture of Hazing?

Universities, as centers of intellectual enlightenment, are more apt to have resources to address such issues as homophobia and sexism than other institutions. Just as the Berkowitz model can be applied to the ability of individuals to change a cultural norm, such as hazing, the model also can be applied to institutions or groups.

Educational institutions must first notice that hazing is occurring and that it continues to be a serious problem. Because fraternities on the national level forbid hazing, and at least some forms of hazing are illegal in most states, most hazing activity on campuses is conducted underground. University administrators may not acknowledge the existence of hazing until after a tragedy has occurred. When administrators receive tips that mild forms of hazing are being performed (i.e., hazing that is viewed by some persons to be mild because the potential for physical harm is small) the information may receive little or no attention. Such inaction on the part of administrators and national leaders, however, can be viewed as negligent if the seemingly harmless activity evolves into high-risk behavior.

In her work as an advocate for bringing an end to hazing, Elizabeth Allan has found that when people with little power are subjected to behaviors such as name-calling and forced servitude, the climate becomes ripe for the activities to turn into dangerous rituals, sometimes leading to physical and psychological injuries.[7] In his story about being gay in a college fraternity,[8] a member of a historically black fraternity wrote, "Many brothers made many antigay remarks during the pledgeship and had even joked that I was gay…. In some ways, I was threatened and tested during the pledgeship to make sure I was not gay." He continued to relay his experience of being threatened with physical harm after he had become an active member and a brother accused him of being gay, leading to such a great fear for his safety that he disassociated from the fraternity for two years.

Other examples of such hazing are found in this book in the stories of Chris Zacharda and John Welles. Zacharda describes his initiation on the swim team when the team captain ordered all freshmen, "Line up, losers. I don't want to hear a word from you faggots. Tonight you're going to prove you're a man." The event led to verbal and physical abuse and excessive consumption of alcohol.

Welles's story includes extensive accounts of hazing, including sleep deprivation and forced standing in place for hours, but he describes a tremendous sense of accomplishment as a closeted gay man when he proved himself worthy through arduous physical and emotional demands. He characterizes his experiences as a source of pride: "Among all these straight dudes, a closeted gay guy had ranked ahead of all but one of the pledges." Whether or not he believed the hazing was intended to be a test of manhood, his feelings of pride clearly were related to an internalized fear of not being able to show that a gay man could be as strong as his straight peers.

A common factor among issues including hazing, homophobia, sexism, and other forms of intolerance is a general lack of respect for anyone who does not fit the image of the ideal member - usually someone who is attractive, athletic, and masculine. Educational institutions must recognize that hazing is linked to disrespect and that disrespectful behaviors can lead to dangerous activities. Understating the importance of disrespectful, intolerant behavior is an indication of denial of the problem. Institutions must acknowledge that homophobic slurs spoken or written in the context of an activity that was to be "just fun" is a symptom of an organization capable of hazing—reducing the value of the individual and thereby subjecting that individual to demeaning and destructive behaviors.

Simply recognizing the problem is not enough to bring about change, however. Again referring to Berkowitz's steps, institutions must recognize that they have both the "responsibility and the capacity" to bring about change. Unfortunately, hazing is currently viewed as an overwhelming problem about which there is much disagreement. The task of changing the hazing culture that experts believe exists in many fraternities is a daunting one, in part because of the resistance to change. Often people being hazed consent to the abuse because they believe it will lead to bonding and strength within the group. In some cases, by the time the hazing has reached a harmful stage, the victims believe they have endured too much to give up.[9] Also, not all victims of hazing are affected similarly, some being traumatized by activities that others find amusing. It is not surprising that university and organizational leaders find it difficult to accept responsibility for activities in which there may be no complainant. The irony here is that until more students who are adversely affected by hazing reveal their feelings, people in positions to affect change will be reluctant to assume responsibility; and as long as administrators are hesitant to accept responsibility, students will be reluctant to come forward to report hazing.

Berkowitz's fourth step—people possessing the skills to address the problem—calls for stepped-up educational efforts. If administrators and leaders have little understanding of homophobia and other related issues, they will be inept at providing training for students in fraternities. As is true for most diversity training efforts, one of the best ways to educate others is to help them see the benefit to themselves of becoming astute about diversity. For fraternities, the incentive for learning can be linked directly to the goal of achieving strong brotherhood. A brotherhood that is based on respect is less likely to haze than one in which individuals are constantly berated for being different.

Developing skills through diversity education and leadership training can provide a solid foundation for Berkowitz's final step, taking action to bring about change. Fraternities claim to be all about leadership development and support for success. Why not challenge fraternity leaders to engage their members in in-depth diversity awareness activities as a step toward addressing hazing? Encouraging students to use campus and outside resources to address homophobia, sexism, racism, prejudice against disabled people, etc., can have the effect of raising questions in members' minds about the legitimacy of traditional practices in today's world. Such encouragement requires time and commitment on the part of students, administrators, and organization leaders, but the end result will be worth the expense in terms of resources, especially if lives can be saved.

A CHALLENGE TO ACT

As this piece is being written, there likely are students being taunted by homophobic slurs as part of hazing practices. Some may even be subjected to activities as deadly as the fraternity initiation reported in fall 2004 in *The Denver Post*[10] in which fraternity brothers wrote slurs on the body of a pledge who was dying of alcohol poisoning. When referring to the writing on his son's body, a distraught parent of the deceased pledge reportedly said, "We still don't see leadership from the university.... They have not proposed any change in the system—but the system is killing our kids." The family attorney summed up the matter by saying, "To do something like that exposes those young men for what they are—thoughtless and perverse."

This article is not intended to accuse any university or organization of overtly encouraging homophobia as a means to destroy young lives. It is important, though, to acknowledge that the ramifications of a failure to recognize a problem and act can be no better than intent to harm. Why not try a new approach to addressing hazing by working to eliminate homophobia and other types of prejudice from the minds of our students? Educational efforts directed toward reducing internal confusion and worries of young men about their own sexual identities, combined with information about homophobia and its role in creating disrespect instead of brotherhood, just might have a positive impact on the methods used to increase male bonding in organizations. Such action could well serve to eliminate some of the major factors that lead to hazing. The messages for students should be (1) that homophobia does not have to be a normal part of manhood, and (2) that persons who respect and accept themselves and one another do not promote traditions that destroy one another. The challenge is here for all of our institutions. Let us not miss a chance to bring about meaningful change and an eventual end to a history of hazing that has gone on for too long.

Pamela W. Freeman *is associate dean of students and director of the Indiana University Office of Student Ethics and Anti-Harassment Programs, which includes the campus judicial system, three antiharassment teams, and the Gay, Lesbian, Bisexual, Transgender Student Support Services. With Shane Windmeyer, Freeman co-coordinates the Lambda 10 Project and coedited* Out on Fraternity Row: Personal Accounts of Being Gay in a College Fraternity *and* Secret Sisters: Stories of Being Lesbian and Bisexual in a College Sorority. *She also chairs the Indiana University Commission on Multicultural Understanding.*

NOTES

1. As defined in *Webster's New Universal Unabridged Dictionary* (1996), hazing means "to subject (freshmen, newcomers, etc.) to abusive

or humiliating tricks and ridicule." While this is a basic definition, the term is further defined by state laws and university policies.

2. Weinberg, G. *Society and the Healthy Homosexual* (New York: St. Martin's Press), 1972.

3. Windmeyer, S.L. and P.W. Freeman. *Fraternity & Sorority Anti-Homophobia Train the Trainer Manual* (available from the Lambda 10 Project, www.lambda10.org, 2002, p. 8).

4. Nuwer, Hank, ed. *The Hazing Reader* (Bloomington: Indiana University Press, 2004, p. xv).

5. Nuwer, p. 258.

6. Nuwer, p. 271.

7. "Is Hazing Harmful?" *The CQ Researcher* (January 9, 2004, p. 6).

8. Windmeyer, S.L. and P.W. Freeman. *Out on Fraternity Row: Personal Accounts of Being Gay in a College Fraternity* (Los Angeles: Alyson Books, 1998, pp. 16-17).

9. "Is Hazing Harmful?" p. 6.

10. Herdy, A. and G. Merritt, "Frat brothers scrawled slurs on dying pledge" (*Denver Post*, October 8, 2004).

Trials and Tribulations of Rushing Openly Gay Brothers

by Kelly Jo Karnes

As more men are coming to college already out and comfortable with their sexual identity, fraternities are confronted with the decision and consequences of rushing openly gay members. Some campuses now have the option of gay fraternities. Other campuses, at the very least, have chapters that have inclusion policies and standards for gay or bisexual men. Most colleges and universities have policies that forbid organizations, offices, and programs from discriminating against individuals based on their sexual orientation. Along with the university policies, some national and international fraternities have begun to put sexual orientation policies into their rules and guidelines for their collegiate chapters. However, upholding and enforcing these rules often falls on the shoulders of the 18- to 22-year-old men of the chapter. Developmentally, these men may not always have the maturity level to see the value of rushing openly gay members. What happens if a man does not have these options on his college campus, or what if a gay man is interested in the "traditional" fraternity options? There are important considerations for both the chapters and prospective gay members to consider and evaluate before making the lifelong commitment of membership in a fraternal organization.

Diversity and inclusion are hot topics on today's college campuses, and it is not any different within the fraternity system. Chapters are striving to break the "cookie-cutter frat guy" image that they once had. Chapters are also seeking to value differences, embrace various cultures, and recruit individuals based on what they can bring to the brotherhood of their organization. We need to explore why students, gay or straight, look to become part of fraternities. Most Greek-letter organizations are founded on four main principles: service, scholarship, leadership, and friendship.

Service: As this is becoming a larger part of high school curriculum, students are continuing to look for chances to give back to others as they enter college. Fraternities provide already established community service and philanthropy opportunities for men.

Scholarship: Fraternities provide many tools to help their members succeed academically in college. Unlike other clubs or organizations, fraternities have national standards for academics that they ask their members to maintain.

Leadership: Along with their class requirements, men are looking for experiences that will help them gain and build leadership skills that will be most beneficial when they enter the workforce. Greek organizations provide these opportunities.

Friendship: Meeting new people and becoming part of a brotherhood probably form the number 1 reason men join fraternal organizations. All people want to be accepted for who they are and want to hang out with people with whose interests they share.

QUESTIONS FOR THE OPENLY GAY MAN ON WHETHER TO RUSH

We hope that these are the reasons that men join fraternal organizations, and we also want to believe that every member will go on to have a great fraternity experience, whether they are gay or straight. However, aside from the positive aspects of fraternity life, potential members who are gay have to consider some other questions before joining a Greek chapter. There are a series of questions that an openly gay man should ask himself prior to joining a fraternity. Some of these might include:

1. Does this chapter seem inclusive of all minorities?
2. Is the climate of the organization an accepting and comfortable one for me?
3. Would I be proud to call these men "brothers"?

4. Could I see myself joining this group as an openly gay man?

5. Could I see myself coming out to the brothers after they have had a chance to get to know me as an individual?

6. Are there other members of the organization who are currently out?

7. Am I willing to confront blatant homophobic comments and derogatory behaviors?

8. Would I be comfortable bringing a date of the same sex to fraternity functions?

9. If asked about my sexual orientation, would I be willing to be honest, regardless of the response of the brothers?

10. Does the national or international fraternity have a sexual orientation policy? If so, does the local chapter abide by and uphold it?

11. Have there been any openly gay members in the chapter before? If so, did they have a good fraternity experience?

Some of the pitfalls that a gay man may confront during this questioning process could include the thoughts of *How do I join a group without sexual orientation being the first thing that is questioned?* or *If I don't come out to the brothers, am I being dishonest with the chapter and myself?* These are common concerns, but they should be fully explored before making the commitment to Greek life. Gay men should not make a life-long decision based on yes or no answers to questions, as every situation will bring new things to consider. However, the above questions will begin the thought process and help explore the readiness of a gay man to accept a fraternity bid and all that may come with that.

QUESTIONS TO GAUGE A FRATERNITY'S READINESS TO RUSH AN OPENLY GAY POTENTIAL MEMBER

There are also conversations that a fraternal organization should have prior to rushing gay members. Fraternity chapters should discuss how, as an organization, they will deal with recruiting potential members who are gay, bisexual, or questioning their sexuality. These questions should *not* be used to choose or not choose a gay prospective member, but used more as a tool to gauge the chapter's readiness for and acceptance of gay members. Many campuses have sexual orientation nondiscrimination policies that they ask all student organizations to abide by. A fraternity could risk losing its recognition status on campus if found to be in violation of university policy. The fact that an organization cannot answer yes to all of the following questions does not mean that it is not ready to ask gay men to become brothers.

1. Do we create an atmosphere that is supportive of differences of all brothers?

2. Is our organization welcoming of all minority groups?

3. Are we prepared to confront behaviors or comments that may be harassing to any minority member?

4. Do we have a history of gay members? If so, did they have a good fraternity experience?

5. Does our national or international organization have a policy or statement on sexual orientation? If so, is the local chapter willing to fully adopt the policy?

6. Does our campus have a nondiscrimination policy or statement of diversity that we could be in violation of?

7. Do we look for men who will be great members and uphold the ideals of our organization, regardless of sexual orientation?

8. Are we prepared to have conversations with members, potential members, or alumni who have strong opinions against asking an openly gay man to join?

9. Are we prepared to support brothers who may come out as undergraduate members?

10. Are we committed to learning more about sexual orientation and willing to participate in educational programs on the subject?

11. Is it the reality that there are already gay men in the chapter, and if so, what can we do as a group to make them feel valued as members and not as if they need to hide who they really are from the very men they call "brothers"?

Some pitfalls or challenges that a chapter may experience as it begins to rush gay members could include being labeled as the "gay fraternity" and declining support and involvement from closed-minded members, potential members, or alumni. As with any decision, the chapter must weigh the positives outcomes with the potential for negative effects.

BENEFITS OF RUSHING OPENLY GAY MEN

Fraternities should not be afraid to rush gay men. There are many benefits for the organization if it is willing to diversify its membership to include gay men. Some of these could include:

• Chapters have the opportunity to confront the unfamiliar. They can interact with, learn from, teach, and affect a minority population that they may have once closed themselves off to. Learning tolerance and understanding of this population will translate to acceptance of all underrepresented members.

• By adding another aspect of diversity to your organization, it may allow others to explore their identity and be more comfortable preparing for life after college.

• Suicide among young men who are gay, bisexual, or questioning is a growing issue. Joining a fraternity just may be the reason that a friend, classmate, roommate, or teammate decides that life is worth living.

• If fraternities choose to become accepting and tolerant organizations, gay brothers and new members may develop a stronger pride in who they are, which could result in higher self-esteem. Otherwise, some struggles with sexual identity could lead men to depression, alcohol and drug abuse, and even suicide.

• Statistics say that at least one in 10 people are gay. Fraternal organizations might now have access to an additional 10% of the campus population.

• Inclusive chapters can make a positive impact in the Greek and campus communities and perhaps encourage others to take a stand against prejudice.

• Chapters may finally begin to live up to the standards of their founders, which include accepting members for who they are without discrimination.

Benefits to Gay Men of Joining a Fraternity

Gay men should also not be afraid to explore the option of fraternities and all that they have to offer. There are many ways in which out men may be able to add to the organization and in which they in turn can benefit from the service, leadership, scholarship, and brotherhood that fraternities have strived to perfect for hundreds of years. Other benefits could include:

• Beginning open and honest dialogues with chapter members about discrimination and what we can do to stop it.

• The presence of a gay member may encourage others in the fraternity, who may be questioning their sexuality, to feel more comfortable in exploring these feelings, rather than suppressing them due to an unaccepting environment.

• The ultimate benefit is having the opportunity to experience true brotherhood and friendship that is virtually unmatched in any other organization on a college campus.

Fraternity Options and Alternatives for Gay Men

Gay men no longer have to feel that fraternities are not a possibility for them during their college careers. There are many Greek options for gay men today, and it truly is up to each man to decide which option he is most comfortable with. None of these options are perfect, and some may be more of a challenge than others. But gay men need to decide which Greek option is best for them, knowing that it may not always be an ideal situation. Some of these options include:

Option One: If a man is not ready to come out of the closet, one option is to join a "traditional" chapter as a closeted gay man. These members may always live with the fear of being outed and not accepted as a gay man in the organization. The con is that closeted members may have to play the role of a "typical fraternity man," which may include taking women as dates to parties or feeling pressured to participate in the mocking and ridicule of other members as being "gay" or "a fag" in the chapter if their actions are not perceived as "manly." The pro is that the closeted member would not have to feel like the "token" minority of the organization. By staying closeted he may be able to have a "traditional" fraternity experience without the added stresses and conflicts that could come along with being out.

Option Two: A second option is joining a "traditional" chapter as an openly gay man, or coming out once you are more comfortable with your identity. Depending on the campus climate as well as the fraternity climate, this can either be an accepting and welcoming experience or one of ridicule, harassment, and devastation. This option can be dangerous but can also have positive outcomes, which might include conversations with the brothers about tolerance and having an open mind. A con with this option may still include harassment and lack of acceptance by members, alumni, and other Greek men. Out fraternity men may have to deal with all of the trials and tribulations that any out man has to deal with, including ignorance, hatred, and painful joking. However, the pros to this option would mean that the out man would not have to hide his true identity and would know that he was asked to be a member in an organization that appreciates diversity or at least is willing to accept types of people they may not be familiar with.

Option Three: A final option would be to join Delta Lambda Phi fraternity or another equivalent openly gay fraternity. Delta Lambda Phi was founded in 1986 as a national alternative social fraternity for gay, bisexual, and progressive men to enjoy the brotherhood of fraternity life in an accepting environment (www.deltalambdaphi.org). Men can join this organization knowing up front what its policy on inclusiveness and tolerance of gay members will be. The pro with this option is that men are joining a group in which members are out and accepting of all sexual orientations. They will not have to educate the members about diversity and inclusion. They are getting the "fraternity experience" without giving up any of their identity. The con may be that they are again segregating themselves in a group to which they most closely relate but which may not provide the challenges and experiences to allow them to grow. Some campuses may also have "local" fraternities with a similar mission or purpose. You can explore this option with your campus fraternity/sorority advisor.

Choosing whether to enter a fraternity openly gay is a big decision for gay college men. Many men have gone on to have successful fraternity experiences after coming out and being accepted by their brothers. Other men may choose the route of staying in the closet during their undergraduate years and then come out only after they have graduated from college. They may not come out to the entire chapter but only to those few select close brothers with whom they remain in contact after graduation. And finally, some fraternity men will remain in the closet years after they leave college, even to the point of getting married and having children.

CONCLUSION

The purpose of this piece is to provide a guide and some questions to start dialogue for both gay prospective fraternity men and fraternity chapters. Each group has a vested interest in exploring both sides of these issues prior to making any decisions. The fraternities may decide that more education is needed for their members before they are able to offer a safe and accepting environment for gay members. Out fraternity men may decide that the "traditional" fraternity experience is not worth the headache and choose an alternative organization in order to get the brotherhood they are searching for. However, each group must come to this decision on their own, only after they have explored the different options.

In an ideal world, all organizations would be accepting and inclusive of differences in individuals. Fraternities would provide opportunities for service, scholarship, leadership, and friendship to any man willing to accept membership. They would treat each other with the dignity and respect that everyone deserves and foster a diverse environment. Fraternities would remember what their founders had in mind as they created these "secret societies" to build men up rather than tear them down. And just maybe the trials and tribulations past gay members may have endured with being closeted or out in a fraternity will help to make the path easier for those to come.

Kelly Jo Karnes *currently works at Old Dominion University as the assistant director for student activities and leadership. Prior to that she was the assistant director for Greek life at the University of Kansas. She has worked with fraternities and sororities for the past seven years and is currently serving as a national officer for her sorority, Sigma Sigma Sigma.*

How to Come Out
of the Gay Greek Closet?

by Tracie M. Massey

Joining a fraternity can be an amazing experience. The men in your chapter are your brothers. You took a bond or vow with them to support and live up to certain ideals and values. Now you are considering telling them that you are gay. Consider completely the fears, acceptance, or questions that may arise from your coming-out. This journey will be filled with a range of emotions, facing tough battles, and conquering the unknown. Where will your journey lead you? My hope is that you will have an experience that is full of brotherhood, support, and love. As a straight female Greek advisor, I have had many men come out to me during their fraternity experiences. I have assisted men in coming out to their chapters. I helped one man come out, although he was afraid to, and he had a good experience with very supportive brothers. Another man I helped had a terrible experience and has been discriminated against, made fun of, abused emotionally, and hazed. These are two examples of how you may experience coming out.

There can be many challenges, rewards, and opportunities in this process. The toughest and often easiest people to come out to are your fraternity brothers. Although each fraternity chapter or community is different, there are similar thoughts to be considered and questions to be prepared for. Below are considerations for taking this journey.

COMING OUT TO A FRATERNITY BROTHER

What to consider:

• Create a safe private environment; your room or house is a comfortable place. Being in a safe environment can protect you and make you feel more confident about coming out.

• Be honest and realize that you may be confronted with a brother who is shocked or may have many questions.

• Assure your brother that you are the same man he has known. You have the same beliefs and ideals that brought you to the fraternity. Tell him that you trust him enough to tell him such a personal truth about yourself.

• Be prepared for both rejection and acceptance.

• Ask for support and guidance if necessary. Ask a brother who is accepting to support you within the chapter.

• Realize your own comfort level of coming out. What are you willing to share? What do you want to keep private?

• Do not assume that a brother will out you to the rest of the chapter. Don't assume he won't either.

• Communicate your feelings and private thoughts, stating who you are comfortable sharing with at this time.

• Visit the Lambda 10 Project at www.lambda10.org. There are many sections that can assist you. This site can help you to discover many resources. There is a message board and even a chat room.

Coming Out to Your Fraternity Chapter

What to consider:

• Create an ally in your chapter. This can be your big brother or a pledge brother, someone you trust and who supports you.

• Provide a safe situation for everyone involved. If you feel a strong confrontation arising, make sure to ask an advisor to be present. They can assist in keeping the chapter meeting from getting out of control.

• Have brothers in the room to whom you have privately come out. This will ensure you are supported by men in the chapter already. It will be comforting to have men around you who support you.

• Understand that there will be a wide range of feelings in the room, from support to rejection.

• Connect with brothers who support you. This will encourage you and facilitate your self-realization.

• Be honest and open with brothers who reject you. These brothers may not understand what being gay means; they may have personal beliefs that it is wrong, or they may just be unsure of how to react.

• Approach brothers who are rejecting you for being gay, if you feel doing so is appropriate or if you are comfortable. It can help educate you both on your feelings. You can help a brother understand your sexual orientation. Hearing why a brother has a different perspective can help you to understand how to deal with the situation. At times you may need to respectfully disagree and choose to stand strong in your brotherhood with a difference of opinion.

• Be prepared for other gay brothers or those who might be gay to confide in you. This could come as a shock to you. These brothers may be closeted and not out yet. If they come to you, they may be looking to share in confidence and trust you to keep their feelings private.

• Be prepared to answer questions about being gay or what this may mean for your membership in the fraternity.

• Do not be shy about bringing a date to any fraternity functions after you have come out to your chapter if the chapter is supportive. Realize not every chapter member or brother will be supportive.

• Ask if your national organization has any resources for gay members. You can look on its Web site or ask for contact information to find out if your fraternity has a nondiscrimination policy including sexual orientation or offers educational support programs.

• Seek assistance from your national organization or local advisors if there is a negative outcome. They can help you deal with confrontations or negative attitudes toward you.

• Encourage your chapter to have a nondiscrimination clause including the words "sexual orientation" in its bylaws if it does not already have one. You can check the list of organizations on the Lambda 10 Project Web site: www.lambda10.org.

COMING OUT TO YOUR FRATERNITY SYSTEM

What to consider:

• Look for Safe Zone materials in a campus or fraternity advisor's office. This person can be an ally for you. If you see Safe Zone materials, you know that this person is someone you can talk with openly and who will assist you and support you.

• Look for administrators or advisors who may be a resource for you.

• Decide whether you would like to come out to the entire campus or let your news stay within your chapter. Realize that others can spread rumors and your news could get out before you choose to share it publicly.

• Be prepared for negative comments about you and your fraternity.

• Talk with your chapter president about how the chapter can support you publicly to the fraternity community. Explain how you would like the chapter to support you.

• Do not be surprised if other gay men or women approach you for comfort or support.

• Lean on your brothers for support and assistance. The response from the community is unknown, and it's better to be prepared.

• Talk to your fraternity advisor about educating the Greek community on your campus through programs and speakers.

• Help create an ally program so that others will feel more accepted.

Coming Out to Student Leaders on Campus

What to consider:

• Research support groups or student organizations that you can connect with to talk about gay, lesbian, bisexual, transgender, or sexually questioning issues you may be facing.

• Consider joining a club outside of your fraternity that can provide support. You will find accepting groups in other organizations on your campus.

• Decide whether you want to come out to the campus, your fraternity community, or even just a few select people.

• Find your GLBT support services office. This office or staff member can answer questions you may have about being gay in college. Not every campus will have this office or resource.

• If you encounter harassment, find an immediate safe reporting method on your campus. This may be calling the campus police or reporting harassment to the dean of students' office. Harassment can be a very serious issue that can lead to physical harm. It is important to be aware if you feel you are in a dangerous situation.

• Seek the counseling center if you need emotional support outside of your fraternity. A counselor is an impartial, trained professional who can listen to your concerns.

• Does your campus require student organizations to include a nondiscrimination clause in their constitution or bylaws? Consider this when selecting or choosing a group to join. You can find this information at your campus activities center.

These are the issues that you may face when considering coming out. Be prepared for many outcomes, ranging from overwhelmingly positive support to the potential worst reaction, rejection. The next listing represents some questions that you may face related to your choice to come out of the Greek closet. The questions are based on real situations from coming-out experiences within fraternities on college campuses. Be prepared for questions such as:

• **Why would you join a fraternity if you are gay?** Talk to students who are not in fraternities about your fraternity experience and what drew you to joining a fraternity. This is a fantastic opportunity to recruit other students to fraternities or even educate them about the positive aspects of fraternity life such as diversity and brotherhood.

• **What is it like being gay and in a fraternity?** Talk about your experience in coming out to your brothers. If you have had a positive experience, you will create new alliances with other students that could look to you for support. You may also encourage other gay men to join fraternities. If you have had a negative experience, you will most likely talk about how you can find a new support group that is outside of the fraternity. You may also explain that you need to follow your own values and find support outside of the fraternity.

• **Where do your loyalties lie? With your fraternity? Or with being gay?** Explain how you do not need to choose one or the other. You can be a gay man and a fraternity man at the same time. Those experiences can coexist and can also be separated as necessary.

• **How long have you known this?** Be honest and explain that this is not a recent decision for you. Explain that the process of coming out is a tough one.

• **Why did you not tell me before you joined?** Explain that you were not sure if you would be accepted by the brothers or that you wanted them to get to know you without knowing you were gay first. Explain you may not have been ready to come out at that time.

• **Does anyone else know you are gay?** Explain if your family or other close friends know. This is all part of your coming-out process. Let your brothers know how important they are to you; this is why you are coming out to them. If your family does not know yet, explain that you would like to keep your privacy and come out to them on your own schedule.

• **Is that why you joined our fraternity? To look for guys to date?** Explain to the brothers what brought you to the fraternity. This will help them to see that you joined because of their values, philanthropy, leadership, and strong friendships—in a word, for brotherhood.

• **Are you attracted to any of the brothers?** Be honest. Explain the reasons you joined the fraternity. You may be attracted to another brother; you can talk about that privately with close friends and brothers if you choose. You may not be attracted to any of them. Remind brothers about your commitment to the brotherhood. There is a difference between being attracted to someone and acting on those feelings. Brotherhood, trust, and loyalty always should be your foremost responsibility to one another.

• **Are you going to bring same-sex dates to formals or other parties?** If the group is supportive of you as a brother, of course! What a great way for your brothers to learn more about being gay. Realize that if they are not supportive of you, this may be a touchy area. Consider your individual situation.

• **Do other fraternities or sororities know?** Brothers may ask this question to find out how to deal with any rumors. They may ask this question to see if you trusted them first or needed outside support. Find out their concern and address it.

• **Do you need support?** Let them know what they can do for you. Suggest a nondiscrimination clause in the chapter bylaws; ask for support of bringing dates to events. Be there emotionally for other men who may come out.

• **What is it like being in the "gay fraternity"?** This is a stereotype that sometimes comes from men coming out in their fraternity. Help to assure people that each man is different and that just because you are gay, it does not mean the entire chapter is. This would be support in return to a group of brothers who are supportive of you.

• **Are you the only gay guy in our fraternity?** Mention that you are probably not. You are just one of the first to feel comfortable coming out. Studies have shown that approximately 10% of people in society are GLBT. This could create the start of a support system on your campus. Depending on the response that others have, they may come out too.

CREATE YOUR PERSONAL COMING-OUT ACTION PLAN

Part of coming out is creating an action plan or as some might refer to as your "gay agenda." Having a plan or an agenda ensures that you have thought out all possible angles and are ready to cope with the outcome. Think about the people you will tell first. Look for signs of support or "safe" people. These could be people who are allies or who have made positive comments about gays. Or they may just be the brother who did not make antigay jokes or who ignored such behavior. Your closest friend in the fraternity may be the first person you tell. You may want to consider your fraternity advisor or your chapter advisor too. Next, think about what you will tell them. Will you divulge detailed personal information, or will you simply state that you are gay, without much explanation? A good suggestion is to practice what you will say. Think about all of the questions you may be asked and how you will respond to them. Next, what will you do now that you have come out? Decide how you will react to comments, both positive and negative. Search for support groups or a counselor if you require further support. More than likely, there are many resources on campus that are welcoming and understanding of coming-out issues. Last, be true to yourself and to your brothers. It is important that you consider that your brothers may not be supportive. Gauge their support level and prepare for both heartfelt support and brotherhood, or, in the worst-case scenario, prepare for harassment and rejection. Keep yourself in safe surroundings at all times. Thinking through each step and forming an action plan can help you prepare to come out with appropriate measures in place ahead of time. Items to ponder when creating an action plan:

• Who will you tell first? How will you tell them?

• Should I tell my brothers? That depends on your comfort level with coming out to yourself, your family, your friends, and your brothers. Seek a counselor if you are not comfortable but would like to talk to an impartial person.

• Why are people upset with me? Sometimes close friends or brothers are scared or confused, or they may even feel betrayed. These types of reactions can be confronted with honest conversations and true feelings being discussed.

• If you are being harassed, contact an advisor or the police in a serious situation. Make sure you are keeping yourself safe. Unfortunately, people can react very negatively when you come out.

• Consider if your fraternity is right for you. Are the men being supportive? Do they hold up the values of brotherhood? Do they support and accept their campus or even their fraternity's nondiscrimination clause, or have one? Is the fraternity a safe place; a place where you can grow, be comfortable, and be yourself? Are the members supportive? If not, maybe walking away from this situation and group of men is the best idea for you.

Conclusion

There is not one way to come out of the "gay Greek closet." Coming out of the closet is a journey that can lead you in different directions. Consider all of your options and choose the best path for you. Some men have positive journeys, and some have negative ones. You might come out to one brother, or you may come out to the entire fraternity chapter and Greek community. This decision is all up to you. Use this as a guide to assist in the process of coming out in the college fraternity. Even if you are not ready to come out, always become prepared in case you are purposefully outed. Sadly, you might fall victim to such a situation before you are ready to come out. Think about how you would respond, and always remember to own your coming-out experience. Determine your choices and make your journey personal, living openly and honestly who you are. The journey will undoubtedly affect you the rest of your life.

Tracie M. Massey *is the coordinator for fraternity and sorority life at the University of North Carolina at Wilmington. She has previously served as the fraternity advisor at the University of Maryland.*

Biblical Passages to Support a Gay Brother

by Doug Bauder and Reverend Rebecca Jiménez

"Love the sinner, not the sin!"

That's what Jonathan Scaggs, in his story titled "1 John 2:10," was told by a fraternity brother when, with fear and trepidation, Jonathan shared with this man the fact that he is gay. And in reading Jonathan's initial response, it sounds like he was relieved by his brother's response. It even sounds as if he felt supported by him! And it may be that when one is taking those first steps toward being honest, hearing "Love the sinner, not the sin!" is at least more welcoming than, "Well, you know you're going to hell!"

That said, the line about loving the sinner and hating the sin still strikes us as an expression of smug superiority! In effect, someone saying that line means, "I know all about living a righteous life—a life of purity. You don't! Clearly your lifestyle is evil, but in spite of your depravity, I'll be your brother because I'm such a great Christian!" That's brotherhood? Not the kind that we would want to claim! And of course, most people who use that line ("Love the sinner, hate the sin") are certain that it's scriptural...something Jesus probably said...something that's in the Bible...somewhere. Isn't it?

An interesting question, to be sure. And it's also interesting the way many of us approach the Bible. In some sense, it is just about the strangest book in the world! (Or maybe it's just the way people interpret it.) While it is still considered a best seller by book marketers, what's really weird is that few people actually read it and, if they do, they fail to understand that it's not one book but many, written over a period of a thousand years by a variety of authors with different writing styles, life stories, and perspectives on God.

Our experience with college students suggests that most of them turn to scripture for one of two reasons: they are facing a crisis (the death of a friend, the breakup of a relationship, a tough career decision) or they are looking for some "facts" to back up their opinion about some issue ("The Bible says...").

You may have heard a friend, or yourself, say something like, "Our fraternity is based on the Bible and Christian principles, so how can we accept gay men into our membership?" Or, "How can I support a gay frat brother when the Bible says that homosexuality is wrong?"

Well...that depends, in part, upon how you read the Bible! Each of us comes to understand scripture (or any holy writing) based on a variety of things, including the religious traditions we come from, the values of our families, our personal understanding of God, and our life experiences, to name a few.

Peter Gomes, chaplain at Harvard and author of *The Good Book: Reading the Bible with Mind and Heart* [1] has some suggestions about how we might approach this task. He spends considerable time looking at the ways the Bible has been used and abused over the centuries to justify racism, anti-Semitism, sexism, and finally, what he calls "the last prejudice," homophobia.

Is it possible that at the heart of the argument that blacks are inferior, that Jews are going to hell, and that women are "below" men is a particular way of reading the Bible? Unfortunately, it is! And Gomes and many other Christians and Jews believe that the Bible is still being used (abused) to view gay men and lesbians as second-class citizens. Some so-called people of faith have even used scripture as a means for advocating violence against those who identify as homosexual or bisexual.

There are others who believe, in effect, that the Bible says nothing about homosexuality as an orientation and that those passages that refer to homosexual behavior are speaking not about loving, consensual relationships but about abusive and idolatrous behavior. [2]

While the controversies surrounding sexuality and spirituality probably cannot be decided in the context of one simple exercise, we would like to invite you and your friends to at least consider the possibility of approaching scripture in some new ways. Chris Glaser, an ordained Presbyterian pastor, is the author of *The Word Is OUT: The Bible*

Reclaimed For Lesbians and Gay Men, a collection of 365 daily medita-
tions.[3] We have chosen two that we would like you to read and to reflect
on. After you do so, we invite you to consider the questions following
each meditation. You may answer them on your own or discuss them
with others. As you do this, we encourage you to think of the Bible as a
compass for your journey and not as a club to beat up on other people.

MEDITATION ONE
For it was you who formed my inward parts;
You knit me together in my mother's womb.
I praise you, for I am fearfully and wonderfully made.
—Psalm 139:13-14

*God wove together our bodies. God wove together our gender and our
sexuality. The tender intimacy of God's personal involvement in our embry-
onic creation is a cause for praise, awe, and wonder.*

*God must have conceived us the way we are: not the way we express our-
selves—that is up to us—but who we are. If we are gay, God made us that
way. If we are lesbian, God made us that way. If we are bisexual, God made
us that way. If we are transgender, God made us that way.*

*Our sexual differences have made us a target for blame, fear, and horror
by those who don't understand. Rather, they should be a cause for praise,
awe, and wonder that we exist. God is very creative and not committed to
one formula of existence. God is not as dull or unimaginative as people seem
to think!*

1. What messages did you receive about your gender as you were
growing up? List several. Were they positive, negative, or neutral?

2. What is one message that you would like to have heard?

3. How did you feel about yourself as a girl or a boy? How did you
express those feelings?

4. What messages did you receive as you were growing up about people with different sexual orientations (homosexual or bisexual)? How did
you feel about those messages?

5. Do you know someone now who is lesbian, gay, bisexual, or transgender? Has knowing this person changed your feelings about issues
related to homosexuality? In what way?

6. Think about your gender identity and sexual orientation and then

reread Psalm 139:13-14. Is there something you need to do at this point in your life to affirm that you are "fearfully and wonderfully" made? What is it?

Prayer: Thank you for intricately weaving me "in the depths of the earth," my mother's womb, Creator God.

MEDITATION TWO
In everything do unto others as you would have them do to you, for this is the law and the prophets.
—Matthew 5:12

Jesus here turned into a positive what other teachers of this time had said in the negative: Do not do to others what you would not want them to do to you.

Until we love ourselves properly, as Martin Luther encouraged, we may try to "feel better about ourselves" by putting down other categories of people. One of my big disappointments when coming out as gay was discovering that the oppressed, who presumably would know better, easily fall into oppressive behavior. Though more sensitive to our own racism, for example, gay men and lesbians can behave in as racist a fashion as the rest of the society. People of color, who might also know better, may be as homophobic. All of us may be hesitant to share what little power we have.

Jesus transformed others' prohibition into positive action: "Do to others as you would have them do to you."

It's not enough to refrain from racism. If we want people of color to support our rights, then we must support theirs, whether or not they do so for us. The Golden Rule, expressed in most religions, does not make our behavior dependent on how others act. Rather, it's based on how we want to be treated.

1. Can you remember a time in your life when the Golden Rule first became real for you? What were the circumstances?

2. As you think about a particular individual or group of people, to whom do you have the most trouble applying this lesson? Why?

3. Imagine that you are struggling with strong emotional and/or sexual feelings for a friend of the same gender. What could someone say that would make you feel accepted?

4. Think of someone in your sorority/fraternity who might be lesbian or gay. In the context of your friendship, what would it look like to "do unto them as you would have them do unto you"?

Prayer: Help me to do for others what I would like them to do for me.

Finally, we invite you to think of one of your fraternity brothers who joined when you did and with whom you learned about the ideals and values of brotherhood. Together you discussed your reasons for joining, discovered your common bonds, and shared your dreams and visions, your joys and sorrows, your triumphs and disappointments. Suppose through this process you became close friends—brothers in the best sense of the word. And now, precisely because you are so close, because of your common experiences through the university and fraternity, because your friend trusts and feels safe with you, because he embraces the same values you do, such as honesty and truth, he confides in you that he is gay. He finally must be honest and open, must unburden himself of the silence and the fear of discovery, and he has to do that with someone he can trust. You are the person he chooses.

1. How do you respond? Can you suddenly change how you feel about your friend? Can you immediately forget the respect and affection you have for your brother? In light of Psalm 139, can you honestly believe that either of you is not created in the image of God?

2. Consider, again, Matthew 5:12. The Golden Rule may be the most concise expression of the Christian faith. Indeed, every one of the world's religions bears this same foundational decree. Just as you wanted to be accorded dignity, spoken to in truth and honesty, treated with compassion and kindness, so too are you called to act accordingly in all of your relationships. Will you allow this calling to be extended to your brother now?

We have seen how interpretations of the Bible and Christian teachings are influenced by various factors, cultural and personal. Every day we interpret our life experiences under the influence of these same factors, based on assumptions that are usually unconscious. We invite you to use the exercises on these pages to become more aware of those influences and assumptions. How have they colored your understanding of

Christian teachings? In what ways might some interpretations of scripture come into conflict with its fundamental theme of justice and compassion? We invite you especially to be intentional about putting into action the Christian values on which your fraternity is founded. How will you express justice and compassion in your daily interactions? How will you seek wisdom and truth?

Ultimately, how we see ourselves and relate to others is deeply rooted in our own spirituality, our own understanding of who God is. It may well be that the issues we have raised, the approach to scripture we have suggested, and the questions we have posed have enabled you to look at yourself or your beliefs in some new ways. Perhaps, in doing so, you found yourself wanting to know more. We have included a list of some additional resources that you might find helpful. Whatever you do, don't be fooled by anyone who glibly says, "Love the sinner, not the sin!" It might sound welcoming on the surface, but such a condescending attitude is about as far from brotherhood as anything we can imagine. Jonathan Scaggs and the brothers of your fraternity deserve better!

ADDITIONAL RESOURCES

Fortunato, John E. *Embracing the Exile* (San Francisco: Harper, 1982).

Helminiak, Daniel A. *What the Bible Really Says about Homosexuality* (San Francisco: Alamo Square Press, 1994).

Miner, Jeff and John Tyler Connoley. *The Children Are Free: Reexamining the Biblical Evidence on Same-Sex Relationships* (Indianapolis: Jesus Metropolitan Community Church, 2002).

Mollenkott, Virginia Ramey. *Sensuous Spirituality* (New York: Crossroad, 1993).

Pharr, Suzanne. *Homophobia: A Weapon of Sexism* (Berkeley, Calif.: Chardon Press, 1997).

Scanzoni, Letha Dawson and Virginia Ramey Mollencott. *Is The Homosexual My Neighbor?* (San Francisco: Harper, 1994).

Waun, Maurine C. *More Than Welcome* (St. Louis: Chalice Press, 1999).

Wink, Walter, editor. *Homosexuality and Christian Faith: Questions of Conscience for the Churches* (Minneapolis: Fortress Press, 1999).

Many other excellent resources are available through Soulforce at www.soulforce.org. We especially recommend the booklet "What the Bible Says—and Doesn't Say—About Homosexuality" and these videos: *Homosexuality: The Debate Is Over. The Verdict Is In. Not a Sickness! Not a Sin!* and *How Can I Be Sure That God Loves Me Too?*

Doug Bauder *is an ordained Moravian minister and coordinator of the Gay, Lesbian, Bisexual, Transgender Student Support Services Office at Indiana University in Bloomington.*

Reverend Rebecca Jiménez *is an ordained American Baptist minister and director of the Center for University Ministries at Indiana University in Bloomington.*

NOTES

1. Peter Gomes, *The Good Book: Reading the Bible with Mind and Heart* (New York: William Morrow, 1996).

2. Daniel Helminiak, *What the Bible Really Says about Homosexuality* (San Francisco: Alamo Square Press, 1994).

3. Chris Glaser, *The Word Is OUT: The Bible Reclaimed for Lesbians and Gay Men* (San Francisco: Harper, 1994).

Creating a PILLAR Support Group for Gay Greeks

by Grahaeme A. Hesp

INTRODUCTION

The significance of a fraternity lies in its ability to influence the attitudes, behavior, standards, and loyalties of chapter members while providing programming that, when taken as part of the total education process, can help members successfully accomplish the development tasks of self-identity, learning about others, and improving the quality of relationships. Colleges and universities tend to mirror the status quo of society, and fraternities are "a microcosm of broader society."[1] In most cases, fraternities have over time reflected the attitudes and changes of both the campus and society at large but without necessarily developing new directions or pathways.

Fraternity members want to change the perception of their organizations by nonmembers by removing the images of exclusivity, reversing the predominantly social image, smoothly assimilating new members into the chapter, and creating intrachapter cooperation rather than competition. However, as change is desired for some things, others stay the same: the roles of providing a home away from home, close relationships, scholastic excellence, and opportunities for leadership and community service.

The change process is very slow in established institutions.[2] To change group behavior it is necessary to change the prevailing attitudes and values held by members of the group. A select number of campuses have attempted to change the established customs and behaviors of their fraternities' members. The successful ones have developed programs that make desired behaviors more attractive and enjoyable. Sadly, the vast majority of campuses and chapters have so far either been unable or unwilling to devote the resources needed to effect a paradigm shift.

They have seminars and training for this and that, so why not have something that you supposedly should strongly believe in? Risk management doesn't make them uncomfortable because it's something that everybody does; not everybody can get it into their head that it's okay for somebody to be gay. You're gonna need to change some people's opinions on that, you know? It would be a lot more difficult and a lot more sensitive subject.[3]

THE PURPOSE OF A PEER SUPPORT GROUP

During the traditional undergraduate college years students face the challenges of having to reconsider "their self-perceptions, develop new skills, and master developmental tasks."[4] This process often becomes especially complicated for those students who are gay, lesbian, bisexual, or questioning. They face discrimination, isolation, and often their own internalized homophobia that their heterosexual peers seldom encounter.[5] A student who submerses himself in an environment that may not offer any support or validation for being GLBQ could make the process of developing a homosexual identity even more confounding.

Fraternities are products of the larger cultural context; they do not exist apart from the societies and institutions that create and support them.[6] GLBQ students who join college social fraternities and sororities therefore face the attitudes, beliefs, and prejudices held by the larger society that are merely reflected in their fraternity and sorority chapters.

I knew that there had to be one [fraternity] for me. I knew from other people, because I have friends in other ones, and I had friends that were girls who knew guys in other ones, and specifically one [female] friend told me specifically to go check out the one that I'm in now. So I did and I ended up loving it. The guys were awesome, very diverse. There was no stereotypical mold. The way that they treated each other and looked at girls was totally different. So I decided to give it a shot, and I'm in it.[7]

CREATING A PEER SUPPORT PROGRAM: PILLAR

The Definition of PILLAR

A structure or part that provides support; a firm, upright, insulated support.[8]

I think when somebody comes out it shouldn't be like a big party [laughs], "Hey, I'm having a couple of kegs, I'm turning gay," you know? I think it should be as seamless as possible. I think if he's in that case where he's already in the fraternity, [and] nobody thinks he's gay, he should probably come out to friends, his best friends, whether they be in the fraternity or not in the fraternity. He should call them, talk with them, and let them know, you know, "I'm gay." 'Cause no matter what, if they're really his good friends, they'll be okay with it. So that will give him confidence to come out to more and more people. 9

PILLAR is a program designed to provide a safe environment for GLBQ students who are in a campus fraternity/sorority community and who wish to receive more information, support, and fellowship about their own sexual orientation. PILLAR provides the option of forming a support network with other GLBQ fraternity/sorority members both in e-mail and face-to-face environments. PILLAR does not serve as a counseling or dating service; rather, it functions as a support and education resource.

*I can pretty much honestly say that there are gay guys in almost every fraternity that are out. I know at least seven or eight fraternities [on this campus] that have openly gay guys in them. And then I know of a couple of others that have closeted or bi, or whatever, but they have feelings for men.*10

To participate in the support functions of PILLAR, a member must:
• be an undergraduate member of a campus-based fraternity/sorority;
• be gay, lesbian, bisexual, or questioning his or her own sexual orientation;
• have a genuine need and interest in receiving further information on sexual orientation and/or a support group regarding this issue;
• be sensitive and supportive of other members and the particular phase of their identity formation;11
• respect the confidentiality of other members; and
• have an initial meeting with a PILLAR facilitator or supervisor.

Any program must contain certain fundamental attributes in order to be successful. When setting up a program similar to PILLAR, several questions will undoubtedly arise and need answering. Answers to these questions are dependent on a number of factors, including the culture of the fraternity/sorority community and the campus, the extent of campus GLBQ needs, availability of resources, and others. As such, specific answers to the following questions are not provided; they should be used as a basis from which campuses may begin the process of providing support.

1. Who advises the group?
2. Who funds the group?
3. How is the program implemented?
4. How are the governing councils of the fraternities and sororities involved?
5. What campus resources already exist that can help with the program?
6. How do you promote the program to every member of the fraternity/sorority community without facing issues of "filtering" of information as it cascades down through the leadership ranks?
7. How does the advisor/facilitator ensure the confidentiality of the identity of the members?

Good facilitators not only are helpers but also share a common interest with the people they desire to help. This does not mean that the PILLAR facilitator needs to be GLBQ, but some affiliation with the fraternity/sorority community is necessary. This could be as the campus-based advisor, as an advisor to a particular fraternity, or as someone who works closely with the campus fraternity/sorority community and who is known to chapter members. The facilitator also needs to be someone who believes that the campus fraternity/sorority community will be a better place through the inclusion, understanding, and acceptance of all people and who will become educated about GLBQ issues, if necessary. The facilitator will perhaps have the greatest impact by simply being a role model and caring enough to listen. However, the facilitator should also adopt the role of educator. Confronting derogatory language and speaking supportively about GLBQ concerns—especially within the fraternity/sorority community—are cornerstones of what it means to be an ally. It is also important to realize that the facilitator may be the only visible person within the PILLAR program. Because of this, others may speculate about the facilitator's sexual orientation.

Financial Feasibility

Financial resources should be considered along with personal resources of time. The program's financial cost is based purely on the number of brochures that are printed and then mailed to campus offices, fraternity members, chapter officers and advisors, and other allies or interested parties. Assistance from the campus counseling center, campus religious ministries, or other such allies could offset costs. Even if other support groups cannot provide additional funding, they should still be brought in as partners, as they are often involved with students questioning their sexual orientation. However, in the 21st century the first stop for research for most students is the Internet. Providing a resources and information page on the fraternity/sorority office Web site would reduce printing costs. Once a brochure or Web site is created, the only time cost is to ensure that the information remains current. This could be as little as reviewing publications once a year (the summer could be a good time for work like this!). If any special activities, such as a pizza party, are organized, they should be the financial responsibility of the individual PILLAR members.

Depending on the needs of the PILLAR program, the demand on staff time for initial inquiry meetings will vary. On a larger and more diverse campus there could be an initial surge in demand once the program is established that might not be replicated on a smaller, conservative campus. Only the campus-based facilitator will be able to assess this initial startup commitment. In addition, an established, strong, and self-motivated PILLAR group may be able to meet without much facilitator guidance and direction after their initial meetings. This can perhaps be compared to a smaller and more reserved group that will rely more on the facilitator to help the students process the various stages of their sexual identity development.

Easy to Replicate

Replicating the PILLAR program can be easy. An option is to create an e-mail address alias whereby incoming mail is forwarded to the facilitator. In addition, an e-mail Listserv allows confidential (and sometimes anonymous) discussions among members. Campus Web-based academic-support programs such as Blackboard and Web CT also allow discussion board conversations and real-time chat options. Education through peer discussion and interaction in a safe environment allows individuals to ask questions, obtain resources, and sometimes find shoulders on which to cry.

The greatest strength of the program lies in the fact that it has a guaranteed impact. Through the drawing of attention to homophobia, all students are able to confront their own fears, stereotypes, and prejudices whether members of PILLAR or not. Although not every student may gain an appreciation or understanding of sexual orientation issues, many will. In essence, there is no failure:

Most sorority girls find out [I'm gay]. A lot of times I tell them, and they ask questions like "do your brothers know?" and I tell them "yeah" and they're like, "Wow! They accept it; they don't have a problem with it?" And I'm like, "No, they love it, you know, because they love me. It's just another part of me, like I have brown hair, green eyes, I'm gay. It's just kind of on the same level." I've actually changed probably a lot of their views, and most of them have come up to me and said so.[12]

CHALLENGES AND PITFALLS OF A PEER SUPPORT PROGRAM

Because of the sensitivity surrounding GLBQ issues, PILLAR respects the needs of its members and maintains confidentiality at all times. Information such as participant names and the times and locations of any meetings are known only to those participating. Respect for individual rights, values, and beliefs are a common courtesy that all members must share. It is for this reason that an initial interview with a PILLAR facilitator is strongly suggested. PILLAR members are also encouraged to seek support from staff in campus departments such as the fraternity/sorority office, counseling office, health education office, and the chaplain, where appropriate or necessary.

A SUCCESS STORY

The biggest success in the history and various incarnations of PILLAR occurred when a student decided to reveal his homosexuality to his fraternity. After a meeting with me he reviewed resources on the Lambda 10 Project web site and read *Out on Fraternity Row*.[13] His fraternity was nearly unanimously accepting of his announcement at the fraternity chapter meeting. Later that academic year the same fraternity issued a membership invitation to an openly gay first-year student. This led to conversations within other fraternity chapters and some sororities about how they themselves would handle a member announcing his or her sexual orientation as gay, lesbian, or bisexual.

Because of this, PILLAR has been a very positive experience for the entire fraternity/sorority community.

I read once that a lot of people don't come out until their, like, senior year of college or until after they're out of college because they want to just kind of have fun while they're in college, you know? There's something like that where they don't want to mess up their college years so they wait till afterwards when they're an independent person and they don't have all this stuff going on with school and social interactions to worry about. I think for some of them, and for some people in general in the fraternity, maybe they are [gay] and they won't say anything just because of the fact that they want to wait. You just have to wait until everything kind of feels right.[14]

Concluding Thoughts

Regardless of how much input, advice, and support an individual receives from a program such as PILLAR, the ultimate decision to reveal a gay, lesbian, or bisexual identity is the student's. An individual must therefore be willing to take an objective look at his or her sexual identity. A structured yet informal approach such as PILLAR promotes and facilitates discussion within the fraternity/sorority community. The ultimate goal is to create an atmosphere that facilitates open dialogue among all students while also creating a support network for GLBQ fraternity/sorority members. The outcome will be a supportive, inclusive, and caring community for all, including GLBQ students within the fraternity/sorority community, and the entire campus.

I think the number of openly gay fraternity members is probably increasing just because more and more every year people are more comfortable with it, like society is accepting gay people more and more every year. And fraternities are just a microcosm of society, pretty much.[15]

Grahaeme A. Hesp *is a member of Sigma Phi Epsilon Fraternity, the Association of Fraternity Advisors, and the NASPA Fraternity/Sorority and GLBT Knowledge Communities. He is a former fraternity/sorority advisor on three campuses and heads a resource, speaking, and consulting agency called Back to Our Roots. He is currently a doctoral student at Florida State University, where the topic of his dissertation research is sexual orientation within historically white fraternities.*

NOTES

1. Bryan, W. A. "Contemporary Fraternity and Sorority Issues." In R. B. Winston Jr., W. R. Nettles III, and J. H. Opper Jr. (eds.), *New Directions for Student Services,* 40 (San Francisco: Jossey-Bass, 1987).

2. Lindquist, J. *Strategies for Change* (Berkeley, Calif: Pacific Sounding Press, 1978).

3. Quote comes from an interview between Grahaeme A. Hesp and an undergraduate openly gay fraternity member.

4. Levine, H., and Evans, N. J. "The Development of Gay, Lesbian, and Bisexual Identities." In N. J. Evans & V. A. Wall (eds.), *Beyond Tolerance: Gays, Lesbians and Bisexuals on Campus* (Alexandria, Va: American College Personnel Association, 1991, pp. 1-24).

5. Johnson, D. "The Developmental Experience of Gay/Lesbian Youth." *Journal of College Admissions,* 152-153 (1996, pp. 38-41).

6. Kuh, G. D., and Arnold J. C. "Liquid Bonding: A Cultural Analysis of the Role of Alcohol in Fraternity Pledgeship. *Journal of College Student Development,* 34 (1993, pp. 327-334, 331).

7. Quote comes from an interview between Grahaeme A. Hesp and an undergraduate openly gay fraternity member.

8. www.dictionary.com.

9. Quote comes from an interview between Grahaeme A. Hesp and an undergraduate openly gay fraternity member.

10. Quote comes from an interview between Grahaeme A. Hesp and an undergraduate openly gay fraternity member.

11. Cass, V. C. "Homosexual Identity Formation: A Theoretical Model. *Journal of Homosexuality* 4 (1979, pp. 219-235).

12. Quote comes from an interview between Grahaeme A. Hesp and an undergraduate openly gay fraternity member.

13. www.lambda10.org.

14. Quote comes from an interview between Grahaeme A. Hesp and an undergraduate openly gay fraternity member.

15. Quote comes from an interview between Grahaeme A. Hesp and an undergraduate openly gay fraternity member.

Out in Front: Questions, Policy Statements, and Resolutions Affirming Sexual Orientation

History tells us that fraternities have been resistant to change. However, the prominence of GLBT issues has taken center stage for many college fraternities in the past decade. The Lambda 10 Project monitors a list of fraternities that have taken the lead and are truly "Out in Front" on the issue of sexual orientation. These fraternities have developed educational steps to address the issue in the college Greek community. Their inclusive educational efforts create a better Greek community and encourage other national and international fraternities to do the same.

FRATERNITIES TAKING THE LEAD ON SEXUAL ORIENTATION

Alpha Phi Omega*	Phi Kappa Tau*
Alpha Sigma Phi*	Phi Sigma Kappa*
Beta Theta Pi	Psi Upsilon
Chi Phi*	Sigma Alpha Epsilon
Delta Sigma Phi	Sigma Chi*
Delta Upsilon*	Sigma Phi Epsilon*
Kappa Delta Rho*	Tau Beta Sigma*
Kappa Kappa Psi*	Theta Chi*
Lambda Chi Alpha*	Theta Delta Chi*
Phi Delta Theta	Theta Xi*
Pi Kappa Phi*	Zeta Beta Tau*

Note: Asterisk indicates fraternities that have a nondiscrimination policy that includes sexual orientation in addition to educational program efforts that specifically address sexual orientation.

Many fraternity members never ask questions regarding the policies and practices of national or international fraternities on sexual orientation issues. If you fraternity does not appear on the list, it is definitely time to start asking questions and challenging the fraternity to be a leader, not a follower. Remember, if you never ask a question, you will never get an answer. Either way, there are still a lot of questions to be asked and answers to be given on this topic. Even if your fraternity appears on the list, there is often a need for much education to be done with local chapters and alumni.

Questions are a healthy part of growth, and by asking questions you encourage the fraternity to take action and support positive change. Several of the changes in regards to sexual orientation started with undergraduate members passing a resolution or advocating for inclusiveness in policies and practices. The more brothers who ask the same questions, the better the chance you will be heard and have a necessary impact within the fraternity.

We offer suggested questions for you and your brothers to ask your national or international fraternity leaders about their position, practices, and policies pertaining to sexual orientation. We believe all brothers—straight, gay, or bisexual—must begin asking the questions and insisting that their fraternities take a proactive stance to affirm diversity, including diversity of sexual orientation.

National and international fraternity resolutions, policy statements, and resources also are provided to assist with such efforts and to suggest potential methods to be inclusive in your particular fraternities and within your college or university campuses. And remember, if at first you do not succeed, try and try again. Let your fraternity leadership know how important this issue is to your chapter and to the ideals of brotherhood. The more people who ask the same questions, the more the "right" answer will be given.

SAMPLE QUESTIONS TO ASK YOUR FRATERNITY LEADERSHIP UNTIL
YOU GET THE "RIGHT" ANSWER

1. Does our fraternity have any written organizational policies deal-ing with sexual orientation, such as membership policies, standards policies, position statements, personnel policies, and so forth? If not, why not?

2. Do we discuss the issue of sexual orientation and being gay or bisexual in any of our educational programs and resources? Do we pro-vide our chapter with any educational resources to help a brother who comes out? If not, what are we waiting for?

3. Do we include workshops or other educational programs on sexu-al orientation issues at conventions or national or regional leadership conferences? If so, what does the program entail? Are there speakers? Facilitators?

4. Do we include the issue of sexual orientation in training for staff (such as leadership consultants) or volunteer alumni? If so, what types of things are covered in the training? If not, why not? Is the issue of sex-ual orientation addressed in any of our resource materials, such as offi-cer manuals, volunteer advisor manuals, and other materials? If not, why not?

5. Would we be open to including an article or resources about sexu-al orientation in our national magazine or other publications? Have we ever done this? If not, why not?

6. What type of advice would our national fraternity leadership give in the following circumstances, and how do we expect our members to know appropriate ways to deal with these situations if we do not have any policies or resources on the topic?

(a) What should our fraternity do if a brother comes out to the chapter?

(b) Can our fraternity president kick out a member because he is gay or bisexual but by all accounts is a good brother? Is this okay?

(c) What should we do if someone openly gay wants to rush our fra-ternity? Can we exclude him from being a member for this sole reason?

(d) Can a member take a same-sex date to the fraternity formal?

(e) How do we stop rumors that our chapter is a "gay fraternity" just because we have an out gay brother? Should we care?

What are your questions to ask? Remember to be courteous, pro-fessional, and brotherly, but you have a right to get an answer. Please share your responses with the Lambda 10 Project to be considered for the online "Out in Front" listing of fraternities who take the lead on sexual orientation issues. Other fraternities can then see the positive work of your fraternity to be inclusive of all types of diversity. Plus, visible change will have a domino effect and spur other fraternities to do the same.

Source: Shane L. Windmeyer, Lambda 10 Project.

Adapted from "Questions, Policy Statements, and Resolutions Affirming Diversity" published in *Secret Sisters: Stories of Being Lesbian & Bisexual in a College Sorority,* edited by Shane L. Windmeyer and Pamela W. Freeman, Alyson Publications, 2001.

Our Fraternity—Chapter Diversity Statement

Our Fraternity *is an all-inclusive society of brothers. It values differences in people and diversity within our organization, the campus community, and society at large. It recognizes the different perspectives and contributions an all-inclusive people can make toward improving the brotherhood of the fraternity and humanity.*

Our Fraternity's *policy is to welcome and reach out to people of different ages, nationalities, ethnic groups, physical abilities and qualities, sexual orientations, health status, religions, backgrounds, and educational experiences as well as to any others who may experience discrimination or abuse.*

Our Fraternity *does not discriminate against any group or individual. In fact, the fraternity will actively oppose any and all forms of discrimination.*

Our Fraternity *also desires to help the Greek community and society at large to develop similar policies and practices that support diversity and assist in making the world a better place for all to live.*

Source: Shane L. Windmeyer, Lambda 10 Project.

Adapted from the diversity policy of the National Society of Performance and Instruction and revised from *Out on Fraternity Row: Personal Accounts of Being Gay in a College Fraternity*, edited by Shane L. Windmeyer and Pamela W. Freeman, Alyson Publications, 1998.

INTER/NATIONAL FRATERNITY HEADQUARTERS POLICY STATEMENT ON SEXUAL ORIENTATION

Inter/National Fraternity *does not judge its brothers on the basis of sexual orientation. Thus, if a brother declares that he is gay or bisexual, we recognize this to be his personal right, free of censure or coercion. Of course, no chapter is required to offer membership to anyone, but it should not use sexual orientation as a reason not to offer membership. It may not expel any brother on the basis of sexual orientation.*

Aside from the fact of sexual orientation, a brother who is straight, gay, or bisexual may have a sexual lifestyle that may be unattractive to other brothers due to various reasons besides his sexual identity. This does not categorize either brother as right or wrong, as long as they are respectful and fair-minded regarding one another's sexual orientation.

Inter/National Fraternity *does follow an ethical code when it comes to sexual conduct. Sexual conduct must always be consensual, not exploitative or coercive, and between equals. Regardless of an individual's sexual orientation, we encourage our chapters to process sexual ethical issues on both an informal and formal basis.*

Inter/National Fraternity *does believe that brotherhood is incompatible with sexual conduct between members that in any way has a negative impact on the brotherhood of the chapter, and we encourage the chapter to have a respectful conversation about this belief.*

The fraternity's position is brief, simple, and clear. Behavior, not sexual orientation, is the basis for evaluating the worth of a brother.

For those who disagree or who are concerned, the fraternity's policy makes it clear that concerns, objections, even disagreement with the policy do not classify a person as right or wrong. Our policy states, however, that such concerns or disagreements do not empower a person to deny membership to other persons because their beliefs or sexual orientations are different or to remove a person from membership for similar reasons.

Our policy respects all sexual orientations as well as individuals who may disagree. It urges that chapters, with the assistance of professionals, talk about their feelings and concerns.

Source: Shane L. Windmeyer, Lambda 10 Project.

Adapted from the Statement of Sexual Orientation of Zeta Beta Tau
Fraternity as stated in the Fraternity Code of Ethics, Section III and
revised from *Out on Fraternity Row: Personal Accounts of Being Gay in a
College Fraternity,* edited by Shane L. Windmeyer and Pamela W.
Freeman, Alyson Publications, 1998.

Alpha Sigma Phi Fraternity Position Statement on Inclusiveness

Whereas, *Alpha Sigma Phi is the Fraternity "To Better the Man" and all of her functions and actions are expected to represent this as listed in our Mission Statement and Code of Conduct, and*

Whereas, *Article III, Section 7 of the Constitution states: "No Chapter shall permit discrimination in membership selection, initiation, chapter operations, or other activities of the Fraternity based on any individual's race, color, creed, religion, disability, or sexual orientation."*

Whereas, *Alpha Sigma Phi's core values, as expressed through our ceremonies, constitution and policies, each express the concept of inclusiveness and respect for all persons, and*

Whereas, *Alpha Sigma Phi Fraternity is an organization based on mutual respect, trust, and honesty where an environment of acceptance and brotherly love exists within the walls of the mystic circle, and*

Whereas, *the value of such inclusiveness has never been greater given the rich diversity of our campuses and communities. Where inclusiveness is not about diversity for the sake of political correctness, but where inclusiveness is a values-based choice, a decision made because it is the right decision to make based on who we say we are as a brotherhood of men.*

Therefore be it resolved *that Alpha Sigma Phi Fraternity, both at the local and national level, is actively working to promote inclusiveness in our membership and will oppose all acts of harassment, and discrimination.*

Be it further resolved *by the Grand Chapter of Alpha Sigma Phi Fraternity that it is the continuing position of our Fraternity that membership privileges are open to any qualified man of character without consideration of ethnicity, race, religion, sexual orientation, physical ability, national origin, age, family status, or cultural background.*

As recommended by the Undergraduate Operations/Alumni Committee of the 2004 Grand Chapter, as of July 23, 2004.

Pi Kappa Phi Fraternity Amendments to be Inclusive of Sexual Orientation

Amend the current statement of position on Sexual Abuse to read as follows:

Pi Kappa Phi Fraternity will not tolerate or condone any form of sexually abusive behavior (physical, mental, or emotional) or discrimination based on sexual orientation. Furthermore, the Fraternity supports educational programming that promotes healthy attitudes between the sexes and acceptance of sexual orientation.

All chapters of the Fraternity must work to provide an atmosphere where proper attitudes and behavior towards sex, sex roles, and sexual orientation will be promoted and a respect for human dignity will be of chief priority.

Amend the current statement of position on Racial, Religious, and Ethnic Diversity to read as follows:

The United States of America is fortunate to have one of the most diverse populations in the world. Here, people of all races, religions, ethnicities, disabilities, sexual orientations, HIV status, and any further protected statuses contribute to the collective achievements of our nation and our colleges.

Pi Kappa Phi Fraternity chapters shall seek out new brothers of all backgrounds. While our fraternal origins are based on Judeo-Christian traditions, the fraternity asks that all members and nonmembers (regardless of belief) join in respect for the beliefs of all.

This fraternity shall only discriminate on the basis of gender.

Whereas, *the 48th Supreme Chapter established new statements of position on Diversity, Sexual Abuse, and Sexual Discrimination on Monday, August 5, 2002. The Resolutions Committee requests that the National Education Committee assess existing awareness and sensitivity programming at colleges and universities where our local chapters currently reside and develop, as appropriate, national, programs to build awareness and sensitivity of the members of Pi Kappa Phi.*

Be it further resolved, *that the National Education Committee's plan of action should be made to the National Council for approval prior to the 2003 Pi Kapp College.*

Approved at the Pi Kappa Phi Supreme Chapter in August 2002.

LAMBDA CHI ALPHA FRATERNITY MANDATORY RESOLUTION
REGARDING DISCRIMINATION

Be it resolved that: *The members of Kappa-Sigma Zeta, with the support of Beta Zeta and Epsilon-Eta Zeta, propose to adopt a new resolution to replace the Mandatory Resolution Regarding Discrimination from the Thirty-Second General Assembly in 1970.*

Proposed New Resolution: A Mandatory Resolution Regarding Discrimination

Be it resolved *that membership selection on the basis of race, creed, color, national origin, sexual orientation, or disability has no place within Lambda Chi Alpha Fraternity. The Lambda Chi Alpha Fraternity, therefore, condemns all discrimination and will actively seek to prevent it in all of its chapters/colonies.*

Rationale: *Every Brother in Lambda Chi Alpha knows well the open motto of our great Fraternity. Vir Quisque Vir*

It is in the spirit of this powerful affirmation that this resolution is presented. We represent the past and the present of Lambda Chi Alpha. We are seeking to bring the nondiscrimination statement of our fraternity into harmony with the nondiscrimination statements of the colleges and universities that host our chapters and the business organizations that provide our future.

Through much of Lambda Chi Alpha, a positive environment is fostered for the growth of all men within the bond. Each man has the opportunity to aspire to take on the responsibilities and privileges of the fraternity upon acceptance of our obligations. The new resolution, bringing sexual orientation and disability into the nondiscrimination policy, will ensure that this opportunity is attainable for all brothers of Lambda Chi Alpha, within and between the Zetas.

Currently, Lambda Chi Alpha Fraternity's stance on the subject of sexual orientation is "home rule." Home rule allows each chapter the ability to choose its own stance on sexual orientation. This position comes from the lack of an official stance by the International Fraternity. Unfortunately, the impact of "home rule" may be less neutral and more hurtful than intended. A brother may find little protection from discrimination within the fraternity with the current policy. To such a man, home rule implies that while he may find acceptance and brotherly love within his own Zeta, another Zeta may legitimately deny him the hospitality deserved by a brother of Lambda Chi Alpha. This resolution will ensure that such a brother may never be received as less of a brother or a man within the bond that is Lambda Chi Alpha.

Many years ago, the fraternity abandoned the open discrimination that once limited the membership of Lambda Chi Alpha to ethnic Caucasians and Christians. The General Assembly recognized that such discrimination is repugnant to the values of the Fraternity, under which even our Exemplar would have been denied membership.

Today, we are calling upon Lambda Chi Alpha to support of the inclusion of all men who share our ideals, values, and principles. We are calling upon the General Fraternity to affirm the sincerity of our open motto. Such affirmation sends a powerful positive message to all of Lambda Chi Alpha and the world, that we are committed to providing a brotherhood that recognizes that the hallmark of a true man is his acceptance of and adherence to higher principles.

This resolution is not anticipated to erase all occurrences of discrimination within the fraternity. Such change can only occur by working to change the perceptions and beliefs that lead to such actions. Likewise, the resolution in no way implies that any Zeta must alter its recruitment. Lambda Chi Alpha should only be open to the most promising individuals, carefully selected based upon their merits and attributes, which would make them good members of the bond. Instead, the resolution is a statement to ensure the respect and dignity of every man who shares those qualities. However, a comprehensive statement may be a vital tool for all Lambda Chi's to prevent and stop instances of intentional and malicious discrimination.

This resolution brings Lambda Chi Alpha's nondiscrimination policy into congruence with that of the majority of our host institutions. Fraternities and sororities across the continent face an ongoing challenge from our colleges and universities to ensure that we continue to provide an atmosphere that is consistent with the ideals and relevant to the objectives of those institutions. The proposed statement follows that of the majority of our host institutions, including Alfred University, University of Maine, and Rensselaer Polytechnic Institute, which have adopted similar nondiscrimination statements. Likewise, many major business organizations such as IBM, Ford Motor Co., Capital One, and JP Morgan Chase & Co. have followed suit. Frequent criticism has been directed at fraternities for being relics of sexism, racism, homophobia, and similar bigotry. This resolution, as a statement by Lambda Chi Alpha, will send a clear message that we stand with our hosts and partners in higher education that we oppose invidious discrimination in all its forms. The resolution also stands as statement that our primary mission is to prepare our members for success in later life.

In 1999, one of our most competitive and similar peers, Sigma Phi Epsilon, adopted a similar resolution to amend their nondiscrimination policy. Lambda Chi Alpha is a fraternity of leaders, not followers. We should not be left behind while our contemporaries take strides ahead. As a fraternity rooted on a foundation of Christian ideals, we ever strive to be the better men. Through the ideals of faith, hope and brotherly love, we find the necessity of this resolution. It is by these ideals that the principles of nearly all civil liberties movements have been based. The truly Christian approach to this resolution may be simplified by the words of our Exemplar, "Do unto others as you would have done unto you."

Brothers across two nations are asking for the support of the General Fraternity to extend the reach of Lambda Chi Alpha's nondiscrimination statement to ensure the inclusion of all worthy men as present and future brothers of Lambda Chi Alpha. This is not only the duty of each and every brother, but it is also, and simply, the right thing to do.

Approved at the Lambda Chi Alpha Fraternity, 49th General Assembly August 1-4, 2004.

Theta Xi Fraternity Statement of Position on Human Dignity

Theta Xi Fraternity *believes that it is the responsibility of the Fraternity, its chapters, and each member to respect and protect the dignity of all human beings. Four key factors are directly or indirectly associated with the degradation of others in Fraternities: substance abuse, sexism, racism, and hazing.*

Whereas, *Theta Xi, in its Purpose, Statements of Position, and programs, has shown a belief in the integrity and dignity of all human beings. This should manifest itself in a mutual respect for ourselves and others, and*

Whereas, *sexual conduct, attitudes toward women, and the consumption of alcohol are all, to some degree, interrelated, since excessive drinking contributes significantly to inappropriate sexual behavior and frequently fosters demeaning attitudes toward women, and*

Whereas, *racism and hazing, in addition to sexism, stem from a basic lack of respect for the dignity and understanding of other human beings, and*

Whereas, *excessive drinking and the use of controlled substances show a basic lack of respect for one's own dignity and a lack of concern for potential negative effects on others.*

Therefore, be it resolved that, *Theta Xi Fraternity hereby states its position on human dignity as follows:*

Theta Xi Chapters and individual members shall not tolerate sexual abuse—emotional, verbal, or physical—of women, shall neither condone nor participate in hazing activities, shall respect the integrity of those of different religion, ethnicity, sexual orientation, physical ability, or political belief; and

Theta Xi chapters shall operate within the guidelines of the Fraternity's Statements of Position on Alcohol, Controlled Substances, Hazing and Pre-Initiation Activities, Risk Management, Fraternity Values and other subsequently adopted Statements of Position; and

Theta Xi chapters shall abide by and enforce the Fraternity's Risk Management Policy and individually adopt policies and procedures reinforcing Fraternity statements and policies regarding all of these matters.

Adopted August 2, 1991.

Theta Delta Chi International Fraternity Statement of Inclusive Membership and Participation

Whereas, *the Grand Lodge of Theta Delta Chi International Fraternity and its Charges are gathered for the 156th Annual Convention of 2003;*

Whereas, *the Fraternity supports the "Resolution on Diversity and Inclusiveness" endorsed in 2002 by the North-American Interfraternity Conference House of Delegates;*

Whereas, *Theta Delta Chi is a single-sex social fraternity "founded on mutual esteem and dependence;" and*

Whereas, *Article IV Section 12 of the Theta Delta Chi Constitution was removed by the 102nd Convention of 1949, eliminating the only socially discriminatory restrictions to have ever existed in the selection of her members; therefore be it*

Resolved, *by the Grand Lodge of Theta Delta Chi and its Charges, that membership in the Fraternity and the selection of her pledges, shall be not be determined on the basis of race, creed, color, national origin, religion, age, physical or emotional disability, or sexual orientation; let it be further*

Resolved, *the Fraternity, its Charges, and its associated groups that perpetuate the values of the Fraternity, are committed to and will actively encourage diversity and inclusiveness in membership, policies, plans, programs, and activities, as fundamental and beneficial to the nature of the advancement of the intellectual, moral, and social being; and let it be further*

Resolved, *that the Fraternity will not tolerate or condone on the part of her Charges, her members, and her pledges, any form of behavior determined to be abusive, discriminatory, or otherwise inconsistent with the respect for individual human dignity.*

Adopted by the 156th Convention of Theta Delta Chi International Fraternity, August 9, 2003.

Out & Online: Being Gay and Greek Resources

Everyone can find something on the World Wide Web. Gay Greeks have found a home at the Lambda 10 Project. There you can find an online community for gay, lesbian, and bisexual men and women and their allies in the college Greek system. The Lambda 10 Project creates a place where out and proud Greeks can be who they are. Where a closeted sister or brother can meet other gay Greeks anonymously and find support from them. Where a straight brother or sister can ask questions on what to do if a member comes out to the chapter. The site provides the most current updates, news, resources, and initiatives to create a stronger Greek system free of antigay prejudice and acts of bigotry. Highlights include the following:

Who's Out? An initiative where out men and women list their names, college/university attended, and their Greek affiliation to create more visibility and to show that there are indeed gay men and women in every college fraternity/sorority. E-mail links also are given to contact these members. The list continues to grow.

Out in Front: A special section devoted to showcase international fraternities and sororities that have implemented programs, policies, and practices on issues of sexual orientation. Section also features gay-positive efforts by local fraternity and sorority chapters.

Chat and Bulletin Board: Regularly scheduled chat room discussions on timely topics with special guests and a bulletin board to post messages for other members. This place is another way to meet other gay men and women in a fraternity or sorority.

Greek Safe Zone Allies: A place to learn how to be an ally and how to start a Greek Safe Zone on your campus. Also, a forum for straight allies to post comments about issues of sexual orientation and what it is like to have a gay brother or sister. Comments can range from serious concerns to humorous anecdotes.

News and Personal Features: Up-to-date alerts on news in the media regarding sexual orientation and Greek life as well as special, in-depth features written by men and women who have come out to their brothers and sisters.

Online Clearinghouse of Resources and Links: A select listing of educational materials, Web site links, and programs to assist in efforts to create change in the Greek system on issues of sexual orientation including the phenomenal "Fraternity & Sorority Anti-Homophobia Training Manual" developed specifically for workshops on sexual orientation issues within the Greek community. The site is also an excellent place to find information on speakers, national organizations, and newly created educational initiatives and efforts.

Source: Shane L. Windmeyer, Lambda 10 Project.
Adapted from "Out and Online: Being Gay and Greek Resources" published in *Secret Sisters: Stories of Being Lesbian & Bisexual in a College Sorority,* edited by Shane L. Windmeyer and Pamela W. Freeman, Alyson Publications, 2001.